INDURÁIN:

A TEMPERED PASSION

INDURÁIN:

A TEMPERED PASSION

Javier García Sánchez

Translated from the Spanish
by Jeremy Munday

Foreword by Sean Kelly

INDURÁIN:
a tempered passion

English edition first published in 2002 by
Mousehold Press,
Victoria Cottage, Constitution Opening,
Norwich NR3 4BD

in association with

Sport & Publicity,
75 Fitzjohns Avenue, Hampstead,
London NW3 6PD

Originally published in Spain by Plaza & Janés, S.A., under the title
Induráin: una pasión templada

Text copyright © Javier García Sánchez, 1997
Translation copyright © Jeremy Munday, 2002

Cover photograph – 'Isola–2000' by John Pierce

ISBN 1 874739 23 4

Printed by Watkiss Studios, Biggleswade, Bedfordshire

*To Miguel, for reminding us of the meaning
of hope, joy and pride.*

About the Author

Javier García Sánchez was born in Barcelona in 1955. He is a well-known novelist and a long-established contributor of sports articles for the Press. For several years he has covered the Tour de France as correspondent for the Spanish daily *El Mundo*. In 1994 he published the critically acclaimed novel *El Alpe d'Huez*, based around one of the toughest stages in the Tour.

About the Translator

Jeremy Munday is currently a Senior Lecturer at the University of Surrey, specializing in translation theory and Spanish–English translation with a particular interest in sport. He also works as a freelance translator for Unesco. His publications include *Introducing Translation Studies* as well as translations of modern Spanish American fiction.

*The Publishers would like to dedicate this English edition to Jackie
and Jill, two of Miguel Induráin's greatest supporters*

Author's Acknowledgements

Benito Urraburu, Pablo Muñoz and Christian Laborde all
wrote insightful books about the Navarran champion before
me. My acknowledgements go to them. And also to those
colleagues who, in the Tour Press rooms – which every day
were a new adventure – often racked their brains to find
the words to explain something as inexplicable and
beautiful as Induráin's cycling career. They were the ones
who put voice and sense to the amazing five years. The
music came from Miguel.

J. G. S.

Publishers' Acknowledgements

The publishers would like to thank Jeremy Munday for his
translation from the original Spanish; Jeremy Mallard for
allowing us to reproduce his limited-edition print 'Riding
into History'; John Pierce and Photosport International for
providing all the photographs we have used throughout;
and Sean Kelly for agreeing without a moment's hesitation
to write a Foreword to this edition.

Publishers' Note

Miguel Induráin was a giant of cycle-racing both in physical stature and in his outstanding performances. However, in our eyes and in the eyes of his many fans he was never given the full credit for his remarkable racing ability and, more specifically, for his aggression and panache throughout his incredible career. The first man to win the Tour de France five times in succession, it was often his outstanding time-trialing ability that made the news and not his frequent dominating performances in the mountains. It was this ability in the toughest mountains of the Tour, unique for so large a man, which prompted Eddy Merckx to say, 'I had to see it to believe it.' But, with the help of a jealous French Press these performances were often disregarded or pushed into the background, and this distorted view was, unfortunately, often adopted by the more cynical and lazy press and media of other nations which could not, or would not, open their eyes to his unique style and unheralded generosity to others which often gave his greatest rivals more than their deserved share of glory.

Specific examples are too numerous to mention here, but they are well documented in this book, and formed a large part of the reason why we wanted to publish it in English. We wanted to set the record straight about Miguel Induráin, the gentle giant of cycle-racing, and his so-called 'lack of panache'. He was a man with an outstanding sense of spirit, who showed great kindness to his team-mates and fellow riders, but who, when the occasion demanded and he needed to prove that he was, quite simply, the best, could be so ruthless with his power and pure talent.

Richard Allchin & Adrian Bell

When they ask me what religion I belong to,
I'll say, to the Col de Marie Blanque …

KENNETH WHITE

You are not so great
Nor so special,
You seem natural,
You are the South,
It is you, it is you…

LUZ CASAL

CONTENTS

FOREWORD

In many ways Miguel was the cool, clean hero of his era on the bike in the nineties. He was a very quiet man, and often only spoke when you made the effort to speak to him. But as a person, he was easy to get on with: in some respects you could even say that he was a timid man. When compared to the other big stars who had gone before him, he never tried to control the peloton and often left the riders to sort themselves out. Whoever was in the breakaway, whether it was the most important or the least important rider, he never shouted or got excited. Miguel had his job to do and he did it with style, together with his team, who often did the necessary work for him.

Miguel was a man who was well liked amongst the riders; you would never hear a bad word about him. All of the other big riders had some bad things said about them and they would have enemies in the peloton. They were not universally liked; Miguel was.

As a bike rider – well, what can you say? He won five Tours in succession and they were as hard to win then as they are now. He was a very good all-rounder which he proved in the big tours and in the many other different types of races he won. Miguel was not a greedy rider: he did what he had to do, no more, no less. On many occasions he allowed other riders to win stages and share in his glory when he could have won many more stages himself. He did not set out to totally dominate the races: on many occasions he followed, and his team did the work, so they achieved the wins without all the fuss and yelling that we had seen in the past. I think that you have to give credit to him for this and not detract from his wins or the methods by which he achieved his goals and ambitions.

Miguel could have won more major Classics like Liège–Bastogne–Liège, the Classic San Sebastian which he won only the once, and, of course, the World Championships, except that he chose mainly to concentrate on the Tour instead. In the World's Road-Race he came very close on a number of occasions, and I particularly remember his team-mate, Olano's, victory in Colombia in 1995 when again his generosity shone though and he came second. This was after Miguel had already won the Time-Trial title. Of course, he won his own country's Road-Race Champion-ship during the years of his Tour supremacy, as well as many other major events throughout his great career.

A nice man from a lovely country, and I hope he is enjoying his retirement.

Sean Kelly

Picture reproduced by kind permission of Jeremy Mallard,
from his limited-edition print 'Riding into History'
© Jeremy Mallard

Allegro con Fuocco

(The Cold)

BOTTLES FOR NEKANE

It was all the wind's fault. Its whistling, its silent calling, which would urge him to fly. Like the mountain eagle.

Or maybe it was the cold, such an unforgiving temperature for a good part of the year, while the rest of the time the heat scorches the fields. It's a land which produces tough and hardy people. They grow up in houses whose roofs are battered in the winter by icy, gusting winds. It was in one of those houses, number 2, San Andrés Street in Villava, that Miguel Induráin Larraya was born on 16 July 1964.

Nothing visibly changed in the neighbourhood, apart from the understandable upheaval within the family, and the nearby roads remained quiet, including the one that runs from Huarte to the Esteribar valley and finally disappears into the heart of the Pyrenees.

And yet the cold must have known that a special child had been born, right there in a two-storey house in a village that's almost swallowed up by the city of Pamplona. A child who would learn in his heart to hang on in there and do his own thing. He was a gangling, dark-haired child who would succeed in composing the perfect poem, in conjuring poetry without writing verses. To get others to do it for him. To get others to gaze at these valleys and these skies, thinking, 'He was born here…'

Nothing changed in the little streets of Villava itself, nor around the San Andrés papermill. Yet the wind must have known. The news must have been passed on by the rustling of the nearby beechwoods, the bone-hard bark of the trees, the dull thud coming from the rocks, the barely perceptible quivering of the moss and the ferns, there, in the darkest, dankest corners of the obstinate wood. Those parts of the forest that choose who they want to reveal themselves to. Wild areas where only explorers and pioneers set foot. That was where Miguel Induráin senior would take his eldest

3

son to shoot wood pigeons. Hours spent silently waiting, and exactly the same scenario would be repeated years later during Miguel's cycling career. To retain your composure in the face of any predicament, that was the secret.

But the ungrateful wind of the mountain would know that: it must have been informed by the terrified fields of maize, the trembling ears of corn, the motionless sacks of grain, the vines which Miguel's father planted and tended with such care and attention. And Miguel, the son, was watching. That gaze would help him learn to be a man. If he gazed upwards he would be able to feel the grandeur of Roncesvalles, that place brimming with disputes and troubles, of suffering and war, but a beautiful place despite its history. And further east the mountains of Aralar. Right there, the mountains of Abodi, of Leyre, of Codés and of Urbasa.

He grew up and lived, then, in the uplands, surrounded by mountains, but perhaps that was how he learned to be as stealthy as a cat, as discreet as those animals of the dark wood who know full well that their survival depends on containing their movements, on their reflexes at a critical instant when predators or birds of prey are attacking. In people, this translates into words and deeds. Miguel was always frugal with words, and he measured his deeds to a fraction of a millimetre. Out of wisdom or shyness, who knows?

Only the wind knows. It always knew. But that's its secret. In a sense, it belongs to both of them. That's why, whenever he can, Miguel goes off to the mountains, with or without his hunting rifle, because, in the end, whether or not he bags a dove is just an excuse. The mountain is most definitely a refuge for him. He goes walking there alone, to be with himself and his thoughts – a ritual he often performs, and will continue to perform, even though, during the crazy period of his victorious Tours, it wasn't as often as Miguel would have liked. There was always a moment for secrets and tranquillity. But it's surely the cold wind of the mountain which knows Miguel and his feelings best. The paradox is, and this may be disheartening when you are trying to put together some kind of biography (and let's not go into whether the aim of this book is a string of juicy anecdotes or a host of outspoken opinions): there's apparently very little to know about this man. I say 'apparently' because his inner world, like anybody's, belongs to a different realm. But on the bike, and away from it as well, Miguel Induráin always behaved with a modesty which sometimes left us stunned and, of course, eager to know more about him. That wasn't possible; we shouldn't have needed to know more. He was what he was. And he was what he has always been – and would always be – a gentleman of the fields. Anything else is lies, rumour or flights of fancy, or all three put together.

Miguel's face is characteristic and defining, like those of the people of northern Spain who have been isolated from other cultures for centuries, or rather who have clung with stubborn and healthy desperation to their traditions so as not to lose their own way in life. It's stony and verging on the expressionless, with bushy eyebrows, a tiny mouth; and with high cheekbones when he was getting towards the end of the Tour. The people of the north don't smile easily. They may frame a gesture which suggests friendliness and a readiness to chat, but even then they find it hard to show it. They are tough, but not rough, people, with cheekbones that have seemingly been chiselled out, and eyes that are imperceptibly sunk in their skull. They have an intense, but not an aggressive, look. They are simple, good and noble people who have withstood the difficult challenge of surviving in a natural environment that isn't always pleasant and comfortable.

These are country people, and teasing a single expression of feeling out of them is often like squeezing blood from a stone. Nevertheless, they can be incredibly warm when you get to know them, when they open up. They aren't extrovert or nervous people, nor, of course, meek and mild. The opposite is more often the case: behind the armour of a lack of facial expression beats a combative heart.

Curiously, the Basque name for Villava is Atarrabia. Yes, Atarrabia, which has a resonance linked to the supernatural and to war: the place inhabited by those who have an irrepressible but tempered rage.

As a young boy Miguel certainly looked in the direction of the Larrau mountain pass, and he didn't like what he saw. Just as he would never like the climb up to Bagordi, with its 13 per cent gradients. Nor would he be on friendly terms with the ascent to the Lakes of Covadonga. Tough mountain passes with an undulating gradient, such as Oropa, where a murderous road constantly checked your rhythm. That's why he loved the Pyrenean passes, the Tourmalet and the Aubisque, immense and unending, or the Alpine climbs, such as Izoard or the Galibier, even Alpe d'Huez, or the solitary and torrid Mont Ventoux, where it's uphill all the way. No messing around with your rhythm.

And, perhaps instinctively, he always knew Larrau was treacherous. Climbing through desolate meadows and wind-whipped gorges, where the July sun beats mercilessly down, the fearsome ascent with treacherous 17 per cent stretches, was something that was never to Miguel's liking. Maybe as a boy, and then as a young man, whenever people started speaking about Larrau, he would frown, as though he were on his guard. 'That's a heck of a climb.' But junior cyclists were not made to climb Larrau, but Badordi, and they all feared it. Soudet or Samport, or Portalet were longer climbs, with more pedigree, but Miguel had less fear of them. There, at least, you could pedal for all you were worth, which would mean the climbers wouldn't take too much time out of you by the summit.

But there was a long way to go before the wheel of destiny would turn full circle and indicate that an era was over. Larrau would have a lot to say in the matter, although on that sad and fateful day in the '96 Tour the wind wasn't blowing on Larrau. A suffocating, baking sun seemed to have laid out the thousands of Spanish fans, mainly Basque and Navarran, who had flocked there to cheer on their hero. No wind, no air, which was something the favourite son of those lands would also feel, as, slowly but surely, he realised he was done for. He had admitted as much shortly before he set off on what could have been his sixth successive Tour victory: 'I think when the time comes when I stop winning, it'll be a liberation which will put an end to some of my suffering.'

He had given notice, like the wind before the storm, that he was physically and psychologically exhausted, but we still didn't want to see it. We just wanted more and more Tours, like someone collecting stickers. And the man himself, the wind's favourite, began once more to experience the anxiety of solitude, and of peace, which the whirlwind of events had made it impossible for him to achieve before.

I asked Miguel once, 'How on earth do you put up with all the hassle?' I was referring to the way he was so relaxed in the face of the huge pressure of people asking him for favours, more than with any movie or popstar, more than anyone involved in culture, or even other sports. By then he had retired from cycling, but he would be constantly stopped wherever he went. 'You simply have to do it,' he told me. 'But back then,' I ventured referring to the immediate past, 'in the middle of a Tour, what with race nerves and all that?' 'Back then, too.'

That's exactly what he said. I realised he had won five straight Tours because it was his *mission*. In the same way as it was for him to be polite to people. Behind that attitude lay the ultimate secret of his victories, although he has been humble enough to deny it. Or at least to shrug his shoulders with the hint of the cryptic smile of a strong, shy man, satisfied with himself and with the life that was his lot. It was the life he chose.

But he was also kind and considerate. I remember one race when someone had asked him to pose for a photo beside him. Him sitting, and the other person standing. At that very moment Induráin had turned to one side to listen to the person on his right, but then realised that the photo would show him looking away from the camera. Miguel called the photographer back and posed again with the fan. All that, to make sure he could get his photo with the Champ.

'Go on, take it again, because I was looking the other way, OK?' he joked. Not even the person who asked for the photo could understand such insistence and treatment. Incredible. A simple, silent detail, but one which probably remains frozen for ever in a frame behind glass, on a wall of someone's home.

You have to have been in a Tour to understand the infinite pressure to which the Yellow Jersey and its pretenders are submitted, for a whole month. Everyone who comes up to you, every movement around you, is always to ask you for something, to remind you about something, or demand something from you. Something as strange and yet as normal as 'You mustn't let the nation down tomorrow.' It's worth putting yourself in the shoes of someone who's under such constant pressure, that sense of being hemmed in which ends up causing you stomach ache, dizziness, vomiting and fear. This, extrapolated to an unimaginable degree, is what Miguel Induráin had to cope with, and he did it better than anyone, because his exceptional character meant he never put up barriers or obstacles to people who came up to have a few words with him. It was a very different matter getting him on his own. He became a consummate master of slipping away, wandering off somewhere or other, like a soul in limbo, like a lost ghost. There again, he always had Francis Lafargue by his side to act as a filter. More than a thousand interviews a year are enough to exhaust anyone.

There's a cliché image of Miguel Induráin, measuring his words on a drip-feed, steering away from controversial subjects, or even any forthright opinion that might be challenged. To a certain extent he's like that, and has never denied it. It's a characteristic recognised by those who knew him when he was a youngster, those who forged the champion's career over the years. That's why it's especially problematic to deal with him in a biography, since he's a young man who really never had a youth, because he devoted it to his bicycle. The cumulative effect of all this may suggest that Miguel Induráin became a legend as soon as he won his first Tour. Every idol has a weakness. Not him. They all have some skeleton in the cupboard. Not him. They all say what they shouldn't at an inappropriate moment. Or the other way round, they keep quiet when what is expected of them is some forthright statement. Not him. He just kept on pedalling. He had a literary mysteriousness about him.

And if very little could be extracted from Miguel himself, to satisfy the voracious appetites of the media, he was lucky enough to be flanked by two men who, though very different in character, were ideal for protecting the legend, for sheltering it in adversity, and for dampening the collective hysteria that seemed to break out during that golden five-year run.

One was Eusebio Unzúe, the man who signed him for the Reynolds team from the ranks of the Club Ciclista Villavés. Unzúe is the perfect gentleman, a man of exquisite manners who was always ready to give you whatever you wanted so you wouldn't get frustrated with Miguel. Eusebio, who followed Induráin's development day by day for years on end and, in fact, was perhaps the first to realise that here was a potential winner of the Tour de France, still acknowledges that Miguel is what he is, and there isn't much anyone can do to change it. He says what he has to say, and no one, not even these two men, can reach his deepest feelings, his dreams. And you simply have to respect and accept that as part of his character. 'Even I am taken aback sometimes at some of the things he does before or at the end of a stage, for example,' Eusebio told me in the middle of a Tour. In a way, you could say that Miguel always improvised. His genius did the rest. The customary absence of words from the champion certainly meant that for more than five years men such as Eusebio Unzúe had to use their wits to fill the verbal gaps, which, when he wanted them to be, could be very sophisticated and complex.

The other man in Induráin's life, José Miguel Echávarri, also played his part in forging the legend of the champion away from his triumphs on the roads. Echávarri is the very opposite of Induráin: talkative, seductive, a lover of the understatement and grammatical turns of phrase; gifted at wordplay, he also spoke for Miguel. That is, he told half the world's Press, and particularly the Spanish fans, what they would have liked to have heard from the mouth of Miguel Induráin. It's only that, with Echávarri, something specific happened which, I think, contributed in some measure to putting the finishing touches to the legend. Until 1993 he tended to restrict his comments about Induráin purely to his sporting achievements. From that year on, and as if after some secret and intimate moment of reflection, Echávarri began to speak about the Navarran champion in somewhat more ambiguous terms. His remarks never went completely overboard in admiration, yet, at the same time, they left some hint of the religious in their wake. Perhaps it all started as a kind of joke when he said that when he approached Induráin he often had the strange feeling that, as he put it, 'he was entering a religious building'. A church, a cathedral. Coming from people with religious convictions this takes on a very important and specific meaning. Before the Tour of Alentejo in Portugal, he said 'It has been by the grace of God that this land of rich pastures and healthy cork trees has enjoyed Miguel's cycling skills.' From that moment on, religious vocabulary such as 'Induráin, the God of the Tour', and so on, began to abound in the Press, and not just the sports magazines. Even in France, one daily newspaper not commonly given to praising things Spanish adopted the religious reference. I particularly remember after the Hautacam stage, when Miguel destroyed everybody in the 1994 Tour, *L'Équipe* carried the headline: 'The Law of the Lord'. In the same paper, they referred to Miguel as *Lui* – Him – with a capital letter, paving the way for that strange, mystical or, if you prefer, inexplicably supernatural feeling which sometimes takes hold of us.

But Echávarri, an able communicator and number-one Induráin fan, merely opened up a path, a particular way of speaking. The tone had mystical and religious allusions, and was never anything other than one of absolute respect. It went forth and multiplied, and seemed completely normal. I recall a talk I gave on cycling, years back, where I was happy to play along with the 'game'. Whenever I was asked about Miguel Induráin the cyclist, I would answer in all seriousness, 'But we're speaking about Our Lord God.' People were rather taken aback, but – and here is the proof that the phenomenon worked – they quickly took up the idea as an accepted commonplace. In cycling terms, seeing him pass by in yellow was as if we'd glimpsed the presence of God. No one was ever scandalised by this. On the contrary, in the last stage of Induráin's career the religious metaphor had virtually become a trademark of some of the media. The truth is, we were witnessing a kind of ongoing miracle, which, in the circumstances, went on an incredible length of time.

The presence of Miguel Induráin on the road customarily did have a touch of the divine about it, an inexplicable yet comforting aura which made us believe that he raced on a higher plane, while the other riders were mere desperate mortals, good sportsmen, struggling to reach his heights. And when I say 'us' I mean not only Spanish fans but fans the world over, starting with the French, through their official organ of propaganda, *L'Équipe*. I remember another joke in *L'Équipe*: a sketch in which a large group of cyclists were strewn over the ground after a real hammering. It was like a scene from the Apocalypse. The sky was slashed by thunder and lightning. A little voice asked, 'Who's caused all this mayhem?' And the reply, '*Lui, évidemment…*' 'Him, of course.' I think it was after the time-trial at Lac du Madine in the '93 Tour.

In one way or another legends develop for very specific reasons. In the case of Miguel, the lack of information or facts contributed to a large extent to consolidating the legend, even when he was still active and had only just started winning. Then, with that eternal glorification of the five straight Tours, even we became lost for words, and also for religious allusions. There was a time when, as a joke, whenever Induráin appeared on TV, I would tell the kids, 'On your knees and pray!' And they would stare at me, not sure if I was being serious or not. On another occasion, travelling in the North of Spain, we passed a roadsign to Pamplona. Once again I told them we had to get out of the car and kneel. They were unsure. It was all part of a series of in-jokes, but I also recognise – and I am sure the same thing happened to a large number of Spaniards – that symbolically we did get on our knees whenever Induráin steamrollered his rivals, and displayed his strength and class. I suppose it was the only way I had of coming to terms, psychologically, with the phenomenon which, by sheer chance, I had been lucky enough to experience at first hand.

In the '95 Tour, which would be his fifth and final victory, and the most spectacular, I promised I would kiss the ground on the Tourmalet if Miguel reached it wearing the yellow jersey. I did so, at the summit of that climb, as graphic proof of my total admiration for the career of the great champion, but also as an expression of emotion because I knew I was standing in a mythical and sublime place in cycling history.

And something deep inside me told me I wasn't the first to make that kind of gesture. Nor the last. Cycling, especially in the big mountains, has a peculiar epic quality that is difficult to explain to those who have never shared the passion, never mind the curiosity, for this beautiful and savage sport.

It's therefore a problem knowing how to construct the human and psychological profile of a cyclist who gave his life to the sport and who, if he did wear a mask, did so when he wasn't racing. That attitude of his was mostly a means of self-defence. I am thinking here of an anecdote that did the rounds during Miguel's victorious tours. Apparently, in the first Tour, a French journalist had seen a book entitled *The Sicilian* in his room. He never finished it. Years later, so they say, he appeared carrying another best-seller, *Goodbye, Baby*. They suggested his reading pace was not exactly sparkling. 'I'm getting through it, gradually,' he replied. Indeed, he must have been carrying that book around, intending to finish it some day, but who knows how much free time a Tour winner allows himself amongst the frenzied dashing from hotel to hotel, and with countless engagements to keep? What might he be reading when he's on his own, in the peace of his home? Who knows? But he'll be reading something, no doubt.

Over time I reached the conclusion that it isn't possible to read and to win five straight Tours as he did. There is a time for everything. Other riders read to relax, normally anything so long as it isn't too complicated. He, apparently, does not. He had enough on his plate reading the daily Book of Life, a book that's a peloton of almost 200 cyclists, each of whom has his own problems and desires, strategies, and tactics. Induráin once said that, yes, perhaps he had 'been born a champion, but he hadn't been brought up as one'. Indeed, perhaps that's something he never fully managed. A champion who wants to have everybody eating out of his hand will say he's reading the 'in' book of the moment (there's always one 'must-read' book if you want to appear trendy), or listening to the current music. It gives the impression he has his own life, that he's more than someone who merely pedals a bike. Miguel didn't do that. He restricted himself to reading the Book of Life, focusing especially on the chapter devoted to the life of cyclists. Each stage was a bloody and murderous war, and it was his responsibility alone to learn the lesson well. The daily reading of the peloton, of the ins and outs of something as complex as the Tour de France, and applying what he'd learned instantaneously in order to achieve the desired end – doesn't that perhaps represent another type of reading? A reading of hidden passions and bitterness, of moves and reactions aborted in time, of dealing with demanding strangers – isn't that the greatest imaginable martyrdom for a person as shy as he is?

It was the same story whenever he was asked about his taste in music. The mask would go up again. First he spoke about the singer–songwriter Serrat, then the pop-group Mecano. Then, for a long time, his reply would be the Spanish pop singer Luz Casal. 'Why Luz Casal in particular?' they would insist. In the end, Miguel would restrict himself to the reply, 'Well, I see what you're getting at.' I remain convinced that it was simply a mask with which he learned to protect his privacy. If you stop and think about it, that limited and restricted privacy was all the champion really had for himself, and even then only ever in small doses. In order to understand some of Miguel's replies which could sometimes be brusque – or terse, at least – you need to reflect on what it means to have no privacy whatsoever.

What could he particularly have seen in Luz Casal? That's the wrong question. It ought to be: why shouldn't he like Luz Casal? That's simple. It's well-written music, and the lyrics are mainly about love. It's sometimes delicate, at other times bitter, and always original. Nostalgic subjects, to wallow in, and to conjure up a sad mood throughout the excruciatingly long hours when you're on the road and living in hotels. To think about Marisa, so far away. Or about the family. But the mere choice of such music shows how warm Induráin could be. Otherwise, his choice would have been different.

Hard, tenacious, and confirmed by his whole make-up – from his physique to his reflexes – Miguel was a man of the north. But, then again, he wasn't: he was also tender and, in his own way, of course, warm. That's the reason for the choice of a verse from a Luz Casal song to open this book. Ideally, the verb tenses would have been slightly altered:

> *You weren't so great*
> *Nor so special,*
> *You seemed so natural,*
> *You were the South,*
> *It was you, it was you …*

And that's exactly how Miguel must have felt amidst all the delirium caused by his successes over the best part of a decade. What else could he do, but flee again, and again, in each new interview when he was asked about his favourite music. It's absolutely certain that he didn't think he was so great nor so special. And in his heart of hearts he was convinced he was a passionate person, albeit with a placid character. You could bet your bottom dollar on that. In spite of everything, the cold and the wind, the ingratitude of the valleys and the inevitable mask, he was a man of the South, because the Pyrenees, the symbolic dividing line between two worlds, was further up, beyond the clouds and the woods. And, as a young man, he would conquer them, even though he was a man of the South.

For the moment, and for a long time to come, he would have to content himself with the steep chain of mountains surrounding his homeland: Iparla, Ortzanzurieta, and all the others. And beyond those, more pointed crests that rise up when the mists part, protruding proudly through a thick white mantle: Montejurra, Ujué, the Higa del Perdón and the Higa de Monreal, another short but extremely tough pass whose inclines make it, perhaps along with Gamoneteiro pass in Asturias, the fiercest challenge for cyclists in Spain.

But, in all probability, he didn't think about the mountains much as a boy. They were simply there, in his blood. He knew, because there are things instinct tells us long before they happen, that he would devote his best and greatest efforts to them. He was a tall, sturdy boy, weighing more than 90 kilos. On a bike he had considerable brute force, but a climb's a climb, especially when it's more than a kilometre long. His problem, therefore, was to maintain a rhythm throughout an ascent. But he was working on it.

There is a story of a couple of waiters who, seeing him struggling up the famous Beloso climb which joins up with the Pamplona road, bet that the big, lanky kid wouldn't make it to the top. They both bet against him! And Miguel made it, although bathed with sweat. 'Imagine the poor kid on Bagordi.' 'Or on Larrau.'

Within a few years the poor kid was to put his home town of Villava on the lips of half the world. Villava, the birthplace of the man who was to be, perhaps, the most complete rider of all time. According to the Sicilian writer Leonardo Sciascia, a man is what his first ten years of life have made him. In that sense, Miguel Induráin was extremely fortunate to have a home life filled with happiness and with people who loved him. He had a brother, Prudencio, who would also become a cyclist and who, throughout the whole of the champion's career, would be a kind of racing bodyguard for him – the centurion-in-chief of Emperor Miguel's praetorian guard, which would have a series of famous names in its ranks: Gorospe, Uriarte, Alonso, Nijboer. And Pruden, of course: he was always there. But, as a child, there were his sisters, too, Isabel, Nekane and Asunción. And his cousins, Daniel, Javier, and Luis. Tere, as well, the owner of a perfume store in the very centre of the village. She was the influence behind Miguel's purchases of Esencia, de Loewe or Cacharel. Later, after he got married, it was Marisa who took care of that kind of detail.

But Tere Uriz touched a raw nerve when she described the psychological pressure on every single member of the family. They were country folk, very open, serious but polite, so that when the house began to fill with journalists, they would offer them all a drop of wine and a bite of *chorizo*. It seems the reporters began to take advantage of this, and there were even cases of them leaping over the garden fence to get into the house, and stealing photos from the family albums. They were constantly pursued by the paparazzi who were willing to go to any length to get an exclusive photo or some indiscreet statement from a member of the family. No way were they going to get that. Tere Uriz herself describes Miguel as a quiet, mild-mannered lad. Although, in fact, there was some age difference between the boys and the girls, they used to play keep-ball together.

Between the four walls and the backyard of number 2, San Andrés Street, Miguel had all a kid could want in terms of amusement and, above all, other kids to play and relax with. Amongst his father's vines and the ploughed fields, they invented all types of games: wars, pretend fights from tree to tree, as well as hide-and-seek, and they exchanged secrets and dreams.

The first classrooms Miguel knew were in the Lorenzo Goicoa school, where he remained until the fifth year. People's memories of that time are a bit blurred, but one classmate, Ángel María Armendáriz, says that Miguel was only an average pupil, that he just scraped through each year because his family would pressure him to study. In addition, after school Miguel would have to help his father with the farmwork. According to Armendáriz, in the afternoons when the children went out to play, running in and out of the village streets, they would sometimes see Miguel driving the tractor. In the games he occasionally played with the other kids, there was still no sign of a bicycle. In autumn they would play a form of conkers, seeing who could throw them the furthest. And they say that Miguel had a special technique, an upward throwing motion used by the shepherds in the area.

There is one fact Armendáriz remembers, however, would be influential in the future: 'Sometimes he would let me copy the homework the teachers had given us.' Hints of Isola–2000 and those hands on the brake-levers, allowing Rominger to cross the line first.*

So that Miguel could go to the same school as his cousins, his parents enrolled him in year six in Larraona school, on Avenue Pío XII in Pamplona; it was a new building opposite the Navarre University Hospital. It's from that time onwards that we have testimony from those who witnessed his outstanding performances in all the sports he tried his hand at. He used to like table tennis, and basketball, in which his height gave him a considerable advantage. Football and athletics too. He ended up playing in defence for Beti Onak, the local Villava football team. As far as athletics was concerned, he loved the javelin and middle-distance running. But, it seems the 400-metres was his favourite event. In the middle distance races he showed good stamina, although he lacked a sprint finish. During this time he even took part in a TV programme, *The Record Way*, in which youngsters from all over Spain participated. He did quite well, and some people claim that that was the first time they saw him on the small screen.

Nevertheless, his passion for sport began to sit uneasily beside his studies and his responsibilities to his father's work in the fields. After finishing his general education he enrolled in the Navarre Professional Training College in Potasas, opting to study Tool Engineering, as ever with a view to helping his father in the fields. Even as a small child Miguel was able to park the tractor with a couple of turns of the wheel, and he never changed. Returning from his second Tour victory in '92, he designed and built the large iron gate for his parents' house, the pride of Isabel Larraya.

Yet the wind continued to call him, whispering sweet melodies in his ear which he alone could understand, since they were coded and indecipherable for any other person. That same wind would push him on to Blois, Luxembourg, Bergerac, Lac Vassivière.

It is said that Miguel was very impressed by the story told him by one of his gymnastics teachers about Lee Evans' 400-metre record in Mexico. Apparently, Evans was incensed because his

---

* A reference to stage twelve of the 1993 Tour de France when Induráin, having resisted all Rominger's attacks, let him take the stage.

friend, Tommy Smith, had been expelled from the Olympic Village for raising his black-gloved fist – a very controversial symbol in the United States at the time, as it referred to the Black Panthers and Black Power. Evans didn't want to run the 400 and it was his wife who almost had to drag him out into the arena, hissing that, if he really wanted 'revenge', he should achieve it by humiliating them on the track. This fired up Lee Evans, who went out into the Olympic stadium in Mexico City and took up his position in lane six. His eyes were glazed, he showed no emotion and his concentration was total. Although he started badly, he soon accelerated phenomenally. He hit the tape at 44 seconds.

This was a true story and not a myth, unlike so many of the anecdotes that have built up over the years around the figure of Miguel. But the part of this story that must have made the deepest impression on him was that, when asked about the secret of his success, Lee Evans had solemnly declared: 'I win because I am able to endure greater pain than the rest.' This was what that gymnastics teacher told him, and, even had the anecdote been apocryphal, it seems certain Miguel would have made a mental note of its message.

So, at the end of the day, it all came down to pain. Not to vital, innate qualities, not to luck or perseverance, but mainly to pain. Pain pure and simple.

Whenever he gained an apparently easy victory he would be accused, even if the criticism was couched in warm words of praise, of giving the impression that he didn't suffer or really have to make an effort, that he dominated without exerting himself. And he always maintained this wasn't so. Perhaps he should have spoken of Lee Evans and his theory of prolonged and excruciating pain, which destroys the senses but grants dignity upon an athlete, and a man. That's something that will never be understood by those who aren't passionate about sport. All the better.

But there's another fact that fits perfectly with that school story of Miguel and the Lee Evans anecdote. He already had three Tours under his belt and he was preparing to go for the fourth, when a French journalist from *Vélo* magazine asked him about the ease with which, up till then, he'd achieved his successes. Miguel politely responded in the normal way. No, he really had to battle for his wins, he said, and behind each triumph there was a whole catalogue of suffering and privation. But the reporter stood his ground. Then Miguel gave one of those replies which, because of their brevity and conciseness seem to mean little, but which, in fact, delve into a whole coded world: 'I've been a very long way down the road of pain,' he said. It was simply Lee Evans's old theory resurfacing, and, in reality, the theory of all the great champions, even if they never actually expressed it. It isn't a case of being the best, but of being able to suffer more than the rest. Of being able to withstand searing pain, when it tears at you, without giving up or lowering your guard.

That route, that road of pain to which Miguel Induráin modestly alluded, is the great secret of his glittering career, as much if not more so than his well-known, and amazing physical qualities. Other cyclists, and other sportsmen and women who battle in other events, possess similar physical qualities, and yet they don't stand out like Miguel. In fact, on one occasion the claim was made that, on paper, in the laboratory, Pruden's physical capacity was practically the same as that of his elder brother. But the role assigned to Pruden was different. Sometimes he was asked to suffer, on other occasions he was allowed a more comfortable ride, but whichever, his renowned physical capacity would always remain there, just waiting to be summoned into action. Pruden's situation, we should remember, was quite peculiar, but that isn't so for the very many great cyclists who, in the gym and in front of teams of medical experts, produce startling results but who go to pieces on the road without anyone really knowing why. The reason for this, what makes some fall apart while others hang on in there in silent torment, is perhaps the main point behind writing this book. Personally speaking, I have less interest in a straightforward retelling of the life story of a leading figure such as Induráin than in an investigation, albeit a modest and tangential one, into the subject of pain, of suffering in sport. The fact that he could hide it better or worse than others is another matter.

As far as pain goes, there's one particular moment ...

Perhaps that is how this story should have begun.

As far as pain goes, there's one particular moment which distinguishes some people from others. Maybe, for those who are unfamiliar with the world of competitive sport, this will seem like overstating the point, but it's true: the only secret is in finding out who will withstand a constant, sharp, lacerating pain the longest. Although, of course, there are tens, if not hundreds of factors which affect the athlete–pain relationship: positive or negative thoughts; lack of preparation; the heat or cold; humidity, or rain; ambition; problems under which each individual silently toils, but which can have a lasting effect on an athlete's performance.

They say Eddie Merckx was fiercely ambitious, and Bernard Hinault, as well. On the road, Hinault is said to have decided who was to make a break and who was to stay. In fact, this is what Miguel ended up doing, too. As for Merckx, the most successful cyclist in history, there's a story concerning a short local race in the north of Spain that sums him up best. Everyone knew that the Cannibal, as Merckx was commonly known, would sprint even for the primes. He wanted to win everything. But that day he mistook a hoarding on a corner of the road for another intermediate sprint, and he raced off towards it. It turned out to be a banner for the Spanish Communist Party, at that time a clandestine movement! Jacques Anquetil, on the other hand, was more cerebral: he knew his limitations, especially in the big mountains.

There's another category of champion, to which Miguel Induráin possibly belongs, for whom ambition isn't the be-all and end-all; indeed, they even have to make an effort to feel ambition. Instead, they are spurred on by the desire to see a job well done, by a generosity of effort, by seeing the joy their victories bring, which surprises them at first, even though they end up getting used to it. That is where the cohabitation with pain starts to take root, to be moulded like plasticine by skilful fingers. They are the modest artisans of suffering itself.

You often hear it said that some sports do in fact resemble a kind of torture, and doubtless competitive cycling would be right up there amongst them. I agree with this view, but at the same time I try not to forget that for professional cyclists that's how they earn their living. It was their choice; nobody forced them to do it. There's no human or social pressure that makes you, day after day, ride up a mountain, pursuing or being pursued, while you feel you're about to cough your guts up. From a very young age cyclists know what awaits them. It's just that some withstand it and others don't. But just as no two people will react in the same way to the same circumstance – to the despicable act of torture during wartime, for example – so also in sport an instinctive reaction triggers some to say 'Enough!' and others to say 'Just a bit more!' This does not mean some are braver than others, but it does mean they are essentially different. From the outset, some allow the presence of pain in their lives; others crack. In spite of seeming to exaggerate, I do believe that the parallel with physical torture is a good example of what I'm trying to convey. Great and brave resistance fighters have gone to pieces with the mere threat of torture. Others, with less ideological commitment, have been able to stand firm at the crucial moment of their lives, when they were about to be deliberately and viciously harmed. It isn't a case of a specific human quality, but of a certain inexplicable quality of spirit, which sometimes comes as a surprise even to those who discover they possess it.

In this vein, one day Miguel had endured the searing but incisive pain of running a lung-bursting 400-metres. He wanted more. He tried a bike. He gritted his teeth. To his amazement, he left almost all his rivals in the village trailing in his wake. Including his cousins. There was always a lot of competitive needle between them and Miguel – the kind of thing that always happens amongst children.

But I know that on another day his generosity shone through. He decided he wanted to take part in and win a local cycle race for youngsters, because he'd discovered that the winner would receive a sandwich and a soft drink. His sister, Nekane, needed the empty drinks containers to use as bottles for her baby dolls, and Miguel wanted to please her. He only ever had one thought in his head: to make his family happy. In the first race he came second. In the next one, which involved two circuits of the village of Villava, he won fairly comfortably. By that time, the boy, with his father's guidance, had signed for the Club Ciclista Villavés, and Pepe Barruso, the boss, had given him some pertinent advice: 'Keep it clean, no underhand tricks or zigzagging. Everyone just rides his own race.' For Miguel his 'own race' meant riding elegantly (even way back then), with his elbows tucked into his ribs, his back bent over and hardly lifting himself off the saddle. He won and got his soft drinks. And Nekane was happy to be able to play at feeding her dolls properly.

In the village there was another lad called Joaquín Marcos who was the best and used to win all the races in Villava and the surrounding area. Until Miguel arrived on the scene, that is, although even Miguel took a year and a half to reach Marcos' standard; Marcos was a year older than him, which is an important advantage at junior level.

Looking back on those early races, it's possible to conclude that, apart from his love of cycling, Miguel rode them primarily to get those bottles for Nekane. Deep down, I have the suspicion that what Miguel Induráin wanted throughout his whole cycling life was one day to win the Tour de France. But it was *one* Tour he was after, not *five*. The reason he then became embroiled in one challenge after another was simply to satisfy the demands of others, the whole mass of people focusing on him and his exploits. At least, that was the case up until the third Tour. After that, if he managed to find time to stop and think about anything – which had hardly been possible before – he realised he was capable of equalling the record five Tour wins of Anquetil, Merckx, and Hinault. His relative dominance in the fourth Tour must have convinced him of that: he had his rivals – several generations of them – running scared. So, it was just a question of making a final thrust, of summoning up one last effort, of working the miracle: then the five Tours, consecutive ones in his case, would be his – something nobody had ever done before. It was a prodigious period.

I maintain, as I did in 1994 after Miguel's fourth Tour, that he was then dreaming of those five Tours. He had fulfilled the aspiration of one day winning the Tour de France – the high point for any cyclist – and then, the Tours just kept on stacking up, one after the other. Events beyond his control led to him 'being in the right place', as he used to say, almost apologetically, using the royal 'we'. He finished the third poorly, and ill, but he still had no real rivals. The other great dream, the record five Tours, which had placed three riders on the Mount Olympus of Cycling, was almost within his grasp, and once that had become a very real possibility, he wanted the fifth Tour win. That is why he swept all before him in 1995.

Yet I believed, and I continue to believe, that Miguel never really sought a sixth victory. It would, in a sense, be defying history, showing a lack of respect for history. So, was he to be sacrilegious or an iconoclast? Perhaps it's an exaggeration to put it in these terms, but there was something of that in his thinking.

I remember another sketch, told as a joke, in a French cycling magazine, a week after the beginning of that sixth Tour which he was never to win. There were Merckx and Hinault, green with envy as they saw that Miguel might be about to outdo the two former greats, and each of them was putting forward reasons as to why they didn't want him to win that Tour. Then, in the final part of the strip, there was the sad, tired ghost of Jacques Anquetil coming along to say that it would be a dagger in the heart of the Tour, almost a lack of respect for tradition. 'We stopped at five, didn't we? So why should you go and mess everything up?' It was all expressed in a curious double language. Almost taking Induráin to task.

I repeat that in no way is Miguel an iconoclast or sacrilegious, and the religion of the Tour, which in itself is a State with a Church which has its own activists and believers, says that, right here and now, five's the maximum. That's the Mount Olympus. What could be higher? To be sure, if he had won the sixth, we in Spain would have put him up against a wall and made him go for a seventh, and an eighth. We would never have been satisfied. And, believe me, when he did finally lose a Tour (because life or sport decreed it), there are some who would have felt just as deflated, almost indignant.

I prefer to believe, then, that Miguel Induráin, like so many of us, dreamed happily and crazily of those five straight Tours, and that anything else was up to the gods. It wasn't about trying to go one better. Having said that, I am not suggesting that he didn't give his all to claim the sixth Tour, especially as he was riding on home territory; rather, he just had a mental block. In his heart of hearts, he arrived at the start physically exhausted and with his morale low; it was not so much that he was defeated, rather he let himself be defeated. By this I mean his fall from glory was his own doing, with scarcely any of his astonished rivals really daring to up the pace. That's what happened that afternoon on Les Arcs: he cracked by himself. It was as if the whole world had changed colour in a flash, on a bend in the road. From that point on they did begin to attack him, although even then not particularly aggressively. They all continued to watch him, respectfully and fearfully, out of the corner of their eyes. Yet, by then, the dice were cast. Something had collapsed inside him, on that cursed curve of Les Arcs, no more than four kilometres from the summit of a not particularly steep climb, the kind of climb which Miguel could cope with comfortably. A spark extinguished itself inside Miguel. Even though there are all kinds of speculation and reasons bandied about to explain or justify the disaster, the truth is that the Tour had just been lost in those few kilometres. In a way, his battle against pain had finally levelled out, and he must have told himself, 'No more. Nekane didn't need bottles for her dolls any more. I've done everything that was expected of me, and more. What, then, is the sense of prolonging this torture?' He must surely have thought something along those lines.

Why is it that he maintained that secret and bitter struggle with pain whilst here in Spain, and perhaps everywhere else, people thought his wins came so easily, 'at a canter' as they used to say. To understand that we need to go back to the beginning of Miguel Induráin's career, although there isn't a lot of information to go on.

As a young boy he got used to winning local races – sometimes Joaquín Marcos won; at other times Miguel came out on top – and he decided he needed to move a bit further afield, although still within the district. José Ignacio Urdániz who, together with Pepe Barruso, was the force behind the Club Ciclista Villavés, recalls that Miguel finished second in the first race he took part in beyond Villava, in the north of Navarre. Then the future champion won his second race, in the village of Luquín. Around that time he was already considering giving up his studies if his prospects in cycling looked good, and they did. Apart from scheduled training sessions, which were not excessively rigorous, Miguel cycled around a lot on his bike. He would be seen taking lunch to his family, who were out in the fields on their smallholding, some twenty kilometres from Villava. He was capable of doing this journey several times a day.

There's a small, and therefore precious, store of anecdotes about Induráin's early cycling exploits at that time. He would travel with team-mates from the Villava Cycling Club, often with his father's Seat 1500, or with his friend Alberto Bretón Mendía. It was on a journey to Barcelona with Alberto, apparently, that their bikes were stolen from the car. Only a pair of lads from Villava would think of leaving their car, with two racing bikes attached, right on the Ramblas in the middle of Barcelona. A naïvety that left them crestfallen.

His old chrome-plated green bike – a *Zeus*.

But life went on, and the story goes that in quite an important event in Navarre, Miguel escaped with a rider called Ibáñez, who had suffered a family bereavement the previous evening. Despite this, the lad still rode the next day. At the end of the race, Miguel allowed Ibáñez to cross the finishing line first. 'The winner's bouquet belongs to you,' he said to his rival.

Nekane's bottles all over again.

Isola–2000 all over again.

He was already like that, back then. A cyclist from Cantabria, who had an outstanding professional career, told me about a race in the north where Miguel had escaped and the bunch had no chance of catching him. He was following two motorcyclists, who then took a wrong turning. By the time it dawned on them that something was amiss, they were in a kind of rabbit warren of godforsaken villages with no signposts anywhere. The minutes went by and the road behind remained empty: they had indeed taken a wrong turning. Distraught, they almost burst into tears. It was Miguel who consoled them, 'Don't worry, it doesn't matter...' And that was the end of it.

It would have been interesting to have seen a young Bernard Hinault's reaction in a similar situation. The fact is champions come in all shapes and sizes, but there's only one who has behaved with such modesty and correctness that when something unpleasant occurred, such as that incident on the Cantabrian roads, his response could simply be: 'It doesn't matter.'

Time passed and Miguel was becoming a battle-hardened cyclist. Especially in the cold, because the races he took part in were all in that region of Spain where the climate is rarely a friend. The cold was a constant companion, and learning to withstand it was the best imaginable apprenticeship, especially for a body like his that yearned for the sun. Miguel's career developed in conditions that were unnatural for him. He was sustained by the sun, yet he was almost always forced to race in unfavourable weather conditions which would undermine the patience of the most hardened competitors, and would repeatedly put them to the test, as if in some macabre attempt to dissuade them from pursuing their passion for the sport. And it leads to illnesses, which, as with the pneumonia that affected Induráin years later, might lay dormant for a long time. It was the same story with his allergies: being forced to race in the spring in pollen-rich areas was unwise, and only served to torture a constitution like his. The lesson life was teaching him, paradoxically, was discipline, which wasn't specified in the cycling manuals but which is all about the pain an individual is able to withstand. The lesson perhaps began to strike home in those adverse circumstances. Eventually, it would be the same story in the Tour, only a hundred times worse.

As time passed it became increasingly clear that sport was going to be Miguel's destiny. Curiously, and this also has something to do with the cold and the adverse climatic conditions, this is where the legend starts. He always maintained that he liked racing in the heat and, yet, according to what we are told by those who raced with him when he was a youth, it was just the opposite. The tall, dark lad grew in stature in bad weather conditions, then vanished in extreme heat. This is exactly what happened to him in the Spanish Youth Championships in Ponferrada, where he was racing alongside the other Navarran riders Daniel de Miguel, Joaquín Marcos and Joaquín Luquín. Induráin caught sunstroke. The weather was to play an important role in Miguel's great exploits, as well as in the sadder moments and the defeats. Later on we'll see how it was the combination of the rain and the sun occurring on the same day, that would end up doing him greater harm than on days when the sun beat mercilessly down or when the race took place in a torrential downpour.

There were many wet and rainy days, but two stand out in the memory: the World Road Race Championships in Oslo, where Miguel gained silver; and that crazy stage up Pordoi and Marmolada in the 1993 Giro when it was teeming, and Miguel was going like a rocket. When it comes to scorching temperatures, you only have to go back to the pictures of the disaster on the way to Sestrière in 1992. But the two occasions when he cracked most spectacularly – ascending Mortirolo in the 1994 Giro and the 1996 Tour just below the summit of Les Arcs – came about on days when the weather had been treacherous. Sudden rain, then intense heat, followed by bitter cold that made him wrap up, then rain again and a high-speed descent from a summit, and finally more baking sun in the Alps. And there was Miguel, wearing his warm neoprene gloves, sweating buckets, with his inner equilibrium shattered: that's exactly what happened to him on Les Arcs. But that's all part of the legend, and the legend ends up resting on rather shaky data, sometimes on stories that are little more than hearsay.

However, one thing is clear: at the beginning was the wind. And the wind in the place where Miguel grew up was always cold and hostile. Later the cold was to become his silent ally, as much or perhaps even more so even than the attacks of his rivals. It was the cold which set out its stall, showing him how to withstand pain, how, in other words, to imitate the sprinter, Lee Evans. So, here we have a quiet, hard-working man who no longer races for Fanta Orange drinks that double up as feeding bottles for Nekane's dolls; instead, he knows full well what's expected of him on a bicycle. His father has always encouraged him, telling him to take the sport as seriously as he can, telling him that if it doesn't work out, at least he has the chance to go back to working the fields with him. That's what's called stress reduction, and it was an enormous slice of luck for Miguel. So, too, was the fact that he was exempted from military service because there were more candidates than places. Joaquín Marcos, his great friend and rival from Villava, wasn't so lucky, nor was Prudencio Induráin: both of them lost more than a year. Marcos's career was simply shattered, and Pruden's was derailed for quite some time. Miguel, on the other hand, was managing to avoid all that. He wasn't even pressurised by Barruso and Urdániz. If he came up with wins, that was fine, but all they demanded was simply his commitment. It was as if the wind of those Navarre mountains had told them in their dreams: 'Don't, on any account, push him too hard, now. There'll soon come a day, I promise you, when he will have to shoulder enormous pressure.'

One of his teachers recounts that, rather like the rest of his classmates, Miguel really couldn't stand mathematics. Yet he ended up being a master of the art of juggling numbers and possibilities within that huge human mathematical operation that is the Tour de France. However much he may have disliked mathematics as a child, Miguel eventually found himself having to do non-stop calculations. On the road he was always instinctively weighing up risks and different possibilities as to whether such and such a rider would make a break in such and such a part of the course. The point is, if you are going to become ringmaster in an arena as nerve-racking as cycling, where you have to take instant and crucial decisions, you need a specific type of intelligence. It's like mental chess, with the pieces in constant motion. But, if you're a champion, you need to make sure of the end result, whatever ups and downs the race might bring.

Keeping your nerve, withstanding pain, learning to suffer to the point where other people have to tell you to stop. That's how a very young Miguel Induráin climbed Leyre as a junior rider in a race in Sangüesa, in terrible pain after breaking a wrist a few weeks earlier and racing before he was fully recovered. The race strategy dictated that someone had to push the pace on the climb. He was the one who set that pace until he could pedal no more.

Induráin always maintained in public that the rider he most admired was Bernard Hinault. Who wouldn't? But, in truth, his idol was Sean Kelly, whom he knew and against whom he competed after he turned professional. And the quality that impressed him most was simply that Kelly 'knew how to suffer'.

There's a story that in another junior race in Salinas de Léniz in Vitoria, Miguel was instructed to really go for it. Some fifteen riders were pursuing him, but no one managed to catch him and take over at the front. Miguel sped uphill like a motorbike and, inevitably, exhausted himself; one of his team-mates even had to offer him his back wheel to pace him up to the summit, because he looked as if he was about to call it a day.

Cold, always the cold. There's another story about a race in the snow in San Jorge. He won at a canter, leaving all the other riders trailing. It's said he arrived with a layer of snow covering his cap.

Those close to him during that part of his career realised that, in every sense of the word, he was a big-hearted lad. When he had to fight for his team, he did so without a murmur, unlike some others who tended to whinge. But, then, Miguel was always like that. He worked for Pedro Delgado and Arroyo when they were at the top. Then they worked for him, but when he had to work for Jean-François Bernard or Julián Gorospe, he did that, too. The same for Mikel Zarrabeitia, José María Jiménez or Santi Blanco. If it needed to be done, he did it.

As far as following orders was concerned, there's a famous anecdote that did the rounds at the time, and is of interest in view of the interpretations that were later placed on it. The bitter rivals of the Villava club were the Club Ciclista Tafallés, whose star was Javier Araiz, a gifted and graceful rider who nevertheless seemed obsessed with sticking close to Miguel Induráin. Wherever Miguel went, Araiz casually followed on his shoulder. In one race on the San Cristóbal circuit, Pepe Barruso drove up to Miguel to tell him that, even if he ended up losing that particular race, he wasn't to worry. He told him to stay right there by the car, to see what his limpet-like rival would do. Things ran true to form: along came Araiz, who then crashed out on a bend, while Miguel remounted and went on to win. In another race, after descending from the summit of the Erro on the road to Huarte, Barruso again told Miguel to wait a while, and that he'd send instructions on later. Almost immediately, Araiz appeared again, to see if he could catch any of the instructions. Barruso says that it occurred to him at the time that if he just left Miguel there, the other guy could well have stayed with them until the end of the race.

And who can forget Montoya 'marking' Pedro Delgado in that ascent of the Tourmalet at a crucial point in the Tour of Spain, while the Swiss rider Tony Rominger was going off down the road in front of them, or Claudio Chiappucci, stopping to relieve himself in a layby at exactly the same moment that Miguel had decided to do so? The fact is that attitudes such as Javier Araiz's merely serve to emphasise Miguel's strength: somehow their intuition must have told them who they were dealing with. And the harsh reality is that, as well as Miguel's great rival in Villava, Joaquín Marcos, there were a lot of other very good young cyclists in Navarre at that time, yet very few of them made it to the top, with the exception of that heavyweight from the region, Javier Luquín, who was later to ride in the Banesto team and help Miguel win his first Tour de France. As Luquín used to say in those days of the first Tour, the only comfort and relief for their nerves was seeing 'that old carthorse Miguel telling everyone to stay calm' while they were all, according to Luquín, flipping their lids.

A very big heart, that's a fact. Just as Miguel himself would continue to maintain right to the end of his career: 'In spite of everything that happened, I still insist I wasn't brought up as a champion.' Javier Luquín remembers José Miguel Echávarri having a go at Miguel once, because he had decided, in the middle of a race, to go back to the team car to pick up a raincoat. He didn't think it was right to ask someone else to do it for him, so he dropped back down the field, himself. It was an error that might have cost him dear. There was a similar, long-standing story about Gianni Bugno doing something similar at the top of the Tourmalet in the '91 Tour, dropping back to his Gatorade team vehicle to get precise information. By the time they'd given it to him, Miguel had gained several minutes' advantage. Bugno's move had lost him the Tour. The constant, never-ending game of chess, which tests your nerves to breaking point. Sometimes it's better not to know, and just to get on with your riding. At other times, the opposite. Who knows? Only the great champions know. Only they can perform this improvised music.

Because, at the end of the day, cycling bears some relation to a symphony. At least in the way Miguel performed his own works, which required a certain cadence, or a rhythm, harmony or tonality. In that fierce, competitive world, the written score is all too easily lost. In 1985, as a professional and, moreover, wearing the yellow jersey that marked him out as the youngest-ever leader of the Tour of Spain, he arrived in Galicia to witness Jaime Salvá's terrible accident, which engraved its indelible and graphic memory on him, with blood pouring down the rider's face and him choking on his own blood because, in their effort to help him, the spectators had placed him face-up. And then there was Ludo Loos suffering a fractured skull. And a little further on, Dejonckheere, of the Teka team, and Martens, of Fagor, coming to blows – goodness knows why. Right by the town walls of Lugo, using their elbows and knees, and shoving each other. Miguel must have thought, through his unflappable composure: 'Is this what being a professional is all about?' A dog-eat-dog world, that's what it is.

In fact, as he came up through the junior ranks, he'd already seen a lot of that kind of nonsense and in-fighting, and the way people repeatedly lost their senses and clashed with each other. In Aragón there were two lads, both good bike-riders – Ara and a boy called Orquín. The two friends' families, and their respective groups of supporters, were at loggerheads. In one race where the Navarre lads took part, Orquín's and Ara's fans were at each other's throats. They hurled bottles through the air at each other, and one brushed past Miguel's head.

He never understood such ill feeling and foul behaviour. He was the grandson of Toribio Induráin, one of three Villava families who pledged themselves to the fields and country life from the pre-industrial era. Miguel inherited the 'carthorse' label from the old man who lovingly tended his vines on the slopes of Mount Ezcaba and who made an excellent *txacolí* liqueur from them. On his mother's side he was the grandson of another living legend, Hermenegildo Larraya, who had a farm in Alzórriz, up in the Unciti valley, in the district of Sangüesa right at the foot of Mount Izaga; tranquillity virtually oozed through that area. Up there, even the sudden anger of the heavens would tail off into calmness. So how could it be that people and, what's more, cycling people, could lose their temper so easily?

It was only in that region that the Great Symphony which was composing itself in Miguel Induráin's heart and mind could ever have come to fruition. It was born and nurtured there, surrounded by the Basque peaks of Ezkaurre, Sobarkal, Auñamendi, and so many more. Almost all these names have warlike connotations. All of them, when translated into French, would end up being important climbs in the Tour.

He grew up in a house where there were always pots of flowers, especially geraniums, a home that was full of love. That made it hard for him to fit into a world where people tore bits out of each other for their living.

Cyclists, and you have to be close to them to really see this, are very different from normal people. Not so much a race apart, as a breed apart. They are made of sterner stuff, capable of adopting a stoical attitude to the kind of pain which gets the better of other sportsmen and women. But it's equally true, as someone in the field of sports medicine once said, that top cyclists are pathological creatures – as hard as nails and yet susceptible to all sorts of illnesses. Sometimes, something which would be easily fought off by a child's ready made defences, might bring down even the toughest of cyclists.

A man like Lemond was able to win two Tours with 60 lead shots embedded right next to his lungs. Pascal Simon led the '83 Tour for nearly a week with a broken shoulder-blade. And the list goes on and on – Miguel himself, with his wrist fractured, suffering on the Fito during a hellish Tour of Spain, with almost every body out to get him.

The great champions really are often pathological creatures, addicted to victory and willing to sell their soul to the devil in order to achieve it. They say that Louison Bobet was psychologically very aggressive towards his own *domestiques*, even threatening them on more than one occasion. Hinault is even known to have vigorously shaken his *domestiques* in public, although later, when he started winning, he would try and make it up to them as best he could. He even invited one – one of those he'd shaken, of course – to spend a few days in his own home. It's the old theory of the good policeman officer and the bad policeman – the one who hits you, and the one who then immediately consoles you to make sure you continue to collaborate.

There is one famous comment from Hinault which outlines his fiercely indomitable character: 'I always like seeing someone behind me when I cross the finishing line. That's why I'll never break the hour record', which is something he no doubt could have achieved in his time. Never was so much arrogance accumulated in a single cyclist. It's clear that Bernard Hinault would never have touched his Campagnolo brakes so discreetly just a few metres from the line at Isola–2000.

But it's also obvious that Rominger had to really fight to get to that finishing line at Isola–2000 in the '93 Tour, and to win his three Tours of Spain. They say that after his first disastrous season as a professional, the Swiss rider sent his CV to fifteen teams, all of whom turned him down, one after the other. Stubborn as a mule he was, and admirably so.

Nevertheless, it was Miguel Induráin who impressed his mark on a whole cycling generation – for a whole decade in fact – just as, years before, Anquetil, Merckx and Hinault had done. Except that he was different from the other greats. Not better or worse, but different. He never seemed to hunger after victory. Victories just came along of their own accord, like the harvest in the fields of the Navarre basin. First the roots were planted, which would then grow and bear fruit. Then it was simply a case of sitting back and waiting to reap the harvest.

From a very early age he was such a down-to-earth person, without an ounce of insincerity in him. Because he was so reserved, his slightest gesture or show of interest could have set rumours going, if he didn't deny it. For example, it was often said that Miguel used to keep a diary in which he noted the details of everything that happened to him on the road, along with the lengthy periods spent in training camps far from home.

As a child he was addicted to *Captain Thunder* comics, but he always admitted that reading wasn't really a major interest; he preferred the cinema. In the same way, he never denied that for years he had carried in his rucksack a copy of *Goodbye Baby*, which he never finished. This was to give rise to more than one rather slanderous joke. And yet he was the one acquiring fame, fortune and general admiration, while other 'better-read' individuals sank into the mediocrity of their lives as critics, passing judgement on the work of others. Unperturbed, he carried on amassing victories and collecting his reproduction model cars. They say that on their honeymoon Marisa gave him a miniature Alfa Romeo. Deep down, he never stopped cultivating his old obsession for tractors, for any traction engine, or any tool. He was captivated by cars, that is true, but that doesn't mean he was interested in showing them off; he simply liked their internal mechanics. Just like the Tour itself. Even when he saw he was going to win back-to-back Tours, he insisted he didn't want to be made to go to the town hall in a Mercedes convertible waving to the crowd, as had happened the first time. 'That sort of thing's for film stars and the like.'

His mask, his protection against the avalanche of popularity he was to suffer, was always to remain respectful to everyone, while, at the same time, demanding that they show similar respect for his private life. His behaviour was outwardly cool: when he was riding in the lower-category races, his team bosses, Pepe Barruso and Urdániz, recall it was common to get to a finishing line and for them, in the car behind, not to know who had won, because the last thing they'd been able to see was that Miguel was merely well placed for the sprint. They couldn't see anyone raise their arms in triumph or express their joy. They would reach the line and seek out Miguel to ask him anxiously who had won. 'I did,' would come the reply.

There are some examples, graphic testimonies, showing Miguel crossing the finishing line with his arms aloft – a couple in junior races, and another as an amateur with Reynolds, winning at Alsasua in the Tour of Navarre. Nevertheless, even allowing for the static nature of the photography, these movements seem to be fairly measured, not at all ostentatious. According to Pepe Barruso, and this is supported by others who have followed Miguel's career from the outset, it was in the stage he won at Luz-Ardiden, during the 1990 Tour de France, when they first saw him openly and clearly express his joy. He punched the air with both fists and there, right at the front of the crowd, were his relatives. Likewise, at the finish in the central boulevard at the end of a San Sebastián Classic, he also showed his huge delight. Again, his family and friends were there. Those victories were more or less home wins.

A year later, crossing the line at Val-Louron behind Claudio Chiappucci, the stage winner, Miguel was also seen to punch the air with joy, although, personally, I can't remember anything like that happening until the World Road Race Championships in Colombia in '95, where he came second behind Olano. There, after a long and fiercely disputed sprint with Pantani and Gianetti, he once again raised his fist – a gesture that he hadn't made for a good five years. What the majority interpreted as an act of solidarity towards his compatriot didn't, so it's said, go down particularly well with the Banesto representatives, who were conspicuous by their absence at Olano's victory celebrations. That should, in truth, have been Induráin's World Championship. He was in great shape and very well placed on the road, but Olano made a sudden break and Miguel never wavered. He would cover Olano's back just as if he had been in the Club Ciclista Villavés.

Really, it was all a matter of the heart. His heart was huge and powerful, but it was not made of stone, nor iron, nor forged of steel. He did, in fact, begin to shut himself off more and more; if he hadn't done so, circumstances would have suffocated him, which is something that not even the Col de Galibier, with its altitude of more than 2,500 metres and its near 40-degree heat, managed to do.

He liked to go skiing now and again, but not often, since top cyclists cannot risk picking up an injury by engaging in high-risk sports. He also likes going out mountain-biking in the hills. And DIY. And slow, serious music. And, above all, Luz Casal.

From his early days he would try and go out in the fresh air, looking for pigeons, or to hunt pheasants and woodcocks with his dog – even as a young child he used to go hunting with his uncle and cousins. They would go to the Mendioroz reserve. There, amidst the laughter and the running races, the Symphony of life that, years later, Miguel would perform, began to be composed in the invisible web of the unconscious. At that time his life was already a healthy and relaxed *allegro con fuocco* in which he was always looking for new and worthwhile experiences.

His life was really to change the day Pepe Barruso said to Eusebio Unzúe, the Navarran from Orcoyen who'd been entrusted with scouting for promising talent for the newly formed Reynolds team, 'I've got something for you.' It's said that Unzúe saw Miguel, and was introduced to him, in a junior race in Obanos. But then again, it's also said that the first time he saw him ride for real was in a race in Olite, which Miguel won in style, and with a determination that quite bewildered him. It's difficult sometimes to play down the legend. So many races and faces, so many hours spent training along those roads in the valley of Baztán, along the road to Elizondo. Even those first memories seem to shine out like stars in the clear summer night sky.

However, Eusebio wasn't wrong in his estimation: the lad *was* an uncut diamond. The other shrewd Navarran in the story, Echávarri, agreed with that impression as soon as he saw Miguel in the saddle. He confirmed to Pepe Barruso that they were prepared to sign him. 'We'll call you,' he said. That was all. And once again courage and patience were needed, and it's certainly true that Miguel became rather nervous, because time passed and still there was no call. Echávarri, the Navarran from Abárzuza, was in no hurry to rush the career of the Villava youngster who reminded everyone of Francesco Moser.

The general observation was that he was extraordinarily gifted, but obviously with the kind of make-up that made him a rider destined to win one-day Classics, or at most three- or four-day tours. They were counting on Induráin's strength and cardiovascular capacity, but they weren't taking into account his heart. Nor his composure. Nor his intelligence.

The legend continues even in the medical data which have been released to the Press over the years. Those who really understand these data are the doctors: Carlos Barrios, José Calabuig and Sabino Padilla, Miguel's personal doctor for years, and the famous Dr Conconi in Milan, who supervised the career of a number of famous cyclists. They were all astonished by the results from Miguel's tests.

Let's continue by focusing on his heart. Certain statistics indicate that, in his cycling prime, the resting pulse rate of that heart was 36 beats per minute. Other sources give this figure as 32. But, it seems that everyone finally agreed to accept the spectacular figure of 28 per minute, because Induráin had 'toughened' or 'trained' his heart with all the racing and training sessions.

It's difficult to believe it, but he was able to go from 160 beats – the heart rate he would have had at the top of an average climb – back to just 60 in only 30 seconds. A diastolic diameter of 7.5 centimetres, as against a normal person's roughly four centimetres, enabled him to pump between 40 and 45 litres of blood per minute. A normal and not especially sedentary person would pump between 25 and 30 litres. But there are other figures that indicate that Miguel was able to pump up to 50 litres of blood per minute, and what is known as his VO2 (Maximum Oxygen Consumption) rate was 88 millilitres per kilo per minute, whereas a reasonable sportsman or woman consumes 55.

So, he certainly had a great heart. But in order to grit his teeth on Val-Louron, or in Luxembourg, or going up Saint-Lary Soulan, or to attack as he did on the way to Liège, he required something more than a huge, powerful heart. What he required was a pact with pain itself, even if that had been signed years before, with pain's disguised emissaries, the cold and the wind, which pierced their way like whispering needles through the harvest, the beech groves and the vines, through the grass and stone, on the way to Alzórriz. What he required was a degree of inner nobility, which perhaps is given only to those who have never sought it. That is the stake. It's the difference between being gifted and possessing a gift. Miguel Induráin was gifted, of course, but he wasn't all that different from a number of others, and on its own that wouldn't have been enough. The really crucial requirement was to cross the pain threshold. Up there where pain becomes neutral and the Symphony begins.

Miguel was preparing to perform the Great Symphony of his life, and amongst the audience there were people deeply moved, even incredulous at what they were about to witness at first hand. But there was coughing in the stalls, too, and dissenting voices: those who were negative towards everything; those who had no patience. Today, now that the Miguel Induráin dream is over, what remains behind is that wonderful flavour of his great triumphs, or perhaps the bitter-sweet epic of his cycling defeats, which, although few, were much talked about. Yet, in spite of everything, from the moment he began to chalk up wins, there was never a second when those critical voices were silent. They were critical of his conservative riding style. Some, I know for a fact, even got annoyed on TV because he didn't seem to be tired when he crossed the line. We don't only want a circus, we want dead gladiators as well.

In the 1990 Vuelta, for example, they slated him when, gripped by flu, he produced a poor performance in Valdezcaray: 'He's not a big-race rider,' they said. And in the Vuelta the following year, when Mauri beat him in a time-trial, it was: 'Induráin has disappointed again. He always seems to do better when he races abroad.' And in Jaca, in the '91 Tour, hours before the devastating coup in Val-Louron: 'And where are the Banesto boys, then? Where are they hiding?' And throughout the Sestrière stage in '92: 'Why on earth is Induráin not attacking, with the lead Chiappucci has built up?' The kind of comments heard during the famous Stelvio and Mortirolo stages in the '94 Giro were: 'He seems half asleep, lacking motivation, and the kilometres are running out for him.' Minutes later all hell let loose in the most exciting stage in memory. And in the middle of the '93 Tour: 'Might he actually be holding something back in an Alpine or Pyrenean stage? It seems he's depriving *us* of the victory *we* deserve.' And during the '94 Tour, in the time-trial up Morzine-Avoriaz, in the rain, and with Miguel totally composed: 'Where's his pride? He's on home territory, he owes *us* the satisfaction.' And it was the same story in Liège in

'95, when Bruyneel won out in the sprint. And on Larrau in '96: 'It's pathetic to see him touring like this; someone should do something.'

There's a lot that could be said on this subject, but it really would be never-ending and tedious to detail it all. These criticisms were a constant and very subtle background music, which for the better part of a decade was a continual annoyance in the more expensive seats. Sometimes they acted as a counterpoint, as a *basso continuo,* to the Symphony. I am referring almost exclusively to certain elements in radio and television, since the written Press, in spite of everything, doesn't go out live; it works at a different *tempo,* with more time to ponder and analyse.

There's one story I must retell, now that time has passed. It happened during the sixth Tour which Miguel never won. We were in the Bordeaux area and the Motorola team invited the Press for a cocktail. The whole Spanish contingent was out in force, ready, since we weren't going to win the Tour, to polish off the exquisite wines and delicacies. Everyone started to tuck in and, more particularly, have a few drinks – and we all know what claret does for you. Suddenly, a Spanish journalist with quite a few Tours under his belt (all of them Induráin wins, of course) and who knew his cycling, said to the gathering: 'Hey, now no one is listening, I'm going to make a confession.' I thought: 'The claret's up to its tricks.' But it was a different story. Days before, Riis, wearing the yellow jersey, had won in style on the summit of Hautacam. He took 42 seconds out of his leading rivals. *L'Équipe* chose what I think was a rather unfortunate and undignified headline. Something along the lines of 'A real champion at last.' 'Come off it,' all the Spanish journalists thought that day. 'Hasn't all Miguel's done over the past five years been champion material? If not, then what the hell was it?' It was an embarrassment. But our comrade-in-arms stated clearly that, in his opinion, *L'Équipe* was right, and that, in all the years he'd seen Induráin dominate the Tour, he had never seen him win like that. 'Like what? You mean winning in yellow on one of the legendary summits?' I asked him in the midst of my astonishment and my temporary, but rising, indignation. That, indeed, was what he meant.

At that moment, I knew I didn't want to be there. I wanted to know nothing about cycling, neither to love it nor practise it. I wanted to stop living. Those words rent my heart asunder. In the darkness, and as the trays of oysters and exotic gastronomic delicacies succumbed one by one at our table, I know I got up and dashed back to the hotel. Then, a few hours later, after I'd calmed down a bit, I reflected on it, although it still left me feeling dejected: 'They still haven't understood what an extraordinary heart he has,' I said to myself. But the worst thing was that there was no longer any time for them to change their opinion. They would never understand.

So I decided I would take myself back in time, back to those years when Miguel was emerging, but when no one was really laying serious bets on him. I recalled my feelings on a bike, riding up Alpe d'Huez in the solitude of spring, and I recalled some strange comments Eddie Merckx had made about Miguel Induráin. What surprised the Belgian, who had only begun to acknowledge Miguel after the third Tour, in '93, wasn't his performance in the time trials. What really stunned the Brabant rider was the way Miguel tackled the toughest ascents: 'With his body and weight, it's just awesome. I'm not talking just about steep little hills or winding drags,' said Merckx, 'I'm talking about the Tour mountains, the Dolomites, the Pyrenees, the toughest paved summits in the world.' And then he let slip a key phrase in that interview, which really forced me to stop and think about an idea which occurred to Merckx, and myself and many, many others. What he said was: 'I had to see it to believe it.'

My memories told me: 'It's true. At first, despite having seen it on TV, you didn't believe it. You needed to see him actually ride past in front of you.' I had almost managed it, but it was still necessary to partially reconstruct the framework of memory.

I don't know for certain what my first memory of Miguel Induráin actually is. Possibly a photo, in his old Reynolds top, maybe a faint and fleeting view on TV, around 1984, in the Basque Country, when almost everyone was admiring other riders. Others had greater 'class'; others greater 'style'; and there were even some with greater 'promise'. Induráin, with his huge body and his proverbial frugality with words, was mentioned as the kind of cyclist best suited to the track, or perhaps the one-day Classics; he had too big a body, too big to drag up mountains. It was possibly sportswriters for the daily *La Voz de Euskadi* who were the first to sing Miguel's praises. What isn't in doubt, though, is that from then on, slowly and gradually, like the reaping of a harvest, Induráin began to attract our attention. He simply began to be there.

Then, years of silence ensued. Even though he was evolving all the time, both as a cyclist and as a person, everything was gobbled up into the mass hysteria surrounding Pedro Delgado. With his outgoing personality, his way with words and his style of riding, Delgado had the whole country eating out of his hand, apart from the usual incorrigible detractors. Pedro, in turn, reaped the harvest sown by Ángel Arroyo, who was such an irrepressible fighter. In the Tours at the beginning of Miguel's professional career, it was Delgado and Arroyo who captivated attention in Spain. If, all those years back, the media had given equal treatment to the likes of Bahamontes, Julio Jiménez, José Pérez Francés, González, Gandarias, Gómez del Moral or López Carril and Fuente, Spain would have reacted much sooner, and equally enthusiastically, but it didn't happen. They sowed and reaped their harvests and, even though they were never aware of it, they were laying the foundations for the Day of the Great Harvest. The only question was who would be the country boy who would come from nowhere to reap it. It was Miguel.

I do remember very clearly that, from a very young age, my dream was to go and see the Tour de France. My cousin did the football pools every week and would try and lift my spirits every now and again: 'Don't worry about it; any day now I'll win a million on the pools and I'll take you to the Tour in a Merc.' Cousin Juan did, in fact, win the pools, but it was a small prize and the truth was I was never able to go to the Tour with him. I had to make do with going, at the age of almost 40, as a journalist in a Fiat belonging to the Spanish daily *El Mundo,* and in one of the organisers' cars they keep for 'special guests'. I was not 'special' in any way at all, but fate decreed that one of the invited guests on that Alpine stage to Val-Thorens in 1994 pulled out at the last moment. Jean-Marie Leblanc, the race director, found it funny that a Spanish writer should have devoted a novel to one of the Tour's legendary peaks, Alpe d'Huez. 'A proper novel?' he asked me. '*Oui.*' 'How strange.' In the 'village' at the start of that stage, Jean-Marie Leblanc asked me if I was familiar with the Tour and the

Alps. I told him that the year before I had ridden up Alpe d'Huez, and the Col d'Ornon, and the Croix de Fer up to the point where the signs prevented me going any higher because of the snows, and the Col de Lauteret. 'You certainly know what it's about then.' 'More or less. But seeing it live, in the raw, has always been my greatest dream,' I said very seriously and directly, and I looked him in the eyes. Monsieur Leblanc receives hundreds of requests for favours before, during, and after each stage, but I realised that at that moment he was about to carry out a complex administrative procedure – substituting one guest for another. As for me, I was, quite simply, about to realise my dream.*

But if the experience of following a mountain stage in the Tour de France in a car was unforgettable and amazingly exciting, the real impact had hit home the previous day, when for the first time I'd been able to see Miguel Induráin in person and in the saddle. The car's mobility, which enabled us to pause at any bend we felt like and await the arrival of the break, did give a certain advantage of perspective, that is true, but didn't really make us live it. On the road to Val-Thorens, with the Glandon and the fearsome Madeleine in between, there was time to watch the spectacle more or less like a TV camera. Stop the car on the penultimate bend of the climb, get your sandwiches out and wait. 'Here they come, here they come …' You would see them in the distance, and then you'd accelerate again, because on the descent the riders are quite capable of catching any car, whatever risks the driver takes on the corners.

That's what occurred on La Madeleine, where the descent was psychedelic anguish: we had reached the summit with a lead of more than a minute over the riders, but by half-way down they were almost treading on our heels. Even the driver of the official car started to get nervous. 'Here they are already. Bloody hell! Here they are!' he bitterly complained as the Fiat's speedometer reached 120 kilometres an hour on several occasions. Flanking us were terrifying cliffs with sheer drops into the void. The wheels screeched on some of the tight bends, and the speedometer

* In Javier García Sánchez's novel, *Alpe d'Huez*, the entire action takes place during one mountain stage of the Tour de France, and culminates in a close finish at the top of Alpe d'Huez.

remained steady, at over 100, but the cyclists really were catching us, and Radio Tour, with Philippe Bouvet's indescribable nasal tones, screamed at the accompanying cars to get a move on! La Madeleine has a steep descent of almost twenty kilometres and it's in situations like that the Tour organisers seem on the verge of losing control. Philippe Bouvet was shouting himself hoarse: 'Car number such-and-such, pull over to the side of the road, please!'

The cars at the front of the Tour caravan must alternate, one on the left of the road, and the next one on the right, but on that particular day, as so often happens, things had got out of hand: the riders were chasing down the organisers' cars. Then it was a case of instilling some order. Hearing the hair-raising screech of tyres endlessly licking the edges of precipices was a strange experience. I recall I was the only one to dare to look behind, and now and again I would see the motorbikes. And the jerseys of the breakaway group. We were pushing things to the limit. Bouvet had seen our car, because the helicopter gives a complete overall view of everything, and he relayed a couple of precise messages. 'I'm going to tell you to stop ... Pay attention ...' One car on the left, one on the right. Always alternating, so that the peloton can pass. With our hands gripping the side of the car, the guests, a Japanese couple and myself, were literally terrified. What a stupid way to die, the Japanese must have been thinking. The husband was the owner of a very large chain of supermarkets in France. VIP guests, they were. On the other hand, it didn't bother me to end my days in such circumstances – descending the Col de La Madeleine at 120! I remembered instinctively that the cyclotourist classic a few months before had seen a rider die in a fall at this very spot as he raced the route based on a Tour stage. He simply went over the side of La Madeleine.

On the flat section from La Madeleine to Val-Thorens we regained our position. But I remember asking the driver to stop the car: I was still suffering from the emotional impact of the previous day and, once again, I wanted to see Induráin actually pass by in person. Someone else would pick me up a few bends further up. My car then went off in the direction of the finish and I lay down on the nastiest bend of the climb to the ski station. The break went past and shortly afterwards came the group of favourites with Induráin dictating the pace. They were flying, watching each other. Their eyes were squinting and the saliva was gushing out of their mouths. Vroom, vroom, vroom. You could hear the noise of the bicycle chains, with a background of sirens filtering its way through. And loads of brightly coloured cars. In the middle of a group of men who were concealing as best they could their agony, I managed to make out once more those shiny tanned ankles that belonged to the King.

Everything was under control. Miguel was supervising. But I asked myself again: 'How on earth does he get so tanned?' They looked like the legs of the Colombian, Rodríguez, who had passed by a few seconds before. It was the 1994 Tour and the great dream was about to be realised. And even then, it seemed sheer madness.

Where did this madness come from? Perhaps the Club Ciclista Villavés people would have something to say about that, since they'd followed Miguel's first victorious Tours very closely, but for me it was something new. I had grasped it only the day before the one during which I witnessed the other VIP guests blanching during that frenetic descent of La Madeleine.

To be precise, it was on Alpe d'Huez, in amongst the crowds. Since I'd been wearing my journalist's accreditation around my neck, the *gendarmes* hadn't hindered me. If you were clever, you could move around freely, even in the privileged area on the other side of the barriers. Along with Chus, the wife of Pedro Blasco, the inveterate cycling enthusiast from the *El Mundo* paper, who was in the Press room with Benito Muñoz putting together the story of the stage, we decided to go a bit further down the mountain to see the race. Deep down, I wanted to see Induráin at close quarters. To feel him. I took up a strategic position between the last two hairpins. That is where the gradients are steep and the cyclists have to make a huge effort to maintain the rhythm of their ascent. The gradient never falls below 10 per cent. Behind them, starting from the village of Bourg-d'Oisans, they have negotiated fully twenty hairpin bends which resemble a snake in its death throes. There could be no other place, or way, to find out if Miguel Induráin Larraya really did exist as a rider or if he was a mirage, a being from some Borges story, a sleight of the imagination, or a trick played on us by our desperate wishes.

Behind, like termites, were half a million people, a vociferous but respectful mass applauding the participants in this enforced route march, and never was that expression more aptly used. Some of them must have been there for days, with their caravans or cars, or in their tents. All to catch a glimpse of their idols speeding past in a matter of seconds. Is there any other sport where people do this? No, just cycling. There must be a reason. When the crowd began to press, I said goodbye to Chus. I had decided to go further down. We would meet up in the Press room. Hundreds of people were listening to the progress of the stage on their tiny transistor radios. Some were watching on miniature TV sets, in their cars or vans parked on the sides of the road, next to the stone walls or on the grass verges formed by the natural shape of the bends.

Suddenly there was the roar of the motorbikes, although the *commissairs'* cars had warned us that the first riders were close, as indeed they were. Roberto Conti shot past, a sinewy skeleton, a brightly coloured rag doll, his eyes red and a grimace on his face that I shall never forget. Shortly afterwards, but unable to catch Conti, came Marco Pantani. And then the minutes ticked by. In theory, but only in theory, Miguel Induráin should appear at any moment with his gleaming *maillot jaune*. But he would need to do so soon, otherwise he would lose that jersey. A Tour can be won or lost on a climb like Alpe d'Huez, as has happened often enough in the history of the *Grande Boucle*, as the French call their race. On those slopes minutes can drip like molten lead from flagging riders. Like mercury in your alimentary canal. At such times, the torment is unending. I knew that, and I also knew how apparently easily Miguel had tackled that legendary summit in two of his other victorious Tours, in '91 and '92. But I hadn't seen it with my own eyes. Yet the eyes of history did remind me over and over again that you can be a strong leader up until the moment when the Alps cross your path. And then they can smash you to pieces, like certain heroes from Homer, plunging you into the bitter darkness of the night.

Suddenly, the whole mountain seemed to shake. People were stamping on the ground, and clapping. Someone shouted in French that Richard Virenque had launched a fierce attack at the foot of the climb and had escaped. The image came to my mind of Induráin cracking, the way he had in the stage at Mortirolo on the way to Aprica, scarcely a month before during the Giro. The second-hand carried on ticking inexorably round. The shouting got louder and louder. The whole mountain was resounding, and Induráin had still not appeared. I saw the faces of the fans uttering a key word, which they repeated again and again as they grinned, although some also looked serious as they said it. At first, because of all the excitement, I didn't understand what they were referring to. Then I understood the clear gesture they were making with their hands, as if they were bringing their hands together and then apart rapidly like an automatic door: '*Fermez!*' they repeated again and again. And like a sinister echo the word spread further and further across the mountain amongst the human tide: '*Fermez-le, fermez!*'

Then it clicked what they were talking about. 'Block him in. Block him in.' That's what those people were shouting. Him, Miguel. I confess, for a few moments I felt something verging on unbearable panic. Any one of those hundreds of fans who at that moment were relaying the message with their shouts and gestures, was going to be, like myself, just a few inches away from the Navarran champion. Any one of them could lose their balance and fall, impeding, even accidentally, the motorbikes or cars, which in turn would block the riders' way. Accidentally, or not accidentally. Such things have happened in the Tour and in other races more than once. Time passed and I was helpless to stop that message.

It wasn't necessary. Induráin himself would do so in a few seconds. The crowd, which had been vociferous up till that point, suddenly hushed, although they continued to clap, when the Yellow Jersey appeared round a bend in the distance. But the road was getting dangerously narrower and narrower. Curt instructions issued from the motorbikes and cars for the packed ranks of people to move back a little. *Gendarmes* elbowed their way through on their motorbikes and in several instances almost lost their balance and fell. But the earlier shouting transformed into long and sincere applause, and into the inevitable ovation. It was directed at that huge man dressed in yellow who commanded a group which had kept the lid on the unruly Richard Virenque. The leader, imposing and sober, rode along one of the sides of the road, and now and again glanced rapidly back to his right, where he had his flock more or less pacified. That was the moment, I recall, when I realised why, even in France, they called this man 'His Serene Majesty', and other similar terms. His formidable progress left the senses dumbfounded, and defied adjectives, praise, plaudits, metaphors and ellipses. Any gloss immediately turned into a contradiction and even an insult. Just seeing him pass by was enough. I would have shouted: 'On your knees, all of you!', but there was complete bedlam.

So, those who, until a few moments before, had still been shouting '*Fermez, fermez!*' now bowed their heads in respect and admiration as their mouths uttered little more than a '*Oooohhh!*' which has no translation in any language. Their mouths closed: '*Oh là là*' and '*Uuuaauu*'. That was the best and only tribute the leader deserved. A single common language as he passed – a spellbound cacophony.

Three things, nevertheless, attracted my attention: firstly, the expression of contained suffering on Miguel's face, protected behind his dark glasses and peaked cap. His lips pressed together and that grin on his mouth which many people interpreted as a kind of smile, and which became famous all over the world. That grin came to signify a whole form of dominance. Lions tense their jaws because they are readying themselves to attack, or because they are defending themselves from an attack. Seeing him pass like that, within touching distance, and with the same grin as had appeared so many times on TV, took my breath away because TV pictures are rarely able to capture the drama of a lone effort like cycling. Even though viewers might think differently. I could hear the half-suppressed snorting from Miguel, his breathing as piercing as a knife wielded in the dark. The pain, not only his own, but also the pain of all those with him in the small group, spattered you, and I mean that literally. You were spattered by the sweat from their foreheads and arms. You could hear the puffing and panting, things that TV cannot capture, all mixed in with background noise and the sirens. But Miguel's face behind his glasses, those white teeth emerging from the mass of people who until then had been vociferous and menacing, that curling of the upper lip and nose, that wish to spit out, perhaps, the saliva you no longer have in your mouth, but which you still do in a reflex survival action, 'just a bit further and you're there, a bit further and you're there ...', this all created a huge impression on me, mainly because the leader's elbows were brushing against the precarious line of fans who shortly before had thought of blocking his path, and who now (presumably they were as overwhelmed as I was) stepped aside as best they could, amidst the shoving and yells of encouragement or admiration. The faces of the people, once Miguel had passed the point where we were standing, were a real picture. They looked as if they were saying, 'Did you see that, did you actually see that?' Or simply, 'Arrogant' or 'imperious so-and-so'. Or they contented themselves with shaking their heads, as though they were indicating that, however many times they saw him, despite the fact they had just seen him go past, they couldn't credit that a cyclist of his size and weight could possibly climb with such lightness and strength, leaving such an impression of dominance in his wake.

The second point which caught my attention was seeing Induráin tackling the most difficult stretch of the Alpe with a totally smooth and comfortable pedal cadence – and at speed, too, of course, while the rest were out of the saddle and struggling to maintain their rhythm. The chain on Miguel's bike was, I think, on the 17 or the 19 sprocket, and he was pedalling with that elegant and ethereal style to which we would grow accustomed, but which he displayed even as a young rider. He climbed 'in the saddle', as they say in cycling parlance, sitting on the seat and using his arms and back. But this is all just an optical illusion, since if you want to tackle a steep climb in this position, all the exertion falls on your legs. He was an impressive sight, and now and again one or other of the cyclists with him would glance almost incredulously over at him. 'How on earth can he have managed the whole climb without getting out of the saddle, even when we have accelerated?' This is enough to dishearten anyone. Ask Bugno, Claudio Chiappucci and so many others.

The third point which caught my attention was something I was simply not expecting: the darkness of Induráin's legs and arms. His skin was a matt colour, dark but gleaming with sweat. They really did look like the legs of a Colombian cyclist! A detail which isn't usually fully conveyed by television. Aside from the anecdotal, this caused me to ponder the hackneyed concept of the 'tanned cyclist'. I thought of the enormous number of hours that are required for skin exposed to the sun and more adverse conditions to acquire that special tone. Those diminutive and lightweight ankles, which looked as if they would fit inside any hand that tried to encircle them, which then stretched into a pair of calves that were as powerful as pistons. One particular muscle, the one which joins the outside of the calves to the thighs, located at the back and side of the knees, was spectacularly tense in riders with Induráin's physique. This is proven over and over again by photography. To an extent, photography enjoys somewhat of an advantage over television or 'live' viewing. Those who wish to verify this could spend their time going through their cuttings and looking at those photos. Induráin was pedalling on two mallets, which were driving straight down on the tarmac like blades, clean sword stokes which those fibrous and muscular legs moved with a musical cadence, with more harmony than rhythm, with more conviction than inertia.

In spite of everything, it's an almost impossible task to attempt to convince some people that Induráin was enduring indescribable pain as he pedalled. They reply by saying their eyes told a very different story. An old cycling hand was interviewing Induráin near the end of his career, and the Navarran rider admitted that the person who can truly understand what it means to suffer on a bike was the cyclotourist who has actually ridden one of the steep climbs and gone through hell. 'Other people,' he asserted, 'who follow cycling because it's trendy or just because it happens to be on TV, cannot really appreciate what it involves. The general public often follow fashion, rather than because they really like something. Take the Tour, for example. The roads are jam-packed, but during the rest of the year there's seldom as much interest in France.'

Miguel's possibly mistaken on that point. Although it is largely true that the general public always believed that the Navarran cruised to victory, there were others who, despite the fact they'd never even sat on a bike, let alone attempted a steep climb, could appreciate how much effort it took for a hefty man to remain unscathed after so many attacks. It's just that Miguel had to put up with the same old story repeated over and over again, for so many years, even when he began to win Tours, that eventually he got a bit tired of it all. Because if winning the great French Tour is one of the most difficult achievements in top-flight sport, maintaining your composure in the face of impertinent interviews, or stupid questions, is something not everyone is capable of. And the Navarran was a champion at that as well. Perhaps the greatest of all time.

Scherzo Vivace

(The Leaves)

FROM ELDA TO VAL-LOURON

He who gives advanced warning does not betray, so the saying goes. The long road from Elda, where, in 1983, Miguel was proclaimed the youngest-ever Spanish amateur champion, to the stage at Val-Louron, where he virtually sealed his first Tour victory in 1991, was full of regular advanced warnings for those who were prepared to listen. Almost a decade. Yet here in Spain many people still did not realise. Even in the middle of the 1990 Tour, on the way to the Pyrenees, many were still expecting an attack from Pedro Delgado. It didn't come and it never would come again. In Spain, we were looking backwards, rather than forwards towards the leaders, which is where Miguel Induráin usually was, waiting for Pedro.

On one occasion, during a special reception held by a group of hunters, I noted that, just as Induráin had been very modest about his cycling victories during the whole of the previous decade, so he adopted a similarly restrained and unassuming attitude about his hunting achievements. Someone reminded him that the area he came from, or perhaps a little to the south of Villava, was full of game.

'You'll bag loads.'

And he replied, 'I'll show you what *loads* means!'

He was presented with a handsome shotgun, and there was another for Pruden, his brother. 'Which of you is the better hunter?' they asked. 'I shoot, but he finishes them off for me,' explained Miguel with a smile.

Later he complained that hunting was good for his chest and heart, but caused pain in his legs. That made me think that he had spent his whole life pedalling a bicycle and doing little else. Something as commonplace as walking in the countryside or the woods was a real chore for the greatest Spanish sportsman of all time.

He had been a slave to his profession, to the peculiarities of his body. But he also used to give replies like that whenever he spoke about his cycling victories. Loads of Tours... 'I'll show you *loads* of Tours!'

Loads of Tours. For Miguel, that already amounted to two. Three was unbelievable. Four, sweet absurdity. Five, paradise. Those wins will provide us with emotional succour for the rest of our lives. He can appreciate what that means, even though it embarrasses him a bit to admit it.

But to reconstruct the day-by-day, month-by-month, year-by-year story, we have to make a lazy jump – which Miguel would appreciate – back to that time in 1982 when Pepe Barruso's telephone finally rang in the Villavés Cycling Club, and confirmation arrived that they were going to sign Induráin for Reynolds. His first wage would consist of expenses plus equipment. Pepe could scarcely believe it: 'You see, Miguel? Patience is always rewarded...'

And Miguel, of course, was no doubt thrilled, but, the fact remains he didn't appear to bat an eyelid, despite his anxiety about this thing that could change his whole life. 'That's fine. When do I start?'

Miguel is like a hundred-year-old tree, and just as silent. He stands quietly in a little corner of the country and not even the wind seems to worry him. His trunk is full of knots, each one a little enigma, a rough edge waiting to be discovered, a mystery that is perhaps a secret unto itself, because if it were not it would no longer be a mystery. The perfect, complex, secretive knots in the trunk are where he finds both his strength and his sense of being.

The world of cycling, ever-eager for progress, sometimes seems as frenetic as a nest of terrified crickets. And the wise tree remains as silent as ever. The barley sways gently, and now and again a bird trills in the pale blue sky, as if it were greeting the quiet tree. But it goes straight past. Its time has yet to come.

At the time when Gorospe, Arroyo and Delgado were making the jump up to the professional ranks with Reynolds, Miguel began riding with the amateur team, which was managed by Eusebio Unzúe. For Reynolds it was a trial season. Echávarri had the idea that a young and combative team could ruffle a few feathers in the Tour, and that is exactly what they would very soon be doing. In their initial year of competition they blew hot and cold. Arroyo looked set to win the Vuelta in fine style, but, to everyone's great disappointment, was given a ten-minute penalty at the end of stage 17 when wearing the leader's jersey. He finished thirteenth overall.

Induráin weighed about 90 kilos in those days, and, apart from adapting to the longer distances at the higher level, his problem continued to be the mountains. He could climb them, but very slowly; his difficulty was in finding a cadence, a rhythm. He raced a Tour of Bidasoa, and that's where the ascents began to hit him – the old ghost of the Beloso climb reappeared. At that time it was still a firmly held belief in Spain that a born climber was small and skinny, didn't allow his backside to touch the saddle in the whole of a big climb, and danced the bike gracefully and rapidly, as if it were his ideal partner in a tango contest. In short, you had to get out of the saddle as you made your way lithely uphill and, most important of all, be capable of just scraping inside the time limit on the flat stages in the big Tours or in the long time-trials. Miguel obviously did not fit the bill.

The younger Reynolds riders used to get together in Cegama, at the *Hostal Manolo*. Lots of riders milled around there – Iñaki Gastón, Arrieta, Pacheco, Guillermo Arenas, Otegui, Eduardo González Salvador, the Valencians Sanchís, Navarro Fuster and Ridaura, amongst others. Álberto Fernández as well, of whom it is said he was an Induráin clone, as like as two peas in a pod. The brave Riojan rider died in a training accident, years later. He was one of the *culones* as the team became known because of their size and power.* Following the trail blazed by the fearsome Belgian and Dutch outfits that were packed with toughened *routiers*, the Reynolds *culones* sowed terror wherever they went. They were able to set a tremendous pace and maintain it as long as necessary. What those in the media term a 'peloton buster', and Miguel, despite his youth, was one of the most outstanding of the *culones*. That's where he would acquire a technique which he would continue to employ later, as a professional – imposing a frenetic pace and not allowing himself to be swallowed up by the main bunch

---

* Reynolds were well known for having a strong amateur development squad. *Culones* literally means 'big bums'.

or caught by a select chasing group. Once he escaped with José Luis Navarro of the Caja Madrid team and they managed to stay out in front – but within sight of the peloton for nearly 50 kilometres – without any of them being able to ride them down. That was at Quintanar de la Orden, during the Tour of Toledo in 1983. A taste of what he would do at Liège in the '95 Tour.

While all the *culones* were very well looked after, Miguel in particular, because of his special physique, was most definitely wrapped in cotton wool. All the same, he still chalked up victories in what was his first year as a senior amateur. He won the Stars of Pamplona trophy, two stages of the Tour of Toledo, and a stage together with the overall classification in the Tour of Salamanca.

On 3rd July he won the championship of Navarre, and, then, while his 'elders' at the time were turning the Tour upside-down, Miguel was giving a real cycling recital in Elda at the annual Amateur Road Race Championships. If you've never seen one of these races, you can't imagine what they're like. Basically, they're a complete free-for-all with constant, crazy attacks and breaks. Unless some kind of prior agreement or pact has been made, tactics often go by the board. So things weren't going to be easy. Eusebio Unzúe still recalls the race as one of the most furious he has ever witnessed, and also one of the most magisterial exhibitions Induráin ever produced. There were numerous breaks, following on one after the other, regardless of the section of the course or the time. There were even people attacking at the feeding-stations. Throughout, Induráin showed amazing composure, tracking each and every escape so they only ever remained 'attempted' escapes. Behind, in his car, Unzúe could not believe what he was seeing. Someone would put in a spurt, and there was Miguel, in supreme command, on his wheel. At the end he had to see off a strong sprint from Jokin Mújica, who was considered a great hope of Basque cycling. Miguel did not react over-hastily. He knew exactly what was going to happen, and he, in turn, attacked forcefully, taking Mújica right on the line. Apparently Mújica's trainers, in a first angry reaction, berated their pupil: 'How did you let *him* pass you?' 'The guy's very good, he's very strong,' Jokin Mújica complained, and justifiably so.

That was the first really big win in Miguel Induráin's career, more important for the manner in which he won, rather than for the title itself. The story goes that the radio gave the win to another cyclist, Fernando Pacheco. All the Spanish Press published the same wrong information, which they were later forced to correct. Among the media there was general surprise, except in Navarre. That exhibition in Elda in 1983, his first big championship, was the launch pad for a glittering career. Apart from a period in '87 and '88, when he didn't always seem to know how to continue his progress, it was to run unhindered right up to the series of Tour wins that began in the early nineties.

The following year, 1984, was a strange, testing year. He was picked for the Los Angeles Olympics, but didn't finish the race. Nonetheless, Induráin being Induráin, he still managed to get on the podium at the Iberduero Grand Prix, the Fuencarral Classic, and the Aragón Week. He won the King of the Mountain prize, and two stages of the Tour of Navarra. He was also race leader for three days in the Tour of Vizcaya, where he made a large contribution to Reynolds' victory in the team time-trial.

In spite of its ups and downs, that year saw a major shift in Induráin's development. His managers decided he needed to spread his wings, to widen his riding experience; so they entered him in the Tour de l'Avenir (which for a couple of years became known as the Tour of the European Economic Community). It is, in fact, a difficult and nervy race, and therefore extremely tough on the riders. The Reynolds rider Carlos Hernández led for a few days, while Miguel was the cornerstone of another team time-trial victory. He also chalked up a spectacular win in the individual time-trial between Lourdes and Tarbes.

There was a lesson to be drawn from that important event: Miguel was certainly a raw diamond, but undeniably he was beginning to cope comparatively easily with Tour climbs such as the Izoard. He was also getting to know those riders who would be his leading rivals amongst the next generation of top professionals: Ugrumov, Konychev, Ekimov, Breukink, Bernard, Mottet, and many others. Although he maintained a natural respect for them, he was quite simply losing his fear of them. It was around that time that Miguel began to win time-trials against Jean-François Bernard, who would eventually be one of his most faithful lieutenants in Banesto. Indeed, it was Bernard who made a huge contribution to his first Tour win, which, for a few moments at the bottom of Alpe d'Huez, was in jeopardy. It was also Bernard who decided to split the group of favourites, once and for all, at the beginning of the ascent of Hautacam in '94, with Miguel shouting 'Faster, faster!'

The next Tour de l'Avenir also saw two Induráin triumphs in the time-trials. He was getting the knack of prologue stages and actually began to tire of winning in that specialism. That was until he came up against Thierry Marie, who was faster than he was over the short distance.

However, what is noteworthy about that far-off year of 1985 is that Echávarri and Unzúe decided to make him ride a few stages of the Tour de France, and also to take part in the Tour of Spain. So Miguel finally achieved his dream of going to the *Grande Boucle*. In the 6.8-kilometre prologue, around the Plumelec circuit, he finished a minute behind Hinault. That was a lot of time to take out of him. In the second stage, ending in Lanester, he finished in 173rd place out of 178 riders. And the following day, a completely flat stage from L'Orient to Vitre, he would again suffer like a condemned man. What Miguel had not taken into account was the brutish nature of the riding: he was now last in the overall classification, 17 minutes behind the leader Vanderaerden! The next stage was the team time-trial, and that day it was taken by the French. Reynolds were the best of the Spanish teams, but they were still two minutes ten seconds behind La Vie Claire, who went like a train driven by the master of ceremonies, Bernard Hinault. Miguel could do no more than tag on to his team-mates and, even at the beginning, was scarcely able to do his share on the front. The Tour was, indeed, a demented world. It was more mad than fast. He continued to maintain his sanity, but the stage between Fougères and Point Audemer, a trifling 239 kilometres, finished him off. He just couldn't deal with the first climb, at Mortain, which was gentle and straightforward enough. Even before he'd reached kilometre 50 the Reynolds doctor decided to call it a day. He was developing bronchitis and it would have made no sense at all to make the lad continue to drag himself around the French roads.

But it was Miguel's first entry in the Tour of Spain, a few months previously, that had been his key point of 1985. His objectives were to reach the pilgrims' goal of Santiago, and to complete the course. Earlier in the year he'd had the experience of being in second place – behind the German Rolf Gölz, in the Ruta del Sol, and, in the Midi Pyrenees, behind Laurent Fignon in the prologue and second overall behind Stephen Roche – but he'd never worn the leader's jersey in one of the big three-week stage races. He was soon to experience that feeling. The Tour of Spain began, that year, with a prologue in the city of Valladolid where Miguel hammered the stop-watch and easily bettered all the other times. Until, right at the end, with the race leadership seemingly within his grasp, the Dutchman, Bert Oosterbosch of Panasonic, powered in and snatched the precious yellow jersey from the Navarran by a mere eight seconds. In the second stage, to Zamora, Induráin managed to withstand the jumpiness of the peloton, which was becoming ever more restless as the kilometres passed. He was even caught up in a mass crash but held on to his second place overall.

Stage three was a killer – 262 kilometres between Zamora and Orense, the longest day of the race. There were three third category climbs, and the Reynolds team were prepared: Bert Oosterbosch might crack there, and lose some seconds. Even just a few would be enough to hand the lead to Miguel, and the whole team focused on making this happen. With Sean Kelly's Skil-Kas team pushing the pace, the leader slipped further and further back as the finish was approaching. Miguel might get to wear gold!* In the face of attacks from Kelly's men, he maintained his composure and arrived in Orense ready to don the jersey that was to fit him like a dream. It seemed to have been made for him, and he slipped it on sheepishly. Everyone knew he was only a temporary leader, because of his youth, and (a point emphasised by the radio reports) because of his size.

It must have been *en route* to the next finish, in Santiago de Compostela, that Miguel came to realise what wearing the leader's gold jersey really meant: those glances over at you; those gestures, and attempts to up the pace to test you out and see how you react; the cameras on the road, and the reporters at the finish. No doubt he found it a pleasant feeling, but it may, perhaps, have been a bit

---

* In the Tour of Spain the leader's jersey is more golden than yellow, and is often referred to as the 'gold jersey'.

too much. He had little comment to make after each stage, and the journalists would seek out other riders with more to say for themselves. It seemed as if Miguel felt, in some way, uncomfortable in the gold jersey, as if he didn't feel he fully merited it. Every day, he made his pithy statement, almost apologising for still wearing it. In Santiago, where the Italian, Baronchelli, took just four seconds off him, he only just hung on to it. And he was up against men who were all experienced cyclists, tested in thousands of battles, men whose legs had ridden several (in some cases many) big Tours, while Miguel had never lasted more than a week at this level.

Stage four is remembered as one of the tragic chapters in the history of cycling. We have already alluded to it – Jaume Salvá's fall, and Loos's injury; Noel Dejonckere coming to blows with René Martens, who had to be treated on the spot by the ambulance staff. And the finish was scandalous: the actual stage winner, Eddy Planckaert, had clearly blocked Sean Kelly, and there was uproar. In the mayhem hardly anyone paid any attention to that young Navarran who had the temerity to continue in gold. In the next stage, ending in Oviedo, and with the mountains looming, Miguel was well protected by his team. They had closed ranks around him, and he retained the lead comfortably, but the following day would bring with it the Lakes of Covadonga and everyone knew the leader would crack there. He knew it, too. Perhaps he'd even accepted it in advance, or instinctively knew it.

Yet he would have a score to settle with Oviedo which would remain unsettled until 1992, when, through those same streets, Miguel won the Spanish Road-Race Championships. What a memorable finish that would be, one of those turning-points in the history of cycling. Jon Unzaga, of the local Clas-Cajastur team, had managed to put a few metres between himself and a string of leading riders, including Miguel, whom Unzaga couldn't have seen, or couldn't have remembered as he readied himself to cross the line in triumph. Then, just as Unzaga eased off the pedals and raised his arms in jubilation, he saw Miguel appear from behind him like a rocket, his chin literally pressing down against the handle bars, and reach the finish a millimetre ahead of him. They had to consult the photo finish. A heart-stopping ending, which some people refuse to believe even when you tell them. I myself have been asked, along the lines of the ending to my novel *Alpe d'Huez*, 'Is such a tight and nail-biting finish really possible?' In the streets of Oviedo, in that duel between Induráin and Unzaga, lay the answer. Yes, it is possible. It's not usual, but it is possible. All this, though, would occur seven years after the events I am currently describing. Poor Unzaga, he was a very brave rider.

Back in the 1985 Vuelta, climbing up to the Lakes of Covadonga, Miguel dropped his cadence; he gave up. Further up the road the favourites were flying, tearing into each other, but he didn't want to know. Not yet. The winner was Pedro Delgado, who was gradually winning over the hearts of the Spanish public, and Miguel came in almost thirteen minutes adrift of him. The cameras showed him, clearly exhausted, although in no way broken. It was just logic imposing itself.

From that moment on, the rest of the race was a case of knuckling down and assisting Julián Gorospe, who seemed to be the one Reynolds man with an outside chance (Delgado was riding for Seat–Orbea at that time). In the time trial on stage 17 he came in one minute 59 seconds behind Pello Ruiz Cabestany, who specialised in that kind of event, but in eleventh place. Then there was that famous penultimate stage from Alcalá to DYC Distilleries, over several first-category climbs. It was the famous stage where Pepe Recio escaped, taking Delgado with him, and Perico*, boosted by being on home territory and in front of his own people, started taking minutes off Peugeot's Robert Millar. Because Millar was incorrectly informed about the gaps and was still the race leader on the road, he remained over-confident. By the time he did decide to react it was already too late, and Pedro took nearly seven minutes out of him. The whole country went berserk at the Segovian's exploits. Meanwhile, an oblivious Induráin remained lost in his own world, and even in the last stage, one of those routine snail's-pace stages, he missed a sudden break at the front and came in off the back of the main group.

But he had worn gold, and knew what it felt like to control a race from that position. Wearing that jersey had been spine-tingling and had made his heart beat to a different rhythm. But that was something he would come to realise only later. It was

---

* 'Perico' is an affectionate nickname for Pedro.

connected to pain and the wind, and was already forming some of those knots which Miguel, the quiet and measured tree, was still struggling to understand fully. Back in Villava his favourite pastime was awaiting him: eating slices of ham and fried eggs, a bit of work on the tractor and then watching the TV with a bag of sunflower seeds to chew. And he could daydream because he had been told that they would let him 'experience' a few stages of the Tour de France.

As far as experiences went, 1986 was to be a year of surprises, albeit without any great discoveries. He won the Tour of Murcia, and was second in the Tour of Burgos prologue stage; he also performed well in the hard-fought Grand Prix des Nations. But there were three trials by fire awaiting him: the Tour of Spain; the Tour de France; and, once again, the Tour de l'Avenir. In the Tour of Spain he did no more than continue his apprenticeship – watching and learning. Fully resigned to playing a mere bit-part in the mountains, he placed all his eggs in the time-trial basket, where he was intent on making further improvement. The Lakes of Covadonga were torture once more, but he endured the climb with his customary coolheadedness. Then, in the short but gruelling time-trial up the Naranco del Bulnes, he came 125th. He clearly wasn't focused.

It is paradoxical that later, in his final year as a professional cyclist, Miguel won that same time-trial on the Naranco, with its torrid, even if short, slopes, and took 20 seconds out of Marcelino García. All that at an average speed of not far off 30 kilometres per hour. That was in the Tour of Asturias, just before the '96 Tour, and it filled us with hope. But just a few months later, on the same slopes of the Naranco, we would see Miguel resigning himself to following the wheel and the pace offered him by his loyal team-mate José María Jiménez. He was saying goodbye to the Tour of Spain, and to many other things. It had to be in Asturias, a land which saw him triumph on several occasions in its prestigious local Tour, but which had also, for years, been the scene of his private purgatory.

In that '86 Tour of Spain, Induráin simply reacted out of pride, spurred on by his own self-esteem after the disaster on the Naranco. On the flat 29.6-kilometre circuit of Valladolid he passed the three riders in front of him, and almost caught the next to finish with the eighth-fastest time. Normal service was resuming, although the truth is that for the whole of that Tour of Spain Miguel was lackadaisical and not concentrating whenever anyone made a break or when the field was strung out. As soon as some hills appeared, his resigned acceptance was obvious. Others could bust a gut, but he wasn't prepared to do so. Quite possibly he was preoccupied with the upcoming Tour de France, in which he was to test the water for a second time, or perhaps the Tour de l'Avenir.

Meanwhile, the whole of Spain was following the duel between the Galician, Álvaro Pino and Millar up in the Sierra Nevada, and they did so with their hearts in their mouths. The final time-trial ended in overall victory for Álvaro Pino, with Miguel a mere 35 seconds behind him on the stage. Then the whole of Spain watched with tears in their eyes as Pino wept at the finish, dedicating his triumph to his former team-mate, Alberto Fernández, who, along with his wife, had died shortly before in a car crash. People lining the roadside waved pine branches in honour of his name as the Galician went past. It was a moving spectacle, and Alberto Fernández, even in his absence, filled our hearts. He had disappeared prematurely and permanently in tragic circumstances, and the people were acknowledging the fact.*

As for Miguel, who'd improved as the Tour of Spain progressed, he approached the Tour de France full of respect, naturally enough, but with few expectations. The prologue time-trial was a little disappointing, not because it saw the inevitable victory for Thierry Marie, but because in just four and half kilometres he took ten seconds out of Miguel, who came home seventeenth; even Echávarri said he had been somewhat 'below par'.

Over the following few days Miguel didn't seem to know where he was. The madness of the Tour was getting to him, but on stage five, between Evreux and Villiers-sur-Mer, he shook off his lethargy and decided to test his strength. With 25 kilometres to go to the finish, Planckaert made a break, and behind him, to everyone's surprise, went Miguel. Together they began to hunt down Van der Velde and Pelier, who had escaped earlier. And it

---

* Spain has been particularly unfortunate in the number of fine riders who have been killed on the road, especially in training accidents.

was Miguel who was doing the driving at the front. As Benito Urraburu, one of our top cycling experts, wrote so lucidly, there is never a single defining moment in the career of a champion; rather, it is a curious and improvised amalgam of moments and usually unplanned events which gradually construct what will later be his highway to glory. So it is possible that on that day and at that moment, one of Miguel's mental chips clicked into place. What is certain is that, with Miguel leading the pursuit, the gap between them and the escape group began to come down rapidly, and at the finish Miguel was fourth on the stage.

Two days later, between Cherbourg and Saint-Hilaire, there were endless attacks, and at kilometre 182 the unthinkable occurred again: after a steep gradient, Miguel attacked strongly, in an attempt to blow the race apart. On his wheel went nine other riders to form a group that would reach the finish with more than two minutes to spare over the peloton. Miguel, having led almost the whole way, was third in the sprint, behind Peeters and Kiefel – both fast riders. Was Liège on the horizon? You bet it was!

Although we were not aware of it at the time, Miguel was developing a liking for the Tour, for its perpetual motion and merciless frenzy of action. In the 61.5-kilometre time-trial, Hinault hammered his rivals. Miguel came in over two minutes behind, in thirteenth place, and amongst the Spanish riders, only Julián Gorospe recorded a better time. The Pyrenean hell was still to come, however, with that epic stage between Bayonne and Pau, which Pedro Delgado won ahead of Bernard Hinault himself. The route took them over the Col de Marie Blanque, and that would spell the end for many riders, Miguel included.

In the future that climb was to be of crucial importance to Induráin's career, and so he made a particular point of studying its features in minute detail. Perhaps he was already familiar with the mountain? Perhaps as a youth he had gone to see a race there with his mates from the Club Ciclista Villavés, who knows? The fact is it was Marie Blanque, one of the toughest mountains in the Tour, which would play a key part in determining the destiny of the Navarran. Although the north face from Escot is a short climb, it is a tricky mountain, to be sure, even for the greatest and most talented climbers. There are those who still recall a distraught Bernard Thévenet screaming at his mechanics for a 23 rear sprocket because the gear he was using had literally made him grind him to a halt. '*Un col terriblement vachard*', as Goddet, the Tour boss, called it. A mean and nasty mountain. And Pierre Chany described it as 'a narrow, winding road, which looks like wounds gouged along the injured back of an old boar'. In 1978 the Belgian Pollentier had been first to the top. It was a treacherous mountain, certainly, but Miguel knew that now – his heart, racing at almost 200 beats a minute, had already told him how and where, and perhaps when as well. It was just a case of waiting. For the moment, though, he withdrew from that crazy Tour, from the craziness that has marked all Tours since the inauguration of the race in 1903.

The time he really came of age internationally, albeit in a race for up-and-coming stars, would be in the Tour de l'Avenir, which, as we mentioned earlier, was renamed that year, 1986, as the Tour of the EEC. Miguel Induráin, together with Marc Gómez and Rubén Gorospe, were Reynolds's trump cards. In the initial time-trial at Oporto Miguel, riding at an average speed of almost 49 kilometres an hour, recorded the best time. The second stage, from Oporto to Viseu, saw the typical, crazy feeding-station break and the La Vie Claire's sprinter, Roy Knickman, opened up a gap of a minute over the rest. The race reached Pamplona with Induráin still some way down the overall classification. At the stage-finish in Pau, Jokin Mújica and Induráin arrived together, but this time it was Mújica who clinched the hard-fought sprint. Yours today, mine tomorrow. The following stage seems now to be virtually identical to the one that would take place two years later in the Tour de France, with Laudelino Cubino powering away towards the top of Luz-Ardiden. Although he lost a couple of minutes to Cubino, Miguel chipped away at Knickman's advantage, and the race leader only just managing to hold on to the *maillot jaune*. Laudelino had made the acquaintance of the mountain which would raise him to the heights as the winner of that blue-ribbon stage in the '88 Tour, but Miguel had also seen each and every turn of that magical col. Luz-Ardiden, like the Puy-de-Dôme, Alpe d'Huez, Guzet-Neige, Isola-2000 and Hautacam, is a mountain of no return with a summit finish.

The second time-trial, 27.5-kilometres at Carpentras, also went to Miguel, and enabled him to make further inroads into

Knickman's lead. Around Gap, with the going getting tougher, Knickman decided to withdraw. Miguel now took over as leader, but with two keen rivals at his heels: the Frenchman Patrice Esnault, and the American Alexis Grewal, the great hope of US cycling after his triumph at the Los Angeles Olympics. They set off towards Briançon, with the Izoard again standing in their way, and despite the constant series of ferocious attacks launched by both Esnault and Grewal, Induráin held his own. In the final stage, from Sestrière to Turin, Miguel contented himself with 'monitoring' – that verb he used so often to refer to his way of watching his rivals' movements, and which, time and again, would drive them to despair.

Miguel's triumph was twofold: firstly, he'd won a race whose previous victors had included Lemond, Baronchelli, Mottet, Pascal Simon, Gimondi and Zoetemelk, the inexhaustible Dutchman; secondly, and perhaps even more important than the podium place, was the way he climbed the Izoard. His team-mate, Marc Gómez, told the Press: 'I've rarely seen a lad of his age deal with responsibility with such composure. He's a great watcher and his race sense does the rest.' Miguel had a score to settle with the high mountains, those legendary devourers of brave men. On this occasion, the high mountains were symbolised by the Izoard, a peak made famous by Louison Bobet when he said that great champions, to prove their worth, needed to cross the famous Casse Déserte in the way he had done. Miguel did not go over the top in first position, but he did reach the summit strongly. Izoard represented a formidable springboard for his confidence and self-esteem.

Paradoxically, it would not be until the Dauphiné Libéré in the late spring of 1996, weeks before the Tour which Miguel would lose, when the Izoard would see him go over the top alone, and in majestic splendour. We could not imagine it at that moment, but it was a farewell parade.

The hot *Casse Déserte* wind knew it, though.

That wind, exactly a decade before, had seen him pass that way, as golden as the wheat, snaking along the winding road. Then, ten years later, in the Dauphiné Libéré, the same Alpine wind saw him pass like Achilles in his bronze armour ready to conquer the imaginary Troy of fame in one of the most eagerly awaited and prestigious events in the calendar. It was, in fact, the last great display Miguel Induráin gave us in the high mountains. That occasion of the Tour of the EEC, a decade earlier, was also the first time that the whole of Villava came out to acclaim him.

The following year, 1987, marked the darkest chapter in Miguel Induráin's career. He was forced to retire from the Tour of Spain, and therefore couldn't offer Julián Gorospe the assistance he'd expected to give him. Gorospe could do nothing to counter the momentum of Lucho Herrera, who ran out overall winner and sent the whole of Colombia wild with joy. In the Tour de France Miguel's goal was to finish, and this he did, although it was back in 97th place. He did renew acquaintance with the tough slopes of Marie Blanque, and the warm breeze of that equatorial plateau must have whispered new melodies in his ear: 'Prepare yourself, for your time will soon come, and it will be right here.' That Tour centred on the historic duel between Delgado and Roche. Although the Spaniard took the lead on Alpe d'Huez, the Irishman didn't allow him to gain too much time in a nerve-racking and memorable ascent of La Plagne.

Miguel and his sixth sense – a gift carefully tuned to recording scenes and situations – must also have noted each and every gradient of La Plagne. That's where the glory of his fifth Tour was awaiting him. But in 1987 he climbed it in his own time, almost touring, trying to keep ahead of the stragglers. And the final time-trial at Dijon, a dark memory for Spanish cycling fans, saw Roche strip Delgado of the yellow jersey. Miguel came in sixth, behind the winner Jean-François Bernard. Even Delgado, who stiffened up quite a bit, produced a better time than the Navarran over those interminable 38 kilometres. Nevertheless, Miguel did win the Tour of the Mining valleys, where he also claimed three stage victories; he won the homely Gran Premio Navarra, as well as stages in the Catalan Week and Tour of Murcia.

He was continuing to learn, and to suffer as well, because even he couldn't see clearly how he was supposedly 'developing'. Furthermore, he picked up a dose of pneumonia, which would plague him for nearly two years. But this machine was not for stopping. He had to ride on.

It must have been around this time that he met the girl who would be his wife, Marisa López de Goikoetxea. She worked in the offices of the Navarre University Hospital, although she is from Lazkao in Guipuzcoa. Naturally their courtship was extremely discreet. It's said that sometimes they would go to restaurants and disco bars in the Iturrama district of Pamplona, although when they wanted some proper peace and quiet they would go off to San Juan de Luz, Hendaye or Biarritz. The importance Marisa would have for him in continuing the 'family' (a notion which seems to have almost sacred connotations for the Induráins) would become most intense at the time of the difficult decision over his retirement.

For the moment, Miguel needed to continue his development as a professional sportsman, in spite of his bronchial problems, his allergies, and the secret fears which no doubt he harboured.

It was clear that he was no longer just a 'raw diamond', but now he had to prove it by doing more than merely confirming his victory in the 'little' Tour of the EEC. The doctors, especially those in the Navarre University Hospital and Dr Conconi himself, knew he was exceptionally gifted, but they couldn't put a ceiling on his possible development. Nor could they state when and how this development would take place, nor even whether it would actually take place. Miguel had high aerobic potential, and he was easily able to cross the fearsome anaerobic effort threshold and recover almost immediately. Although no biopsy was carried out, they knew that his muscle mass had a higher percentage of slow rather than fast fibres, which is generally down to genetic factors. The slow fibres are less susceptible to acidosis – that is, muscle saturation caused by lactic acid and, therefore, fatigue. For this reason, his muscles worked best at middle and long distances.

All this, however, remained pure theory. The reality was that one moment Miguel would be suffering, as in the 1988 Tour of Spain where he abandoned at kilometre 52 of the final stage, just as they were approaching Madrid. He was suffering from a heavy cold that had been pummelling him for days. The next moment he would be performing miracles that would astound his own team-mates. Ángel Arroyo, for instance, tells the story of a climb up Cerler where he saw Miguel looking very relaxed. He asked him how he was, to see if he could push the pace on a bit, more just to liven things up than anything else. Miguel replied with a worrying and ambiguous 'Mmm...' But he pushed on so much they practically had to tell him to hold back because he was beginning to drop some of his own team-mates. In the '88 Tour de France Induráin finished in 47th place, although he helped Pedro Delgado as much as he could, on the flat, on the false flat, in the small mountains, and also in some of the high mountain stages, such as the Aspin and Peyresourde. However, you never saw him on television, because by the time the live TV link-up began, he had already performed his role to perfection. Throughout the whole Tour, and for weeks afterwards, Pedro was constantly thanking him for his generous efforts.

It was that grim toil as a *domestique* which Miguel performed with never a murmur of complaint. Just as he had always done, really. Javier Luquín tells a story of the night of Perico Delgado's triumph in the Tour, a controversial triumph because of the awful Probenecid issue. This was a substance permitted by the UCI but not by the French Cycling Federation. What a mess. In the end, Pedro swept to victory, and the whole of Spain, which had felt slandered by the doping accusation, was ecstatic. That night Miguel was more talkative than Luquín had ever seen him; they even drank a little champagne and played the fool. Incredible. A generous heart, a big heart, a pure heart.

It was the following year, 1989, that marked Miguel Induráin's definitive and spectacular leap on to the stage of top-flight international cycling. It was a gentle but firm leap, silent, and yet as emphatic as a space shuttle leaving its launch-pad. In making this move it was to his advantage that everybody's attention being centred on the versatile and captivating personality of Pedro Delgado. For a couple of years, when Miguel was beginning to offer us complete recitals of cycling, we had the ridiculous situation in which the only question that seemed to concern Spaniards was: 'What's Perico done?' Or, in similar vein: 'When's Perico going to attack?'

There's no doubt that 1989 also saw Induráin's view of himself changing. He was second in the tough Subida al Naranco, thus showing he could indeed climb. He won the Criterium International (held that year in Avignon) and in the time-trial stage he was devastating: he even caught Laurent Fignon (a feat he would repeat several times) – and don't forget that was the year when the bespectacled Parisian had almost recovered his outstanding form of 1983 and 1984. Fignon made a comment that day, in the city of the Popes, to the effect that 'Induráin murdered me today'. But this was nothing in comparison to what would befall him in front of the eyes of the world in the famous Luxembourg time-trial in the '92 Tour.

Here then was Miguel, reaping the harvest, according to his own particular philosophy of life. He had a number of minor triumphs, but, against that, the ever-thankless Tour of Spain punished him once more: following a crash, he was forced to retire on stage 17. Many people believe Miguel didn't like the Vuelta, but that's a mistaken view. He always said he would have loved to have won it, on home ground, amongst the Spanish people. More appropriately, it could be said that it was the Vuelta which wouldn't accept Miguel – for instance, the cold and the snowy, hellish weather conditions which caused him to crack notoriously on the climb to Alto Campo; and then there were the illnesses and the falls. At times, several of these misfortunes occurred together. This was too much even for Miguel Induráin Larraya. So when, in 1992, he chose the Giro d'Italia rather than the Vuelta as preparation for the Tour de France, this just got under the excessively patriotic skin of certain people. It had been just the same with Delgado: there was an enormous uproar when Echávarri decided that, rather than race the Vuelta, Pedro would use the Giro as his preparation for the Tour. This was a Tour he would subsequently win in classic fashion, overcoming all his rivals as well as the cloak-and-dagger conspiracies of certain sections of the French Press, but it made no difference whatsoever: saying 'No' to the Spanish Vuelta was a mortal sin. With Miguel, this decision not to ride the Vuelta opened up wounds which would have lengthy repercussions and which, in fact, never fully closed.

Going back to 1989, his performance in the Paris–Nice that year refuted once and for all the old fallacy that Miguel Induráin could not climb because of his size; it swept away any doubts and opened up a world of hope and expectation. The place where we'd see Miguel attacking in the mountains was on the much-feared Mont Faron (and it was to occur there the following year as well). At the foot of this legendary mountain, with its difficult inclines of up to 12 or 13 per cent, Miguel attacked with superhuman conviction. Only the stubborn Bruno Cornillet was able to follow him. That attack helped Miguel to move to within just 45 seconds of the leader, Marc Madiot. Then on stage five Induráin escaped again, along with the Frenchman Gérard Rué, on the Col de Vignon, and further increased the advantage on the descent. He allowed Rué to win the stage, while he himself donned the leader's white jersey. Just like the following year, everything was decided in the time-trial climb up the Col d'Eze. Roche ran him very close, but Induráin managed to survive. He was already 'conducting'.

One year later he would again win the Paris–Nice classic, and the blue-ribbon stage would again be Marseille–Mont Faron, a distance of 164 kilometres. What was that about Miguel not attacking in the mountains? He attacked with a harsh, ruthless pace and, by the summit, Stephen Roche himself had lost more than a minute to him. Over the following days Roche closed a little, so once more they were neck-and-neck by the time of the time-trial up the Col d'Eze. Miguel lost just seven seconds to Roche, but retained the white jersey.

It was around that time Induráin became the man to watch, and for the first time *L'Équipe* paid homage to the Navarran. 'A raw diamond', they wrote. Not very original, since Barruso, Urdániz, Unzúe and others had been saying the same thing seven long years earlier. And similarly, Philippe Bouvet, on *Antenne 2*, was speaking of the 'stunning possibilities lurking in those legs'. Nevertheless, the 1990 Spanish Tour was another disappointment. The astute Marco Giovannetti, superbly supported by his Seur team, monopolised all the attention. Miguel was again left trailing. Even in the 1991 Vuelta, in which Induráin was second in the overall classification behind Melchor Mauri, all his plans collapsed when the principle stage in the Catalan Pyrenees was suspended due to adverse weather conditions. That came as a great relief for Mauri, and there was nothing Miguel could do about it. The Vuelta had a jinx on him.

But let's retrace our steps, to that uncertain and emotional year of 1989, with Pedro out to retain his Tour title, but where he blew it by taking a wrong turn on the way to the start of the prologue stage in Luxembourg. This left the Segovian nearly three minutes behind the leader. And this after only 7.8 kilometres of the Tour! It was a disaster which would continue the following day when, in the second part of the stage (a team time-trial) Pedro would crack spectacularly. That afternoon all the nervous tension which he'd accumulated from the previous day, when he had produced an exceptional time in the individual time-trial despite his initial error, came to the fore. It was painful for us to watch, helpless and confused, as those pictures showed practically the whole Reynolds team coming to a halt and waiting for their leader.

Delgado waited for the mountains to arrive to recover some time which, he did, in amazing fashion, day after day. The die was cast; it had been a crazy race from day one, but now it seemed that an order had arrived for them to pump up the craziness even more. Now it was all or nothing – the Reynolds riders having to turn the screw, in a bid to deliver a surprise knock-out blow. But it was too much to hope that both Greg Lemond and Laurent Fignon, the two other big pre-race favourites, would allow themselves to be surprised at one and the same time. Indeed, the excitement of the event focused on the ultra-tight marking of those three star riders, with everything else shaped by that complex strategy. At first, Fignon, as lippy as ever, dismissed Pedro's chances completely, but by the time they'd left the Pyrenees, he would find himself having to contend with him again.

As they reached the Pyrenees Induráin's great day was about to materialise. The eighth day was a Sunday, and the stage 200-odd nervous kilometres between Bastide d'Armagnac and Pau, with sudden bursts of acceleration and a watchful eye kept on rivals. There was a lumpy final stretch – and two blue-ribbon stages ahead. The first had its finish in Cauterets, and the second in Luchon-Superbagnères.

Superbagnères was a better-known and charismatic mountain. Hinault had won a time-trial there, although years before he had suffered a serious *défaillance* there, too. Top-rank victors such as Massignan, Bahamontes, José Manuel Fuente and Lemond all attested to the toughness of that 1,804-metre summit. Cauterets, on the other hand, had only been climbed once, in 1953, and it was another Basque cyclist, Jesús Loroño, who had triumphed there. However, the stage Loroño rode, from Pau to Cauterets, was 103 kilometres long, whereas in 1989 they would ride 147 kilometres with several other climbs as an apéritif. One of these was the much-feared Marie Blanque and another was the

Aubisque by its steepest face – from Laruns to Eaux-Bonnes, which has no false flats.

The stage had a lively start, and there was a feeling in the air that something important was going to happen that day. Between Oloron Sainte-Marie and Gurmençon, the riders were on their guard. Some distance still from Escot, the village located at the foot of Marie Blanque, three riders decided to break from the main bunch in an adventure that was doomed to fail. Suddenly, the mist loomed over the valley. That area has a special microclimate, with big contrasts in temperature between the ascent and descent. The road is steep, seemingly hewn out of the side of the rock, and it twists and turns in hairpin bends. The movement is circular, disorientating, dizzying, as if the road is searching for itself.

And then a miracle occurred, right up there in the mist. On the orders of the wind, no doubt. The Symphony Miguel Induráin was to play was already a forceful and lively *Scherzo*. Up to that day he had produced a few Haydneseque touches in the symphonies that others had created by pedals and sweat. Always monitoring, hardly ever taking a risk, except in that first ascent of Mont-Faron. But that was at the finish of a stage and this, apparently, defied sense. Pedro saw he was restless and told him to go for it, to build up a lead if he could on the Aubisque. He'd join up with him later if he could.

The wind and mist saw Miguel sprout wings. He went away from the main bunch, which was going at a good pace, at the very start of the toughest gradient of the Marie Blanque, a mountain where I personally have seen very fit cyclotourists forced to get off their machines despite all the training they'd done. A brutal four-kilometre-long cliff-face, unrelenting even on the few bends, and with a 14 per cent gradient the whole way up to the summit. That was the road along which Miguel flew.

There was a poet called Kenneth White who wrote:

When they ask me which religion I belong to,
I'll say: to the Col de Marie Blanque.

Miguel's poetic *Scherzo* merged into the thick layers of mist along the side of the narrow road with its less than perfect surface. Over the top he went and soon he was giving chase to the breakaway group. This was his home territory: he knew the landmarks; he knew that his people were waiting in Cauterets. The beech groves spoke to him once more, and history too, but after a short moment's truce in Bielle, he realised that if he wanted to lead into Cauterets he'd have the fight of his life on his hands: the fearsome Aubisque. He began to climb it – less rapidly than the Marie Blanque – but still without giving his heart a rest. This was his day. That afternoon he was really going to test his relaxed heart. He was relaxed himself, because he knew Pedro had Rondón and Palacio with him. And he reached the top of Aubisque on his own.

And then the gentle but treacherous Soulor slope. And then, when his leg muscles had loosened, there was the Col de Borderes, and after that, pedalling on automatic pilot, he was faced by the small but terribly untimely Côte de Saint-Savin. It is scarcely higher than the Erro Pass, but must have seemed like a calvary, one of those little peaks you look at on the map and disregard, but which end up weighing like lead in your legs as if it were a special-category climb.

And, finally, he reached a place called Pierrefitte-Nestelas. From there, all that remained was the ascent to Cauterets. Not to the village of Cauterets itself but a little higher, to Cauterets-les-Cambasque. The place of the Basques.

And he flew on, although he was gradually weakening. He kept his composure and his elegance, but did begin to lose a little of his speed – like the injured swallow in the poem by the great Spanish poet, Lope de Vega – and behind him, Perico Delgado was closing, locked in his personal duel with Fignon and Lemond.

By that time, Miguel could no longer see anything. All he wanted to do was to fly, even though he felt as if he were treading water. He had won a Tour stage! Years later, whenever anyone insinuated (if they did not actually rebuke him) that he had never won a big mountain stage, he would smile and reply: 'Well, I won one before I started to win Tours.'* The wind of the Aubisque, the mist of the Marie Blanque and the deathly yet beautiful paleness of that final ascent to Cauterets must have whispered to him, his face blue from the effort he had expended: 'You can go higher. If

---

* In fact, he won two: at Cauterets in 1989, and at Luz-Ardiden in 1990.

you managed to get here, then the heavens are yours for the taking.'

There were hardly any cameras to record it, which seemed to be Miguel's fate at that time. However incredible it might seem, all eyes remained on what Delgado, Fignon and Lemond were doing, or should have been doing, back down the road. But Miguel did not need cameras, although no one deserved them more than he did for that stupendous solo procession. Exactly a year later he would get his just revenge.

A year later, the 1990 Tour was riven by controversy surrounding the supposed hierarchy in the Banesto camp: according to the backroom team, Perico was the leader, and Induráin was there to help and also 'in case something happened'. An ambiguous and delicate situation. First off, there was an escape which no one expected. Once again the typical madcap feeding-station break which is what can happen in any big, three-week tour. A substantial lead developed and everyone's plans went out the window. After his back-to-back Paris–Nice triumphs and his phenomenal win at Cauterets the previous year, Induráin had posted a further warning, just to remove any lingering doubts. In the long time-trial at Épinal he recorded the best time until Alcalá came in with a truly phenomenal ride. The Mexican would never reproduce another performance to match it. Miguel was second, but you could see just how eager he was.

It is curious to look back at photographs of that Tour, in the Alps and, above all, in the Pyrenees. They normally show a small group of cyclists, the favourites and their lieutenants, but, a few metres ahead is the tall, dark, cap-less silhouette of Miguel. Propelled by the wind, he again turned the screw to see if Perico would jump off the front so that they could go for broke together. But Delgado was struggling to conceal his serious gastro-enteritis, and to keep up with the group of favourites.

We saw Miguel's face, looking over his shoulder on La Madeleine, seeking out Pedro, and again on the Glandon. The approach to Alpe d'Huez saw another of Induráin's recitals: out on his own, without anyone taking over from him, he forced the pace like a man possessed at the head of a group which included Delgado, Bugno, Lemond, Claveyrolat and Eduardo Chozas who had managed to get on to the back on the descent towards

Allemont. Just after Bourg d'Oisans, around Prédes-Roches, as soon as the road leading to Alpe d'Huez begins to get a little steeper, Induráin lifted his foot off the pedal, his mouth gasping from the effort. He lost almost twelve minutes on a stage where Perico was unable to finish off all the good work. Even Bugno, the stage winner, showed his admiration for Miguel's effort. Days later, in the stage between Villard-de-Lans and Saint-Étienne, which was won by Chozas, Miguel had to give Delgado a tow because the breakaway group contained Lemond and Breukink.

By then they were nearing the Pyrenees, but first lay the stage between Le-Puy-en-Velay and Millau, a short but fairly tough climb. Marino Lejarreta made a break, because he thought there was another rider in front of him, and Induráin was immediately on his wheel, with the idea of taking Perico with him. But when he turned round, he saw Delgado wasn't there. This time Miguel had no doubts: he wouldn't hang around for him. Lejarreta came home first and Miguel finished second 24 seconds behind, but better than his own expectations. That day Delgado confessed to *Marca*, the Spanish daily sports paper: 'Because he stayed behind with the main bunch I think I deprived Miguel of the stage win. I hold my hands up to him. He's my right arm, and left arm, my legs as well. I owe him so much and he provides me with all the protection I need.' No comment.

Fate has many twists. Just a few months later, as he climbed Jaizkibel in the San Sebastián World Cup classic, Marino Lejarreta would see Induráin forcing a pace which not even Marino, an expert climber and master of such tough events, could live with. Miguel's advantage just kept growing, and he won by more than two minutes from Laurent Jalabert in the city's central boulevard. According to eyewitnesses, a stunned Echávarri took several minutes to react after seeing what his pupil had done.

However, getting back to the Tour, the most amazing exploits were still to come, in the stage ending in Luz-Ardiden. Miguel's soul still bore the scars of Épinal and Millau, and of Alpe d'Huez, of course. On the road up to the summit of Luz-Ardiden, where it seemed that the whole village of Villava was gathered, race leader Claudio Chiappucci, the combative Italian who'd made a surprise solo attack on an earlier mountain, cracked disastrously. Delgado was also flagging, and still out in front was Martínez Torres, the

ONCE rider, who had led over the Tourmalet. Then, suddenly, Greg Lemond, who knew that this was the day and the climb which would decide the Tour, launched a ferocious attack. He was followed by Marino Lejarreta, and Miguel Induráin. Lemond made what was possibly the ascent of his life. Literally hunched over his bike, he vented all the rage he could muster on each thrust on the pedal. Like motorbikes, they zoomed past an exhausted Martínez Torres and soon afterwards Marino Lejarreta dropped off the back, blown away by the American's pace, but on his wheel, like a shadow, remained Induráin. The long corridor of spectators became increasingly narrow, and Lemond's rhythm became increasingly devastating, with his smooth and extraordinarily rapid cadence. It looked just as though he were freewheeling on the flat. It was that famous *souplesse*, a word the French use to describe a fluid and rapid uphill motion, moving the sprockets with a very fast pedal speed, which rends the heart of any rival. It is simply that the pursuing Miguel was not just any rival. No one really knew yet who he was. Maybe he himself didn't, nor did the wind on Luz-Ardiden, bursting that day with people and the heat of the sun.

Induráin's life had recently passed through a kind of early autumn. It was the season which marked the completion of his apprenticeship, the last occasions when he would have to suffer the role of a *domestique*. Now he was performing music as he pedalled, and his *Scherzo* began to overwhelm friend and foe alike. These were bars of music nobody else had ever before been capable of putting together. Now, as he climbed Luz-Ardiden, there was a touch of Beethoven in his pedalling, whereas Lemond's cadence suggested an exultant and excited animal scenting blood. It seemed impossible to climb any faster.

And then the miracle occurred again: on a bend in the road Miguel accelerated. His wheels whirred ever quicker. The thousands and thousands of Spaniards crowding the lush slopes of Luz-Ardiden couldn't believe their eyes. But it was true. A special force, a wind concentrated on his back, was propelling Miguel towards the summit, towards glory once more, on a mountain stage in the Tour. He outstripped Lemond as easily as someone ripping up a thin sheet of paper and scattering the pieces to the wind.

The wind. There was no wind on Luz-Ardiden, everything just seemed bathed in sunlight. But it was there.

It was the beginning of a new era. And that man who raised his arms, who was applauding himself and was almost laughing with joy, was to be the master of that era. He always knew the heavens of the Tour belonged to him. And its lands, and its peoples. Nonetheless, he was ready to be a Good Lord.

Andante Maestoso

(*The Sun*)

THOSE FIVE GLORIOUSLY IMPROBABLE YEARS

In his gentle way Miguel always rejects anything that could be seen as presumption on his part. One day I put it to him: 'You know the descent from the Tourmalet as well as anyone does.' I was convinced that he did – both via La Mongie and the road to Barèges, and via Luz-Saint Saveur, which is perhaps the rockier, wilder and more inhumane side. That was where he hunted down Rominger in 1993. But Miguel denied this at first. Later he accepted that, yes, it was a dangerous descent that he did know well, and one on which he was forced to brake on 'three or four bends'. So, not on the others, then?

'You're always gambling when you're descending!' he told me, 'and it's better not to see what's on either side, those sheer drops and the like, because otherwise you'd probably stop the bike there and then.'

That was a modest way of expressing his Theory of the Descent, on the greatest of the Pyrenean giants. Touch the brakes on four bends. Don't look. It sounded almost like an excuse for having clinched the '91 Tour in such rampant style, when he launched himself down towards La Mongie, or for having caught Rominger on the road to Barèges in the '93 Tour. And this, coming from the rider who is remembered for the most spectacular descents (perhaps the most effective, rather than necessarily the fastest descents) in the history of cycling.

The decade up to the summer of 1991 had seen a dramatic shift in Spanish cycling. At the outset there hadn't been a single rider capable of making a showing in the big foreign competitions; by the end of the decade the Reynolds team had burst on to the scene, shaken up the peloton and raised everybody's expectations. That was the heyday of Pedro Delgado and Arroyo, and the performances of Marino Lejarreta and Chozas in the Giro. Riders like Pello Ruiz Cabestany and Julián Gorospe even won stages in the Tour de France. Those were 'magical moments' in the lives of thousands of Spaniards. It was something akin to a mass phenomenon – whole families glued to the TV waiting for French television's broadcast to Spain. The hysteria, which was heightened in no short measure by the media and the charisma of the leading figure, Pedro Delgado, had three phases. The first was the 1987 Tour, which Pedro almost won, but then lost by a few seconds in the individual time-trial at Dijon. Second, there was the '88 Tour which he did win, and this was even more highly valued because, halfway through, the issue of the alleged doping scandal reared its ugly head. With Delgado already in yellow, one of the Tour organisers' vehicles drew up alongside the Reynolds car to 'suggest' to the team bosses that Pedro should feign a fall and that they should claim he was injured, or ill. They wanted him to retire with his 'dignity' intact. Not on your life, not with the pain it takes to win a Tour! It was all or nothing, and it was all.

The third phase was the following Tour, in '89, which went from the ridiculous to the sublime: it began as a disaster and ended as one of the epics. It was the Tour when Delgado took a wrong turning going to the start in Luxembourg and was last on overall classification at the end of the first stage; and on the Champs-Elysées he was on the podium in third place. The French Press didn't give due credit at the time for the historic way Delgado had battled up the classification because, naturally, they were more focused on the fierce, private duel between Fignon (a Frenchman who was never loved by the French) and Lemond, an American who seemed to be half-French and about whom France was divided. On the one hand Lemond had demonstrated his undeniable qualities as a champion, since he was the man who had 'granted' the almighty Bernard Hinault one final Tour; on the other hand he was to be his executioner shortly afterwards, depriving him of his sixth Tour.

So for Hinault, too, the limit of five Tours seemed to be sacred. Exceeding it was like entering an unknown world: it wasn't simply a question of fame, but of whether it was really proper to win more Tours than Eddy Merckx. And yet Hinault gave his all to win a sixth Tour, launching attacks in the face of team orders, which made manager Paul Koechli increasingly neurotic with each passing day. Hinault was failing when least expected and winning where it didn't seem possible. The climb at Alpe d'Huez in tandem with his junior partner, Greg Lemond, his team-mate in La Vie Claire and the race leader, was memorable. Their arrival together at the finish, shaking each other's hands (Hinault won, of course) was merely a deceitful lid on the tensions that were boiling over within the team, where some riders supported Lemond and others Hinault. That, too, has passed into history. It was in '86, and soon afterwards Perico Delgado's time would come.

Then, in 1990, the Tour ran an equally strange course for Banesto: again it was a matter of the team hierarchy. Some said: 'Of course it should be Perico; he's still got what it takes to make an impression in such a demanding event as the Tour.' At that time Delgado was one of the most experienced riders in the French Tour. But other voices spoke of the need for the leadership to pass to Induráin, even though he, himself, frowned whenever the issue was raised. A third approach, which, as things turned out, was the most practical and sensible, proposed that the race itself should decide. It should be emphasised how well the Banesto management dealt with this delicate issue. Nevertheless, while letting the race decide was all well and good, it should still be remembered that in the previous Tour of '89 Delgado, despite his spectacular and commendable recovery – 'a real bullfighters performance', as the French said – had not gained a single stage victory. Miguel, on the other hand, had won in one of the blue-ribbon stages of the race, at Cauterets, even though the public impact of that feat was partially eclipsed by Perico's incessant and astonishing recovery – the seconds and minutes he was clawing back, day in day out, like some workaholic ant.

In the end it was the 1990 Tour that settled matters once and for all. Miguel was always ahead. He was constantly at the front on the big climbs in the Alps and in the Pyrenees, and always having to wait for Delgado to catch up. That is, until that one unforgettable day when Miguel had had enough, and shot off like an arrow on Luz-Ardiden, and on to victory. In the time-trials as well, his progress was spectacular: he was now on a par with the very best. It could be said that, given this overall picture, the prospects for the '91 Tour should have been crystal clear. But they weren't. There were still people who continued to believe that Perico was capable of sweeping all before him once more, as he had in '88, and, secondly, and even more surprising, there were those who maintained that Induráin definitely couldn't 'climb'. His two Paris–Nice wins, clinched on Mont-Faron and the Col d'Eze, counted for nothing, apparently; nor did his San Sebastián classic sealed on Jaizkibel. Cauterets and Luz-Ardiden, they, too, counted for nought. Generally speaking, people in Spain continued to place their faith in Delgado's lightning ability to break. We had still not grasped that the Tour, to quote the author Lapeyrére in a thought-provoking book entitled *Comme faire le Tour*, far from being a simple test of speed, is, in fact, a test of character and style. And that's where they would be up against Miguel. Delgado was a great watcher, but Miguel was even greater. His vision on the road might be described as 'multiple'. He had that exceptional quality which insects possess to 'see' images fragmented through a series of compound eyes. Each rival, each movement, everything was computed and registered. And all this information would end up being used at the least expected moment.

In 1991 we were about to enter the Kingdom of the Sun, and there was certainly a lot of sun in those Tours, that's for sure, even though there were bad days in all of them. We were getting to the most fantastic and unforgettable part of the Symphony which Induráin was offering us, up now on his conductor's dais. Earlier I said that Hinault gave his all to achieve a sixth Tour win, but failed. So did Merckx, who was broken as he attacked like a wounded animal on Pra-Loup and the Col d'Allos, and was finally superseded by someone younger, a new rider named Bernard Thévenet, who managed to rid himself of the 'Merckx complex' that was ruling the peloton at that time. Eddy Merckx's last victory was in '74, but his increasingly laborious attempts continued right up to '77. It was a similar story with Jacques Anquetil, whose last Tour triumph was in '64, but who was still there in '66 and even the following year was still the leader of the BIC team, which contained a very young Jean-Marie Leblanc (later to become the Tour boss) and José Miguel Echávarri.

Hinault, though, was unconcerned about revealing his deficiencies on the road. He had the good fortune still to have the class to register the odd win and, like Merckx, he was able to do this at the age of 32. He retired rather discreetly. Induráin was to be the most decisive of all in that respect. After his incredible five-year run, and despite it being commonly accepted that physically he was still fit enough to attempt a sixth Tour, he said 'adiós'. A gentleman until the very end. This served merely to add to his legend.

In spite of everything, he did prepare conscientiously for that last Tour which he could not win, the Tour that brought the magical era full circle. This was witnessed by the roads of Valcarlos, by the road that leads to France, by Burguete, the Ulzama, the Erro mountain, and so many other places that saw him train (alone or accompanied by Pruden) with his sights set on that longed-for sixth Tour. The story goes that, in April '96, after a reception given in Induráin's honour by the King of Spain, Don Juan Carlos de Borbón, Miguel arrived back late in Navarre. The aircraft is said to have touched down at Pamplona airport at nearly four in the afternoon, yet that day Miguel still did a 100-kilometre training stint, wearing his thermal jacket, because at that time of year the Navarran evenings are quite chilly. He wanted to win that sixth Tour and was physically capable of doing so, but his head was another matter. Maybe he was exhausted from so much constantly monitoring his rivals, and that huge single focus on the Tour de France no longer had the same attraction.

Going back to the real beginning of the dream, though – the year 1991 (although for Induráin it had started two years earlier, as he ascended the slopes of Cauterets) – it was obvious that a change in the Tour hierarchy was imminent. Pedro Delgado's physical condition seemed to have declined; Fignon had not recovered emotionally from his disappointment at losing the '89 Tour by eight seconds on the final time-trial in his home city of Paris – that sort of experience weighs on you for ever; and a question mark remained against Lemond – his recent victories, deservedly gained by eking every second out of the stopwatch, still did not mark him out as the man to beat. And, finally, Roche was injured, and did not appear to be in the best of form. So, in short, the race was wide open. Anything could happen.

It is strange that in the days leading up to that '91 Tour, the French started to backtrack on themselves. They were excited by the possibility that Induráin might play a major role in the race, especially since up till then the Navarran's major achievements had been on French soil – in the Paris–Nice events, Tour stages and the Tour of the EEC, which they really hyped. He was looked upon as a top-class rider, with impressive pedal power, and one who broke the mould of the classical gritty Spanish battler, equipped only for making his mark in the high mountains – although that, of course, is no mean feat. However, as I say, the contradictions were beginning to surface. Cyrille Guimard, one of the most prestigious directors in French cycling, refused to recognise Induráin's worth. He considered him to be too 'cold' to win a Tour. Guimard, himself, who had been a powerful sprinter and had troubled Merckx on several occasions – even on mountain stages – had coached Hinault and Fignon in their heyday. Naturally, compared to such hot-blooded brutes, Miguel must have seemed an icicle. And he was.

It was just as well that Guimard, with his sixth sense for anything to do with cycling and especially for spotting new talent, did not realise that inside this great and serene man there beat a tempered passion and a devastatingly firm, man-of-the-soil conviction that he would win the Tour. Not even Guimard, a real genius when it came to discovering uncut diamonds, sensed that this tall, shy, incredibly strong young man had his eyes on the Tour, and the roads of the Tour, and the people of the Tour, and the fateful happenings of the Tour. For all his passivity, he was brimming with vision. The French Tour was to be his harvest, and Guimard did not see it. So, when asked why he hadn't listed Miguel among the favourites for the '91 Tour, he replied: 'The fact that he's won two mountain stages in the *Grande Boucle* and the last two Paris–Nice races doesn't necessarily mean we are at the start of an Induráin era, does it?'

But he was to be his own betrayer. However much he disliked the prospect, and without even being prompted, Cyrille Guimard was the first to coin the term 'Induráin era'.

After Miguel had won that '91 Tour in magisterial style, Guimard predicted, before the following Tour, that 'Induráin is in for a hard time this year, because last time out I saw him really suffering on some of the mountains.' In 1993, he was at it again: 'I've always said, and I'll say it again, that Miguel Induráin is never going to be a cycling great. You only have to look at his record to see I'm right. Hinault, Fignon and Lemond all had a much more glittering and extensive list of triumphs by the time they were 24. Right now Induráin is the best, but remember: he's had two or three shots at the Spanish Vuelta, and flopped. And that's despite having the full support of Pedro Delgado at his disposal.' It is amazing how much nonsense can issue from the mouth of an individual who knows his cycling, and the only explanation I can think of is that such statements were prompted more by commercial interests than by patriotic motives.

Those five gloriously improbable years were littered with sideswipes and shameful comments from French cycling experts. Guimard never changed his mind, even when Miguel clocked up his Giros, the third Tour, and the fourth and the fifth. No. He was pigheaded. Eventually he limited himself to saying that, personally, he did not find Induráin's riding style pleasant to watch and that Induráin needed to put the icing on the cake as far as his image was concerned by winning a few classics. Raymond Poulidor, who was more sincere and generous, as well as having been an infinitely better cyclist than Guimard when it came to suffering in the saddle, laid to rest any further criticism about the Classics, in which Induráin often preferred not to compete simply so that he could focus on the Tour. One day, tired of the way the French sporting Press kept harping on about it, Poulidor remarked: 'Why should Induráin want to win a Classic? Every single day in the Tour is equivalent to a Paris–Roubaix.' This time they didn't pay too much attention to these comments by Pou-Pou*, who never won a Tour de France but did claim one Vuelta a España and several Classics.

The contentious issue of the Classics was first raised by Merckx and Hinault. The Belgian remarked how much Miguel's climbing impressed him, like a high-speed train, but he couldn't understand how Induráin did not feel somewhat frustrated at not having a Classic under his belt. Later, Merckx retracted this and admitted that times had changed and that nowadays it seemed to be

---

* 'Pou-Pou' – Poulidor's nickname.

essential to plan the season more carefully. If Induráin's aspirations centred on the Tour, that was good enough.

Hinault was more of a bruiser than the Belgian, although he, too, eventually retracted some of his initial criticism. At first he emphasised what he termed 'panache' – anger and fighting spirit – to detract from Induráin's achievements. Hinault was always a very compulsive sort of guy, who regarded a wild Classic such as the Paris–Roubaix, with its miles of cobbled roads and endless mud, as an 'event for goats'. Nevertheless, 'for the hell of it' – to use his own words – and just to shut a few people up, he entered. And he won it, of course. On the other hand, he never wanted to take part in the Tour of Flanders, whose infamously steep climbs, cutting across it like sharpened teeth, make it extremely tough. Because of peaks such as the Mur de Grammont or Berendries, and especially the very steep, and much-feared Kwaremont (which he seemed to bear a real grudge against) he refused to go to the Belgian race. He would say: 'I'm a cyclist, not a crazy goat, ready to clamber up those madcap cobbled hills. Yes, the favourites do cope with them relatively easily, but you also see a good handful of pros get off their bikes and walk the last stretch. That's degrading.' That was Hinault – Miguel's idol when he was young, presumably simply because he was famous, since Hinault's style was actually nothing like Induráin's. Miguel was a man more in the Sean Kelly mould. Suffer in silence, never complain. And if there was some vendetta in the heart of the peloton, he would try and carry it out it discreetly and tactfully.

There is one memorable and amusing remark from Bernard Hinault shortly after climbing Alpe d'Huez. He was buttonholed by a particularly intrusive journalist, who scarcely gave him time to recover his breath. The cameras were rolling and the whole of France (and viewers round the world) was watching. The intrepid reporter could only think of asking Hinault how he felt after such an effort. 'Awful,' he panted. And the reporter went on: 'How on earth do you manage to cycle at such speed up a summit such as the Alpe?' Hinault looked him up and down, put his right hand under his jersey, then opened his shorts a few inches to reveal a glimpse of his genitals: 'With a pair of these,' and he spun on his heels, leaving the dimwit standing on his own, having shown neither respect for Hinault's exhaustion, nor the professionalism to prepare a few sensible questions.

By contrast, the Irishman, Roche, was generally more refined and laconic. Another famous question, also broadcast live on French television, was from a sharp-eyed reporter who inquired as to how the day had gone. Roche, who, like the rest of the severely decimated peloton, had just taken a hell of a beating from several Pyrenean mountains, pondered for a moment and then, with a childlike grin, replied: 'Great. I've been out on my bike all day.'

But that damned panache issue would dog Miguel for years. In fact, it never let go of him, although eventually the giants of cycling, especially the duo who gradually saw their record five Tours come under threat, did relent. Even so, *'Il manque de panache'* – 'He lacks panache' – was one of the most odious phrases which accompanied Induráin during his victorious career on French soil.

Philippe Bouvet, who ended up being one of the characters who most typified the French race, would go on and on about it at every opportunity. And Pierre Chany, himself, the man who had followed more Tours than anyone, said shortly after Miguel had won his fifth Tour: 'Induráin will never enter the pantheon of great cycling champions. Even winning a sixth Tour would not change that.' When the surprised journalist asked the reason for such a dogmatic opinion, old Chany argued: 'I saw Merckx and Coppi cry, Coppi in fact in the Vigorelli velodrome, and I can't imagine Induráin crying.'

Crazy. And especially absurd because the same Pierre Chany, the man who has published the most comprehensive books on the Tour de France, its legends and history, was the first to laud the 'majestic and unbeatable' figure of Induráin. 'Extraordinary and untouchable,' he wrote in his key reference work *La Légende du Tour de France*. At the end of the day, those are the observations that remain as a record, and we ought to regard some of the other statements as having been made at unusual moments. They may even have been shamefully manipulated, because from my own experience I know that the Press might commission a one-off article from you on Induráin, and then plonk a provocative or petty-minded headline on it. Whatever the case, statements about 'lacking panache' were a long way from the reality.

And yet the stigma of panache dogged Induráin and, strangely, was in evidence amongst the whole group of people who, in one way or another, were linked to Monsieur Cyrille Guimard and his entourage, whether in the La Vie Claire or Système-U squads. First into the breach was Guimard himself, followed by Hinault, and finally along came the relief column in the shape of Laurent Fignon, who in turn ended up having a rude swipe at the Breton: 'Il me fait rigoler.' – 'He makes me laugh'. The fundamental mantra of all of them was: Induráin wins because the other riders don't attack him enough. Coming from Fignon, who had competed against the Navarran for over half a decade, it smacked of sheer stupidity. Why on earth didn't he attack him himself, instead of merely droning on and on about how 'il manque de panache,' and how the rest of the peloton seemed to be spellbound or disabled?

Induráin never bothered to respond to any of this. Why should he, since his results showed that he was right, and made his veiled detractors look ridiculous? Doubly ridiculous, in fact, because Fignon himself often acknowledged that he'd never, in the whole of his cycling life, witnessed the power and dominance shown by the Navarran in the Tour (although he never saw Eddy Merckx race). Remember, too, that this was the same Fignon who, having been caught by a very young Miguel in the Criterium International time-trial at Avignon, confessed to the local Press: 'Induráin murdered me.' And, to cap it all, this was the same Fignon who was passed by Miguel with a couple of kilometres to go in the fantastic Luxembourg time-trial in the '92 Tour, and who, through the haze of his exhaustion, merely panted: 'I saw a missile fly past today.' The front page of all the magazines, even L'Equipe, portrayed a serene Miguel flying to glory having ridden past several riders, and behind him, trying to stick to his wheel to avoid losing too much ground, was Fignon, whose face showed he couldn't believe what was happening.

First there would be praise, but then, always between the lines, a kind of insinuation, complaining about certain 'technical innovations' which Miguel allegedly used on his Pinarello. Something about the weight of the frame, the hubs, the special forks. This was the same Fignon, who, as Ángel Arroyo correctly said, should have been attacked in the mountains by Pedro and himself, backed by climbers such as Peter Winnen and Robert

Millar, since other worthy climbers like Pedro Muñoz and Lucien van Impe were at the veteran stage by then. We should give Fignon credit for his two consecutive Tours, but he should really have won the '83 Tour without needing the injury to that great fighter, Pascal Simon (who was leading at the time), or the absence of the Badger. In spite of that, he was always speaking of panache, which he apparently possessed but which other cyclists, like Miguel Induráin, didn't. Perhaps it was his panache which made him spit at the TV cameras.

Induráin's response to all this perhaps reflected the fact that he was becoming rather tired of this refined, but scarcely veiled, tedious criticism from the French. Following his third consecutive Tour win in 1993, when Hinault stated that, with the exception of Rominger, the peloton had scarcely broken sweat, his reply was just perfect: 'I'm not racing against the sick and the lame.'

Gradually we would see the real merits of the Villava man as he achieved each of his victories, because in each of them he had to suffer in his own way. Year on year, there were new and fresher rivals who set out to attack him at every point. The history of the Tours is there, and the history demonstrates it. But what sent me into a fit of rage that I could scarcely contain were the comments Raphaël Géminiani made in the '95 Tour. This was Induráin's fifth consecutive win and he'd produced further recitals in each and every aspect of the race. Géminiani, who had been the 'patron' and sponsor of Jacques Anquetil for several years, was a combative and strong-willed rider, certainly, but he was also over-excitable, and had his limitations. He'd had his chance in the 1958 Tour, at a time when the teams were organised along national lines: the French team contained the veteran, but expert, Bobet, and a young and ambitious Anquetil, who had triumphed the previous year. But Charly Gaul, one of the best climbers of all time, launched a furious attack on Géminiani, on Bahamontes, and on all the French favourites, in the Chartreuse massif. And he did it in a terrible storm, which was so much to the liking of the flying Luxemburger. Géminiani was the leader, and was scuppered, so he said, because his French team-mates 'abandoned' him. At the end of that diabolic stage to Chartreuse, Gaul had gained twelve minutes on him, taking over the leader's jersey in the process, and going on to win the Tour. In tears, Géminiani shouted over and over again: *'Tous de Judas!'* – 'You are all Judases!' Who knows?

Paradoxically, it was Géminiani who taught Anquetil the *colmatage* tactic, which involved accumulating minutes in hand on stages that were suited to the Norman rider (i.e. the time-trials) in order to give himself breathing space later in the high mountains. Despite the enormous admiration there was for Anquetil's class (Adorni used to say it was worth being a cyclist just to place yourself behind Jacques and watch him pedal his refined style, almost as if he were a ballet dancer), he was never really loved in his home country. People loved Poulidor, the battler. In France, because they are Latin and Mediterranean, they also like thoroughbred cyclists, the kind of brave little bulls on wheels who tear into the attack, sometimes without rhyme or reason, even if they do generally end up losing out because they've overdone it. Completely the opposite of Induráin. As a result of all their bragging about the odious quality of panache, the French seem to think they are the only ones who can officially declare a cyclist to be one of the greats. And this all follows from an article that Géminiani wrote in 1995, called 'On tiptoe'. Although the 'Big Gun', as Géminiani was nicknamed, is not part of the official Tour de France organisation, he has commentated on all the Tours for one media outlet or another, and his opinions carry considerable weight.

In his article, Géminiani was talking about the Cauterets stage in the '95 Tour, which Virenque won, while Miguel kept a tight hold on his rivals. Géminiani gave free rein to his 'rage' at the fact that the Yellow Jersey had not massacred the field in this great Pyrenean stage. What he had seen that day 'annoyed' and 'exasperated' him, he said, since Miguel had had everything in his favour. It was a long stage, the slopes thronging with Spaniards, and he was stronger than his rivals but, in the end, he merely contented himself with coming home ahead of the next rider in the overall classification, Alex Zülle, and this despite having Zülle gasping for breath on the ascent of the Tourmalet and Cauterets. The key sentence in Géminiani's article was: 'You don't become a legend on tiptoe.' For me, this really was the limit: he was talking about a fifth consecutive Tour win! The same old story, then. In this respect, the French were like termites, like woodworm, like colds in winter and the tax return every year. Induráin had dominated the toughest and most important race in the word, perhaps better than he had ever done. As very few had ever done in Tour history. He had given an exhibition of tempered calm, of strategy and, when the occasion warranted it, of aggression. He'd destroyed everyone's morale, the morale of the French Press to start off with, and then the Tour organisation's, and finally the morale of his stricken rivals. Miguel got on their nerves, Miguel the inscrutable, the immovable. And what really seemed to alarm them was that in his steady accumulation of Tours Miguel didn't give the impression of someone fulfilling an historic duty, or a titanic feat, but more like someone who was simply going about his daily bread-and-butter work. Cowered by the apparent ease with which Induráin achieved his Tour victories, they did not realise that he embodied the whole epic nature of cycling. His dominance was simply such that even the very concept of 'epic' became relative.

Elsewhere in his bitter article, Géminiani, just as he had done on previous days, displayed blind admiration and total respect for Induráin. Until, that is, the fateful day on Cauterets – the very day Fabio Casartelli perished – and then all the Big Gun's patience seemed to crack. His mask shattered like a Murano-glass table service. According to Géminiani, you should always please the fans, and apparently the fans love a certain kind of gratuitous effort – panache for panache's sake. I thought about what would have happened to Géminiani, if he had ridden a stage like the man-eating (and deadly) 1995 Cauterets stage. He asked why Miguel did not treat us to more displays of the kind of genius he had shown at Liège. He never understood, and I think many French cycling fans never tried to understand, that, though Induráin was no tyrant like Merckx or Hinault, nor an illustrious and artful despot, skilled in a thousand and one tricks, like Anquetil, he still dominated the Tour. He was His Excellency in the Tour, His Majesty, His Most Serene Highness. Perhaps more than anyone else before him, Induráin *was* the Tour. He knew its sewers, its pressures, its rhythms and hidden neuroses, its fears, its most intimate secrets. He lived peacefully with them and, when the time was right, he acted ruthlessly. Each July, at just the right moment, he acted ruthlessly. Deep down, it was a problem of perspective: people still thought of Induráin as a man who won Tours by going flat out for one day (always in the lonely battle against the clock) and then spending the rest of time doing little more than cruising along.

They were thinking of the Induráin who had faced down his rivals in the time-trials at Alençon in '91, Luxembourg in '92, Lake Madine in '93, or in the awesome suffocation of Bergerac in '94; they were thinking of the Induráin at Maçon in '91, or at Blois in '92 or at Lake Vassivière in '95. They overlooked the fact that it was in the high mountains that Induráin had turned the screw, and blown apart each and every one of his Tours. At Val-Louron in '91, Sestrière in '92, Galibier in '93, Hautacam in '94 and La Plagne in '95. The first day in the big mountains and he'd knocked out all his rivals. Wasn't that panache? When someone has always triumphed in this way – and the specific details of those different stages are there to remind us – does he deserve to be told that he'll have to tiptoe into the world of legends? Or, as the elderly Chany suggested, that he would never become a legend like the other greats because he couldn't cry? As soon as they could, the French would shoot, that was for sure. It reminded me of Goya's painting of the Third of May Executions in Madrid, where in 1808 the French had shot Spaniards who had dared to rebel against their rule. Except now it was happening in July and, most of all, in the weeks leading up to the Tour.

The worst thing was that those kinds of poisonous, spineless remarks of Géminiani who, like so many other French cyclists, was great until he decided to open his mouth and spout this nonsense, would have been made just as openly even if Induráin had been French. The proof of that was the case of Jacques Anquetil; in his homeland he was never really forgiven for never having had a fall, for not splitting his nose and arriving at the finish with blood pouring down him, like Pou-Pou, or for not having had as much bad luck as Pou-Pou, or for the fact that he had not been fated to be the eternal runner-up, like Pou-Pou. People love a winner, but they begin to hate him when he wins too much. Then they decide to love the losers.

All well and good: criticising is an implicit part of human nature, and, in that respect, the French are the bearers of Descartes' legacy. But the naked truth is that for five long years, while there were some who never won a Tour and never would win a Tour, someone like Miguel was achieving the highest qualifications. He was gaining a doctorate and the rest were doing their run-of-the-mill exams for goodness knows what minor position, perhaps just to be allowed to be his leading opponents. Miguel contented himself with collecting Tours. In Cartesian terms, he achieved what nobody else had achieved: five straight Tour wins. And for that reason alone, he deserves to be considered among the greatest.

Contrary to what was said by those who advised Induráin throughout his racing career, and contrary even to what he said himself on numerous occasions when he was asked about how and when he clinched his Tours, I still believe he won them less in the time-trials, and more in the high mountains. In the time-trials, he 'deterred' his rivals; in the mountains he chewed them up and spat them out. We can think of cases such as Bugno, or others who were gifted time-trial specialists, who saw how Induráin took one, two, three, and even four or five minutes out of them every time they rode against the clock.

But what then about the mountains, where the time losses can be huge, and where struggling on just the final climb can lead to the loss of a very many minutes in just a few kilometres (as Miguel himself was to prove)? The problem, for Bugno in '93, was not the *two* minutes Miguel took out of him at Lake Madine, but the *ten* he took on the first Alpine stage, up the Col du Télégraphe and the Galibier. Bugno knew better than anyone that one bad day for Induráin on the Galibier would have meant the loss of several minutes which he would never have been able to claw back in the time-trials. If we think of the '94 Tour, where Miguel produced what was perhaps the time-trial of his life in Bergerac: he took two minutes out of Rominger. *Only* two minutes. What difference does that make, if you then crack on Hautacam where, in terms of time lost, your whole world can cave in? This is what Miguel would demonstrate so painfully, just two years later, against Riis.

Let's turn to the time-trial at Huy-Seraing, in the '95 Tour. Miguel took just a dozen seconds off Riis. The same thing happened in the time-trial at Lake Vassivière, where his advantage over Riis was less than a minute. So, in all, he gained a minute against the clock. Whereas, in just six kilometres of hard climbing at La Plagne, Induráin managed to open a huge gap of fully *six* minutes over the rider who, the following year, was to be his 'executioner'. It is always the mountains that create the gaps, opening up bottomless chasms of time between cyclists. And there needs to be a set of very special circumstances, involving strong all-round riders, for the time-trials to be as decisive as some people think.

Another point is the psychological factor, and its function as a deterrent: 'Why should I try and go for something which is not even going to get me a stage win if, when the mountains come, Induráin is going to climb more or less as well as me (assuming he isn't in the mood to actually attack), and if, when you add it up over the time-trials, I'll lose another three or four minutes?' That is how they were 'deterred'. Those memorable time-trial stages were useful, not only in amassing substantial advantages over his rivals and in calming down the hens clucking in the ever-agitated Tour backyard, but in actively reminding them of Induráin's formidable form. They eat away at their hopes almost from the outset, although there was always someone, somewhere, who hoped to be around for Miguel's 'bad' day in the high mountains. Up until Les Arcs in '96, several generations of cyclists had hoped to be there to see it. And several of them disappeared in the attempt, or just got old waiting. Those generations were scalded, in the sense of being taught a lesson or defeated, in those same high mountains.

I must reiterate the mathematics which translated into five Tour victories: if we were to count up the real time advantage obtained over, let's say, Miguel's ten closest rivals in each Tour, that advantage was obtained not so much at Alençon, Luxembourg, Madine, Bergerac, and Vassivière as on the cols of Val-Louron, Sestrière, Galibier, Hautacam, and La Plagne. In the time-trials he restricted himself to impressing quite a few, demoralising many, and basically giving them all a metaphoric clip round the ears. In the mountains he laid into them.

He did this year after year, which makes it all the more perplexing to recall the other type of veiled – and sometimes blatant – criticism to which Induráin was subjected even at the most brilliant moments of his career. When he was about to gain his fifth consecutive Tour win, Bernard Hinault was at it again with his usual tactic of trying to stir things up before the Tour started (and in a chat-show programme in Pamplona, of all places). After making the obligatory flattering comments, he actually said, 'Induráin's been fortunate not to be riding at the same time as me, because I'd have found it relatively easy to ambush him.' It is embarrassing, not only that Hinault should have thought like this – and doubtless he did – but that he should have actually dared to express it publicly.

In Spain, too, there were plenty of barbed tongues ready with their back-stabbing comments. For instance, one famous ex-rider (who could be accused of many things, but certainly not of lacking panache) came out with a comment that made us squirm with disbelief and embarrassment, and then with indignation. What he actually said was that yes, Induráin was the strongest and most complete cyclist of his generation, but that sometimes he tended to 'be a bit of an exaggerator'.* That retired rider used the term because he had the impression Induráin more or less cruised along, and could doubtless have claimed many more victories if he'd shed this *globero* attitude.

My own experience of former riders, all great battlers, especially in the mountains, was much the same: at first, they all showed their admiration for Induráin – they agreed he was a phenomenon – but then, one way or another, they would tend towards the Hinault Syndrome. 'I'd have had him in my time,' they would say, because they were better climbers, etc., etc., than today's riders.

Sometimes you think that what people want is pure circus rather than an epic cycle race. Fortunately, time is the one judge whose verdict will endure for generations. And history tells that, pre-Induráin, the Spanish riders who went to the Tour, the most important race in the world, were no more than snipers. During his reign, however, we seemed to be living a dream. We certainly were. We still don't know what will happen in the coming years, though: the figure of Miguel may have boosted the number of youngsters taking up cycling (and increased the number of armchair fans), and the whole delirious five-year period from 1991

---

* The word he used was *globero*, which in Spanish cycling parlance refers to that kind of not-very-serious cyclotourist, who has a tendency to inflate his exploits. To describe any professional racing cyclist as a *'globero'* is something of an insult.

to 1995 was a kind of sweet intoxication of triumph. And yet, just as Miguel was giving up cycling, a list was published of the number of young Spanish riders who were moving from the amateur to the professional ranks: a mere six, and two of them were going to foreign teams. That is the situation, and it's impossible to avoid the conclusion that although Spanish cycling has some fine riders, life is very hard for those who are bidding to earn their living on a bike.

In the same year that Miguel retired, honoured by huge crowds, and amidst oceans of print and pictures, many other riders also departed from the cycling scene for ever without receiving so much as a passing mention except in the specialised Press. Among them were Jean-François Bernard, Gilles Dellion, Thierry Marie, AndyHampsten, Jelle Nijdam, Steve Bauer, Franco Vona, Sean Yates, Cassani, Jean-Claude Colloti, Eric Van Hooydonck, and many others. Quite unjustly they went in silence. So it remains to be seen whether all the expectation aroused by Induráin and his glittering career translates, even in a small way, to an interest in cycling. Miguel would like it to. That's what he worked for.

But the huge edifice of victories he constructed, that majestic Symphony with which he would delight us for far longer than we ever dreamed possible at the outset, began in the July of 1991. Up till then, we knew of him, but who really was he? A simple guy, an excellent *domestique*. Someone, just like the majority of riders, who hated sleeping 130 nights a year in a hotel bed, in different places and among different people. But that is what professional cycling is all about. Induráin liked going back to his parents' home and sitting on the sofa all afternoon watching the TV, and devouring huge quantities of nuts and dried fruit. He loved the short winter break when he could eat almost anything he liked, including butter beans and chorizo sausage! But what was this man like inside, this man who, they said, was super-gifted, whose lungs were able to move eight litres of air? What could be said of a cyclist who, on an exercise bike in the labs, achieved a power equivalent to 550 watts? To get an idea of what that means, a child of ten or twelve years of age would scarcely be able to move that wheel for more than a couple seconds, even if he or she actually managed to set it in motion in the first place. Was his ability down to a question of cardiovascular capacity, of breathing, of brute force? No, there was something else involved – his philosophy of life. Sow, pick; climb, descend. Fight, fight, have faith.

And what does Miguel Induráin's face tell us at the time? Few faces can have been so photographed in so many ways, especially faces that are so difficult to fathom. Several times, during the first victorious 1991 Tour, he was seen to smile broadly. And when he smiles, and does so like a timid child, earnestly and ever so slightly turning his lips. He smiles like a lad who is used to being affectionately reproached, as if he were immersed in a perpetual process of inner learning. But generally we had to get used to his serene and, somewhat expressionless face.

Despite everything, his is not a stony face, nor is it eclectic or closed, although, for all kinds of reasons, this has often been insinuated. It is a noble face. It is not a mask or the face of a statue, but the face of a man who knows what he wants, yet has never been inclined to make it easy for anyone trying to paint an over-simple profile of him. Many of his victories were as relaxed and imperturbable as they were eminent; so too were the key lines of his face and his character.

On one occasion, a reporter from the *Miroir du Ciclisme* asked him if he was aware that he had become the *'bête noire'* of sports journalists the world over. 'Me... a *bête noire*?' 'Yes. You've had so many startling successes, we've run out of adjectives to describe them. You've drained us dry. We don't know what to write any more.' But Miguel cleverly evaded the trap. He answered in vague terms, maintaining that actually it was in their best interests. Eventually he put the ball back in the journalist's court: 'I bet you've already thought about the day I retire.'

There would be a void, or at least a weary grey interlude until another star appeared who was bright enough to dazzle everyone, as he had done.

Induráin's star had always shone somewhat tenuously. That time he came to the castle of Montjuich in Barcelona as a junior to tackle that short but savage climb along the walls to the castle, he set off 120th out of a total of 130 participants. And then gradually, no doubt in secret collusion with the gentle Mediterranean wind, he ended up in 45th position. Only three or four years earlier, they had laughed at him whenever he climbed the slopes of Beloso. No doubt, years before that he would have seen, out of the corner of his eye, those people who had watched him struggle so painfully on the famous gradient that runs from Pamplona to Villava smiling sarcastically or naïvely. What the hell. It didn't matter what they thought. This was a country full of aspiring football coaches and tacticians, but soon there would be just as much respect for cycling.

Despite the proliferation of Indurainophiles and Indurainologists, the man himself always remained a mystery. The only thing that mattered was that he thought about the Tour: and the fact that he wanted to win it, and was capable of winning it. Up until that point he had contented himself with working, and watching.

Miguel loved watching the faces of the other riders in clinical detail, studying their expressions in the saddle, the gears they used on each specific stretch of the road, the pedal rate at which they changed the gear ratio, the way they moved their necks, their arms. But above all he would scrutinise his opponents' legs. He could read them like a book, through the veins that were visible, and the special texture the muscles took on as they reached maximum exertion. In this way, together with his sixth sense, he would acquire his profound knowledge of the Tour, even before he started winning the race. He got to the point, he claimed, where he could tell when a man like Rominger was tired, merely by looking at his legs.

Those cyclists' legs, dark and smooth ever since an Italian called Giovanni Gerbi took to shaving them. He did that for a variety of reasons: firstly, to stop the sweat sticking to them, which could produce hypothermia with the sudden changes in temperature, for example when climbing and then suddenly descending a mountain; secondly, to avoid complications in any fall, since hairs harbour microbes which can quickly lead to an infection, which could be delayed if a clean wound is washed quickly in water; thirdly, massage – it's not difficult to imagine what it must be like smearing cream on hairy legs; and, finally – the point people find most amusing and strange – for aesthetic reasons. Gerbi first shaved his legs in 1903, and although at first he was laughed at, the others soon understood how practical it was. Hair and cycling have always tended to be at loggerheads. There have been very few instances of top cyclists sporting long hair: Brochard,

Anderson, Theunisse, but certainly not many. Copious sweating, at times for six hours on end, and a long head of hair cannot be the perfect match.

It is a similar story with moustaches: cyclists have permanently runny noses, and the skin above the mouth must be clean. Since the heroic times of Petit-Breton, or Trosselier, or Lapize, or Scieur, or Faber or Garin – the winner of the first Tour de France in 1903 – a moustache has not been a common sight in the peloton. Once you reach a reasonable level of cycle-racing, you don't tend to see beards, either. And the answer is obvious: it is hard to imagine someone suffering like hell in the burning sun for hours on end if, on top of all that, he's covered in hair like some bear. They say that Octave Lapize, who, at the top of the Aubisque, squared up to the Tour organisers, calling them 'murderers' and hurling his bike to the ground, was frightened by the bears on the Tourmalet and even more so on the Aubisque. They were wonderful animals who had lived in peace for thousands of years, in what is known as the 'Cirque du Litor' and the 'Circle of Death', until some very odd creatures began to arrive on bikes zigzagging in and out among the mud and the boulders.

Watching, watching. Miguel would always be watching as he climbed the mountains. That was his natural habitat, the environment where he had struggled for years because of his weight, but where he was destined to discover himself spiritually. In a way, the mountains are like the dead daughters of the wind, who return to life every two or three hundred years, and stir ever so slightly. They beat, deep down beneath our feet, and beneath the tyres of cars and bicycles. They have their own voice, which is like the song of sirens muffled by millennia of inertia. But they beat, and the ability to listen to this rhythm is a gift Miguel possessed. He knew how to take the pulse of each mountain: 'Now you go up, and later you'll have to come down. It's as simple as that.'

In this way he learned to respect the mountains and, in doing so, to lose his fear of them. Hardly ever was Induráin seen staring fixedly at the metallic power of his handlebars, or at the two or three metres of tarmac immediately beyond his front tyre. The photos are there to prove that his head was always up, if possible gazing far upwards, challenging the mountain. Before that, however, he would have been studying the places and people around him to size up everything.

Merckx also used to watch his rivals' faces, with undisguised insolence, to see the right moment to deal them the *coup de grâce* and judge how hard he needed to strike. And Hinault was the King of the Gaze, the Bully Boy of a film called the Tour de France that has been running for almost a hundred years. You could think of the Breton as the Taris Bulba, the Genghis Khan or the Tamberlain of the *Grande Boucle*. Fierce and implacable towards his enemies and demanding of his *domestiques*, Hinault could perhaps have passed on a thing or two to Induráin about looking, although, as would soon become evident, the Navarran had a very different approach from the one the Badger had adopted over the years. In short, Hinault used to issue threats, sometimes coloured with highly sophisticated obscenities. He would frequently accelerate and then inexplicably slow right down as he looked challengingly round at his opponents. On occasions he even went as far as confronting them verbally, to the embarrassment of the race stewards and onlookers. 'So, do you want today to be just a boring old, run-of-the-mill day, or do you want to come out and play?' he might say to them after launching a furious attack. And they would be terrified. No one would leave the peloton without his permission and, indeed, hardly anyone was capable of leaving it.

While Merckx and Anquetil used to offer some crumbs to other riders, the temperamental Hinault counted on a select band of *domestiques* such as Quilfen, Bernaudeau, Vallet, Jourdan and Vigneron, who were extremely efficient. Years later, one of them told the story that on a certain day in the Tour, the Raleigh riders, all top-notch cyclists, had been causing non-stop trouble. They were beginning to wreak havoc amongst Hinault's *domestiques*. In response, he did something that was unthinkable, and which had never been seen before in a Tour stage. There was a strong headwind which all the cyclists were trying to shelter from. At the speed the bunch was going, the first man to try and leave the compact group would have been destroyed as soon as the wind hit him head-on. All well and good, so Bernard Hinault, throwing challenging looks at the Raleigh boys, moved over to the other side of the road on his own. On one side of the road was the whole peloton, and on the other, riding into a gale, was Hinault. He kept his eyes glued to them as he pedalled. The Raleigh riders, clearly infuriated by this, really started to shift. The peloton was now riding at close to top speed. So what did Hinault do? He shouted: 'OK, then…' and shot off ahead. He left them standing, and for a good minute they were struggling to keep up, until he called time. A pair of Raleigh cyclists parleyed with the Breton and things returned to normal. They would not step out of line again for the remainder of the Tour.

The psychological control exerted by Induráin was, as I said, just as important, if not more so, than Hinault's, but the means he employed were completely different. He used his elegance, and a system of 'permits'. Before anyone launched a proper attack at crucial moments, they would look over at Induráin. He could cruise along comfortably in the main bunch because there was a tacit understanding among the peloton that you always had to make way for a leader like him. He only had to whistle and everyone, not just his *domestiques*, moved aside. The sight of Induráin was at least as imposing as Hinault's warlike countenance. It was well-known that Hinault, especially in the later part of his career, sometimes attacked precisely when he felt bad, just to shake everyone up a bit, to discourage any strange idea they might have had of pushing the pace too much when he wanted a nice quiet stage. Merckx used to do exactly the same.

Induráin's look would be the thing that triggered the first step of that magical five-year period. Or, to be more precise, not his look, but his fleeting glance. Let me explain. In 1991 Induráin blew the Tour apart on the descent of the Tourmalet towards Sainte-Marie de Campan, near the walls of La Mongie, which had been placed there as snow-breaks. And he didn't look over his shoulder until some way further on. For a long while, he gave it everything, without bothering about what was happening behind him. He couldn't afford to lose even a fraction of a second. It was the day the wind had sung its song: 'Today.'

And, by now in yellow, he sealed the Tour on the way up Alpe d'Huez. However, at no time did he openly look at Bugno there either, not even in the challenging Hinault-style – for him that would have been the height of bad manners. It would have altered the destiny of the legend. It was simply that, whenever Bugno tried to accelerate and shake him off, Miguel would draw alongside, or slightly ahead of him, and throw him a quick glance out of the corner of his eye. Every time, a perfect and serene gesture, as if silently to tell the Italian: 'You see? Here I am again. Why don't you just accept it?' In fact, he didn't look at Bugno but at his front wheel, as if he were trying to depersonalise him.

During the first stages of that race, from the prologue in Lyon, won by Marie, to Reims, Le Havre and Argentan, which, of course, the sprinters won, things remained quiet. The first alarm bells were sounded by Induráin in the time-trial between Argentan and Alençon. It was very long, 73 kilometres. Lemond had high hopes, and, in fact, the American came home, totally exhausted, just eight seconds behind Induráin. Jean-François Bernard, the hare recently signed by Banesto to set the pace for Miguel in the time-trials, was almost a minute behind. Quimper and Saint-Herblain were exciting finishes and brought victories for the *rouleurs*, but it was *en route* to Jaca, over the Pyrenees, where things were to happen. That is where Miguel started to watch. And he saw that the French idol, Charlie Mottet, was restless, as was a young blond rider in the Castorama team, Luc Leblanc. There was a battle up Soudet. On the short but steep Col d'Ichère, Mottet gave chase to a break-away group, and embarked on a solitary adventure along the valley of the Aspe. That day Miguel was wearing a helmet, goodness knows why. Could he have been thinking of launching himself like a madman down one of those descents? At a very critical moment, Lemond, who was in the yellow jersey at that point, found himself surrounded by five Banesto riders: Perico Delgado, Jean-François Bernard, Abelardo Rondón, Fabrice Philipot and Induráin. It was surely the ideal moment to attack. Ahead, the riders were strung out, with Lemond's overall lead now being threatened by Leblanc, yet the disconcerted American still had the cheek to suggest that they lead him up – which showed that his game was finished. They were climbing the Somport. I know that mountain, and it is a gradual climb. You need to find a rhythm and it didn't seem the ideal place to launch an attack which Lemond, with his class, would have neutralised even on his own. No, it was better to keep watching.

Miguel looked at Greg Lemond's legs, which were extremely swollen and with new veins showing. That was an indication of something. His demands that everyone should give him a tow were not only a give-away, they were alarming. In the end, Mottet won, while Leblanc took over as leader and offered his yellow jersey to Raymond Poulidor, who had never worn the prized garment, not even for a single day. Of course, that day the French were already thinking of Luc Leblanc as the Tour winner. He was young, ambitious, and a battler; he had a slight defect in one leg (it was shorter than the other) and for training he used to fell trees in the woods, like Pou-Pou, his master; he had lost his younger brother in an accident. In short, he was ideal hero potential.

No one expected the move that was to take place one kilometre from the finish in Jaca, and when the first finishers had already completed the stage. The main bunch was racing at full speed. When this happens, because they are desperate to make an impression, or because they are just anxious to finish or simply because of the momentum, they all accelerate and, if you aren't a specialist climber, it is very difficult in those circumstances to make a break. Induráin's family were all gathered there, just as they had been at Luz-Ardiden the previous year. So, almost casually, Miguel pulled away from the group, gained a few metres and arrived at the finish in Jaca out on his own. He waved. Seeing him pedal so freely you would have been forgiven for thinking he'd escaped from the bunch merely so he could come home ahead and wave to his family, and that he'd triumphed the previous year at Luz-Ardiden for the same reason.

It was the Nekane syndrome all over again, but in a profoundly symbolic sense – perhaps all Spaniards had now become Nekane, and we were anxious and sad because no one was bothering about our toys. Nekane still needed bottles and the finish at Jaca, though a modest and apparently pointless achievement, was another bottle. But Miguel's burst to the front had demonstrated the strength he carried in his legs.

And very possibly he continued to think about the aching legs of that gladiator who was about to bite the dust – Greg Lemond. And perhaps he also remembered Hinault, who said that a quick glance was all he needed to know how well his rivals were feeling. In the Badger's opinion, Joop Zoetemelk was the one who was least able to hide it: 'When he reached his limit, his right leg would bend at right angles,' he said. 'I read a book about Coppi where he taught that cycling was not only a matter of strength. Coppi had observed that Magni became vulnerable whenever the veins in his legs swelled. So he got a team-mate of his to watch him, and when the team-mate shouted "Vein!" Coppi would launch an attack. I've done the same. Watch them all the time.'

Those legs of Lemond, that out-of-the-saddle style, even on mountains where he could have ridden in a more relaxed stance, that frenetic looking out for who was boxed in, that shuttling back and forth to the Z team car. On the road to Jaca these were all tell-tale signs.

The Spanish media, however, were outraged. How could Banesto possibly have failed to go for the jugular, with Lemond isolated? Some of them were practically calling for heads to roll: they considered it to have been an insult that Echávarri's men had not made a move, especially with the stage ending on Span-ish soil. People like that can be terrifying when they get into posi-tions of power; they cause harm simply for the fun of it. But when all was said and done, the Pyrenees were *two* days, and only one had gone. Outwardly, Induráin seemed exhausted, but in one piece, despite his exhibition over the last kilometre. His reply was spectacularly concise, arithmetical and ingenious: 'The important thing is the Tour as a whole. The Pyrenees last 48 hours,' said Miguel, more relaxed than anyone, to the chagrin of reporters, especially those from the radio, who wanted somebody's blood and guts there and then.

Anyone who had endured Pedro Delgado's nail-biting Tours might have thought: 'Now we'll hear the old cliché that there's a lot of Tour left to ride.' But no, what Miguel had told them in a gentle code, sketching out in his own words the *Andante Maestoso* which he was preparing to initiate the following day, was: 'There are still 24 hours to go.'

In those 24 hours they would have to climb the Portalet, the Aubisque, the Tourmalet, the Aspin and the finish right up at Val-Louron. More or less the Apocalypse, and in a sweltering, near-40-degree heat.

Between the town of Jaca and Val-Louron there were a mere 232 kilometres and five high mountains to contend with. Not a single metre on the flat – much has been said, in the secret liturgy of the Tour, about the *faux-plats*, or false flats, on the roads surrounding the Aspin. And the stage began under an intense, unforgettable sun. Leblanc and his team manager, the ever-present Cyrille Guimard, were euphoric, although you could also see they were concerned. They had reason to be. All the inexperience in the world was laid on the shoulders of the new Yellow Jersey, an idol in a country that was already raising him (a few hours into his reign) as the successor to Jacques Anquetil. It was too much. Too much even for Cyrille Guimard.

They were riding in a compact group, looking at each other, the Portalet up ahead. Miguel didn't need to look: the decision had already been taken. The river Gallego lay behind. The road to the Aubisque, from Eaux-Bonnes, seemed like the Kalahari Desert, with nowhere at all to hide. More or less all the favourites were there, Ronan Pensec and Eduardo Chozas, fighting harder than ever at the front, going hell for leather on Soulor, the peak preceding the summit of the Aubisque. Then they started the rapid descent towards Arrens and Argelés-Gazost.

That was when, for many, the dream began – and the nightmare. Pensec, looking like a mischievous punk, was still giving it all he had. This was how they were when they reached the foot of the Tourmalet. A boiling inferno. Climbing via Barèges, which, according to Perico himself, the master of these Pyrenean heights, is the more difficult face. Barèges has been described as 'a sad village suffocated by the mountains'. So true. Its waters are also known to be ideal for treating nervous exhaustion, and the fact is, as the writer Raymond Escholier put it, there are more than enough reasons in those parts to turn the 'most jovial of men' into hypochondriacs.

It is a climb over pure, mute rock, a climb for the hardmen, who don't understand the word 'disheartened', who know how to watch. Leaving Barèges, something occurred which was outrageous, yet also expected: some leaders, when they are feeling bad, even when they are feeling very, very bad, especially psychologically, attack like crazy. Lemond had learned the lesson of Merckx and Hinault. But Induráin knew that lesson.

A brutal attack from the American, as if he were trying to wrap up the Tour on those first kilometres of the Tourmalet.

Miguel was observing his swollen legs and those eyes distilling cold desperation. He must have thought: you're a dead man.

And he simply waits. He climbs at his own rhythm, a common-place yet nonetheless worrying phrase for generations of cyclists who know full well what it means when Miguel 'climbs at his own rhythm'. This can be translated as: a stretch that could be climbed at 15 kilometres an hour, or at 20 in bursts, is climbed at a steady 20-plus kilometres an hour. Even if, as in this case, we are talking about a distance of almost 20 kilometres. The sun beats down mercilessly on the bends of the Tourmalet. Miguel snorts.

He can't see him, but possibly he finds out from the Banesto team car that Lemond is showing signs of nervousness: he's talking to his coaches; he's unzipping his top flamboyantly; and, even better, his head is swaying from side to side, from left to right. Induráin doesn't need to see Lemond's legs any more. There are five or six kilometres left to the summit of the Tourmalet, and Miguel's group comprises the leader, Leblanc, Mottet, Rué, Hampsten, and Bugno – the ever-dangerous Bugno who had stunned the whole world the previous year by winning the Giro, leading from day one – and his key rival, Chiappucci. Miguel has what he needs. They've caught Lemond. They all know what this means – his death knell. The winner of three Tours had been unable to initiate a break at the foot of the Tourmalet, even though he'd clearly been increasing his effort over the last kilometres. In competitive cycling, if you show signs of weakness for a single instant at the supreme moment you will be repeatedly stabbed, like Caesar.

When they pass Lemond, Miguel checks just how bad he is. For the moment Leblanc doesn't count. It remains to be seen if descending a peak at nearly 100 kilometres an hour, risking your life at every bend, is his cup of tea.

Greg Lemond's failed break seals the fate of that Tour, and of history. There are just 500 metres to go to the summit. There's a tight curve where the gradient increases. Rivers of sweat are pouring, but this isn't the time to weaken. The hairpin bend, between the rocks, encircled by vast and bottomless drops, claims a victim. And it's Lemond! He's lost the wheel of the last rider in the group. This is his grave. Up ahead, Chiappucci, who's also a good watcher, mercilessly turns the screw. The American slips back and drops behind. On Radio Tour, they begin to get nervous. They're backing Leblanc, but as Leblanc looks none too good either they're staying with Lemond, a professional from top to toe. A group of riders reaches the summit of the Tourmalet and, indeed, Lemond isn't among them. I must emphasise again that while it is of no great importance to lose two or even three minutes in a time-trial, losing them on a mountain takes on a different meaning. It means double that time will probably be lost on the next one. Simple, crude arithmetic.

Chiappucci reaches the top, but Miguel has made him suffer. He has quickened the pace, aware that Lemond is cracking back down the road. They go under the banner and there are those few seconds of rest when the cyclists attempt to wrap up to protect themselves against the wind on the downhill section. They never wear raincoats on such a sunny day, but they do stuff a newspaper down their top. Miguel focuses. It's now or never. You have to be bold and, of course, to risk your life if you're going to deliver a *coup d'état*. As soon as he reaches the summit of the Tourmalet, Induráin takes a deep breath and speaks to the wind, perhaps: 'Don't fail me now.'

In little more than one kilometre, he is free of all the other riders. They don't dare descend so quickly, at 80 or 90 kilometres an hour. It's madness. The Navarran pushes to the limit.

The wind. It's blowing favourably. Miguel has selected a 12 sprocket and won't be changing it at all on the descent. The key lies in the way he comes out of the bends – with strength and rage. A terrible rage. So many years dreaming of an opportunity like this. Maybe it's not worth risking your life? 'Careful,' your head is saying. 'No', or 'Brake'. Of course it's not worth risking your life.

But, what is the harvest? Is it worth risking? Is it worth risking a whole life's harvest because you're a bit scared when you come out of a few bends? And what about Nekane, and Marisa, and Eusebio, and Pepe Barruso? You must descend without touching the brakes. For them. Miguel never descended with the kamikaze fearlessness of a Frans Maassen or a Konychev, but he flies. Not even Chiappucci manages to link up with him, even though he strives to do so for twenty kilometres.

Not for nothing is the Italian known as the Devil. He gets close, and Miguel is told to wait for him. Ahead are the false flats of Aspin, the Aspin itself and Val-Louron. Miguel hasn't looked back once. Why should he? He knows full well no one can catch him on a descent as nerve-racking as the one he has just produced to Sainte-Marie de Campan. Around La Mongie, the speedometer was touching a hundred.

Claudio makes the junction. They speak. The stage for you, the yellow jersey for me. There's no further discussion. A terrible rage. He dons his cap, tenses his jaws, and his gaze is liquid.

The sun was beating more ferociously than ever on the climb up the Aspin, a well-paved road with its sides covered with lush green where the sun's rays appeared to reflect, bouncing up at the cyclists, like a kind of natural magnifying glass. They took turns on the front in textbook style. This was one of the most synchronised escapes in memory. There was no need to speak, or even to look at each other. On the ascent, logically perhaps, Claudio did the greater share at the front, but once over the top, and on to Arreau, Miguel went for broke again. All that was left was to skirt Peyresourde and make one final effort. The Banesto and Carrera cars were shuttling back and forth updating their men. Echávarri still couldn't believe it. Lemond was destroyed. Destroyed! Apparently, he had even fallen when he ran into the Gatorade team car, but it wasn't serious – just another sign of how exhausted he was. The climb to Val-Louron, where there were more Spanish and Basque *ikurriña* flags than at almost any other time in the history of the Tour, was frenzied. People were unsure who was keenest to reach the finish: Miguel to don yellow; or Chiappucci to claim victory in this, the queen of stages. They were going flat out, gasping for air and elbow to elbow, yet still not looking at each other. Either of the two would have found a lone climb infinitely more painful and unbearable. The euphoric Italian crossed the line first, a metre ahead of Induráin, who raised his arm in joy. That, as we have said, was an almost violent gesture. It was the first time that finishing second had caused him to make that victory salute. The only other time would be at the World Championships in Colombia, when he saluted as he followed in his team-mate, Olano.

They'd taken one and a half minutes out of Bugno, and almost four out of Mottet, although only two minutes 50 seconds out of Fignon, who had regained strength and passed Luc Leblanc, his young team-mate and leader, without even looking at him, without asking if he was OK or offering him assistance. Is that panache? From that point on, I must admit, although we recognised his qualities as a cyclist, many of us felt disappointed with the Parisian. Lemond had come in around eight minutes back, and Luc Leblanc, poor man, was shattered when he arrived.

All of a sudden our eyes were glued to the ceremony on the podium. We were speechless and full of pride. The Crédit-Lyonnais hostesses pulled the yellow jersey over Miguel's head. That was emotional, but in reality it seemed as if it had been happening for years, as if it were the most normal thing in the world. That jersey was his – his – and the wind of the Pyrenees knew it, had always known it, as it blew, cool and snaking, through the valleys of Navarre!

On that first podium on which he wore his yellow jersey, something occurred that was strange and endearing. The beautiful Crédit-Lyonnais girls were there, well-versed in such matters. They seem to be devious experts in sleights of hand, softly groping the riders: their ribs, arms, and sometimes, so it's said, even their back and bum. This is never recorded by the cameras, of course. After the donning of the yellow jersey, when the leaders of the different classifications, or the stage victor, are up on the podium, along come the PMU girls, or the Coca-Cola girls, or wherever they're from, but the general consensus is that the real stunners are the Crédit-Lyonnais girls. They're chosen for this job after a very rigorous selection process, which isn't hard to imagine. Anyway, they dressed Induráin in the yellow jersey and he had to take out his black Banesto baseball hat (the smart, flashy one). That was when it happened, before anyone realised what was going on. One of the girls grabbed his Banesto cap and, simultaneously, and without checking with him, placed the trademark yellow Crédit Lyonnais one on his head. Miguel must have seen someone near the podium gesturing at him and reminding him very clearly of his advertising commitments. For a moment the new leader gave a confused smile. What an embarrassing situation, and the other girls were smothering him in kisses and groping him as they pretended to adjust his *malliot jaune*. Banesto, like Credit-Lyonnais, is a bank with interests in France, so the cap incident was especially delicate. Within a matter of seconds, Miguel, with a broad smile on his face, had put his black Banesto cap back on. And perhaps that was the only time, if ever, that they attempted to pull a fast one on him in the Tour. It is well known that those hostesses are experts at using their hands, arms or bouquets of flowers to cover the trade-names and logos the riders sport on their jerseys. Amidst all the smiles, kisses and the odd bit of touching-up.

For Miguel, the best thing that came out of the day, apart from gaining the lead, was that he had also 'seen' Bugno's legs. Not in the final part of the stage, because the Italian had been behind him, but certainly in the earlier stages. He'd spent the whole of the previous tour studying them. And the data was recorded in his mind.

Induráin phoned home the day of Val-Louron. In Villava there were fireworks and everyone was going mad with excitement. His mother, Isabel Larraya, asked about the details of the stage, but Miguel wasn't interested in speaking about it. He asked how the barley harvest was going. Later, in an interview after his fifth consecutive Tour win, he would still insist: 'In the countryside there is a philosophy, a whole way of thinking. You sow and you harvest, and you're always dependent on whatever good or bad weather might come. This is the kind of philosophy I also find useful in cycling.'

For the moment, the sun was shining. And it would continue to do so for some time.

The following days were, on the surface, calm, but only on the surface, since in the Tour you can receive a blow at any moment, either symbolically – that's to say in the sporting sense – or quite literally. Years before, the Italian cycling team had been assaulted at Saint-Gaudens, and in the '75 Tour Eddy Merckx himself received a punch from a spectator while climbing the Puy-de-Dôme which almost put him in the broom-wagon.

The Tour brings together ten million people to the roadside, and in the mountains all these people are in a position to grab or shove you as you pass by them on a bike at low speed. Even if you are in a car, it can be quite frightening. You see some over-enthusiastic hands banging on the bodywork. Sometimes you run over someone's foot, but it's impossible to stop. The Tour caravan never stops. The Press cars tend to travel at top speed, sometimes mixed up with the cars of the publicity caravan, which are obliged to alternate – one on the right and one on the left of the road – enabling anyone to pass them quickly. On more than one occasion, from inside the car, we have seen the wheel run over a foot or heard someone bang on the side of the car. That's the Tour, and you just have to keep going. You have to bear in mind how hard it would be to stop that gigantic worm-like creature which wiggles its way round the innards of France.

I often had the feeling that the caravan was like a giant alien wriggling from inertia in the country's intestines. Echávarri defined the Tour as a tremendously complex being, and Cyrille Guimard once explained that if the Tour seemed big it was precisely because of its inhuman dimension. He was right there. Indeed, that segmented worm, comprising anything up to 1,500 cars, motorbikes and various accompanying vehicles, of which nearly 300 belong to the world of advertising, is strung out over nearly 20 kilometres of road. There are normally around a thousand accredited journalists, although, as far as the Spanish are concerned, more attended once the Induráin phenomenon began. Three thousand mobile police officers guard each crossroads, each street, each roundabout, each tiny turning from any local lane out in the country, which is why it is not uncommon to see several *gendarmes*, arms crossed and expressionless, in the middle of uplands which appear to be endless wastelands. Fifty motorbike riders from the Republican Guard accompany the race each day, apart from the many other bikes belonging to the Press and the Tour organisation which are the ones normally closest to the action on the road. Seen from the air in helicopters that are specially equipped by *Antenne-2* to give a better view of the human and motorised worm, the cyclists must look like little jelly-babies dancing to a single tune inside a screwed-up plastic bag. When you think of a peloton of 200 men, you have to remember that it generates around 90,000 watts of pure power each day. In the stages that take place each year in Belgium alone, there must be an average of 600 roundabouts, each and every one of which breaks the riders' rhythm. And, to repeat the terrifying figure, if we bear in mind that, in the course of a day, the muscle fibres of the heart pump blood to the different parts of the body around 90,000 times, and then if we multiply all this by 200 sportsmen pushing their bodies to the very limit, we have one very bloody situation. All of this is all part of the Tour, in addition to the spectacle.

The '91 Tour, in particular, seemed to prostrate itself before Induráin, although both the foreign and the Spanish Press were uncertain about the Alps. How would Miguel deal with the challenge of those high mountains? It seemed as if they continued to distrust his abilities, in spite of what he had just done at Val-Louron. Climbing when you're in yellow must be different. Anyone who doubts this should ask Luc Leblanc, who, make no bones about it, went to pieces like so many others have done, simply because he was in yellow. Whereas, for another kind of rider, the yellow jersey gives him wings – and this isn't just a cliché. Delgado always maintained Induráin would be that kind of rider. If he got the lead, he would fight tooth and nail to keep it; he would draw strength from where he had none, and it would be a hell of a job to drag the jersey off his back.

And Miguel was still thinking about Gianni Bugno's legs, because he knew how much they would make Bugno suffer in the coming days. That was what he was thinking about when he committed his second mistake of that Tour, after the naïve and quickly corrected mistake with the Crédit-Lyonnais cap. He opened his mouth. His famous and controversial comment '*Je me moque d'être espagnol*' (which translates, more or less, as 'I couldn't care less whether I'm Spanish or not') brought inevitable controversy, especially since it was reported in the Holy Bible of the Tour, *L'Equipe*. Miguel retracted it, but by then it was somewhat too late.

How was he supposed to explain to his team that he was from the earth, the wind, the sky? People yearn for categorical definitions, irrevocable stances. But with Induráin they were in trouble. After that comment he was no doubt given some advice by Francis Lafargue, and he never slipped up again. Quite the reverse, in fact – he became more reserved in the statements he made. He never actually reached the point of scarcely concealed semi-autism, but he verged on it. All the better for him. I am one of those who maintain that anyone who's too concerned with shouting his mouth off, or such like, is not concerned with winning Tours. It's true, nevertheless, that over time Induráin did open up a little more.

Now the race's own dynamic was preparing us for yet more surprises. Between Alès and Gap, there was a fright. A break, which included all the favourites, was instigated by the tireless Chiappucci on the fourth-category Saint-André climb. Fignon and Bugno were up there, always looking for their opportunity. It was important to get back on, and there were only 60 kilometres to the finish. The Banesto squad had to work extremely hard to reduce the dangerous minute the favourites had put between them, and there was a memorable and heroic effort from Perico Delgado, who thereby returned his team-mate some old favours. All this was in one of those stages, incorrectly termed 'transition stages' – incorrectly since everyone is really waiting impatiently for the high mountains to arrive – when Induráin went up to Perico and told him he was in trouble. 'I'm in a bad way.' This had to be covered up, come what may, and cover it up they did. It was one of those fleeting but worrying episodes that occur in every Tour and which the public never hears about.

And then came the most feared stage: Alpe d'Huez. Once again the ghost of the mountain reared its head and the question marks resurfaced about how Induráin would react. Those doubts had scarcely figured in the Paris–Nice races. At Cauterets, in the '89 Tour, he had broken away on his own from a long way out and, actually, his lead had decreased alarmingly towards the finish. At Luz-Ardiden, in 1990, he spent almost the whole climb on Lemond's demonic wheel. On the Jaizkibel, in the San Sebastian Classic, it was Marino Lejarreta himself who almost dropped Miguel. And on the day of the Val-Louron stage, the Navarran had attacked on the dizzy *descent* of the Tourmalet, and he would enjoy the priceless help of Chiappucci when, later, he came to tackle the Aspin and Val-Louron. Doubts. There remained plenty of doubts.

The main bunch was practically intact when they reached the foot of Alpe d'Huez. And that was where we experienced some of the most unforgettable moments in Miguel's career. There, amidst those devastating slopes leading to Le Ribaut, La Garde or the village of Huez-en-Oisans itself, an epic duel was fought out. On the first kilometres of the ascent Jean-François Bernard attacked harder than he had ever done before. His top was unzipped and his eyes were bloodshot, and he forced a hellish pace. Even so, Bugno kicked two and even three times, and remained just a few metres behind him. That was where our hearts skipped a beat. That was where Induráin was supposed to make a break. And that's what he did. Whenever Bugno accelerated Induráin drew up alongside, and even increased his rhythm a little (a psychological move which shows your rival who's in control) and then went back alongside, relaxing his rhythm. Bugno was suffering. He could see his last chance of winning the Tour evaporating. Behind them, a stubborn Luc Leblanc seemed to be on a piece of elastic; no sooner did he drop off the back, his chances apparently disappearing down the drain, than he would join up again with the two leaders. And, to everyone's surprise, as well as to our specific relief, Jean-François Bernard managed to get back on, fighting like a hungry wolf until he was once again in the group with Bugno and Miguel. That must have thrown the Italian, who still managed to accelerate on a couple of occasions. But there was Induráin on his wheel, glancing out of the corner of his eye at Bugno's legs, always at his legs, never at his eyes. Five more bends, just five, and the torment would be over, although Miguel seemed to be climbing comfortably, so comfortably we couldn't believe it. He even led Bugno right up close to the finish, as if he were a *domestique*.

And there were two choices: to round off that fantastic ascent in spectacular fashion and sprint it out with the Italian, or win him over, once and for all. Induráin reached the final straight intact. He could have won, he told himself, but he crossed the line half a metre behind Bugno, just as at Val-Louron where he crossed a metre behind Chiappucci. The same Chiappucci, incidentally, who had blown up on the first of the Alpine slopes. No doubt Induráin made the instantaneous calculation that it was preferable to have Bugno as a rival in the present, but as a friend for life. To the Italian went the joy of carrying off the most attractive stage in the race, and Miguel was even more firmly ensconced in yellow, complying with the tradition that says that whoever leaves Alpe d'Huez in yellow will arrive victorious in Paris. Something which was not true for Perico in '87, though it was the following year.

That was the day, I believe, when we discovered a new Induráin, the powerful man who climbed like the angels and put

1989 and a foretaste of what was to come: Induráin climbing towards his first Tour stage win at Cauterets after a long solo break through the Pyrenees.

1996 and the end of the dream: Induráin after the stage into Pamplona.

'The stage and the polka-dot jersey for you; the yellow jersey for me.'
Chiappucci and Induráin climbing in tandem towards Val-Louron, 1991.

Prudencio leading Miguel on the Champs-Elysées, 1993.

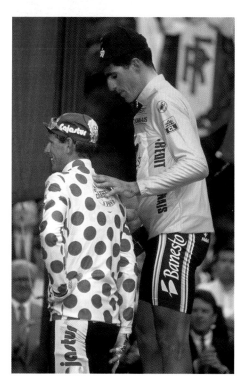

'The Hand of God.' Induráin and Rominger on the podium in Paris. Their battle was the essence of the 1993 Tour.

Towing a strung-out group in pursuit of Ugrumov on the Col de la Colombière in the 1994 Tour. It was performances like this in the mountains that prompted Eddy Merckx to remark, 'I had to see it to believe it.'

Liège–Bastogne–Liège, 1994. It was over these roads that Induráin sprung his outrageous surprise attack that took almost a minute out of all his main rivals in the 1995 Tour, even before the first time-trial.

Beating Pantani to the Silver Medal in the 1995 World Championships in Colombia behind his compatriot, Abraham Olano.

Induráin on the vicious climb to Mende in the 1995 Tour, cutting back the dangerous gap that Jalabert had opened up. Riis struggles to hold on.

Exhausted, isolated, and dropping further back with every turn of the pedals. Les Arcs was the graveyard of hopes for a sixth Tour victory in 1996.

Second, behind Ullrich, in the final time-trial of the 1996 Tour – a result that encouraged Induráin to go to Atlanta where he won the Olympic gold medal.

The supporters were everywhere – on the roadsides of France …

… and in the Spanish Pyrenees.

(Sunada/Photosport International)

Miguel and Prudencio, and parents, before the start of the eighteenth stage of the 1996 Tour: Pamplona to Hendaye.

fear into his rivals not by his gaze, as Hinault did, but by his very presence. However, we have committed a slight oversight here. We have forgotten that the following day saw another Alpine stage, finishing at Morzine. And prior to Morzine they had to climb the feared, though often overlooked, Joux-Plane, a ten-kilometre ascent on roads that were well-surfaced but which did not allow the riders a moment's respite, with their average 10-per-cent gradient. Tying in with my earlier theory about how much time Miguel gained in the time-trials, if you had a bad day on a mountain like Joux-Plane you could lose half a minute or more per kilometre without even necessarily blowing up. That's where Delgado had fallen on the descent years before. Even though it was not often climbed, it was a mountain marked by the aura of the 'ogres' of the Tour.

On the day we were unable to follow the Joux-Plane stage due to the heavy rain and terrible weather conditions that prevailed throughout the ascent. Of the 225 kilometres, virtually the only bit we were shown on TV (and a very fuzzy picture, at that) was the arrival at the finish of Thierry Claveyrolat, an excellent *grimpeur* whose hairpiece was all askew. He was followed home by the lanky Thierry Bourguignon, a rider who, years later, was to be very seriously injured in a training accident. He spent several days in a deep coma, from which it was feared he'd never recover. But luckily he pulled through, and the first thing he said was that he wanted to carry on racing. He had almost lost his ability to speak, but he soon recuperated and was riding the roads again. There is no doubt about it, cyclists are made of stern stuff.

On Joux-Plane, although we were unable to see it because of the terrible weather, Induráin suffered another awkward moment. On a bend in the road, Bugno, who was not beyond making one last effort to win the Tour by a technical knock-out, accelerated strongly, and Miguel lost a metre, then two, then three. The Italian was pulling away, but it wasn't a big, clean break. That wasn't his style, which was just as well. We sighed in relief, for Bugno was merely increasing the tempo. It was that which saved Miguel, who was once again well protected by his phalanx of bodyguards. Bugno had contented himself with turning the screw to see what would happen, but it wasn't in Chiappucci's interests for his compatriot to pull away, since he was defending the polka-dot jersey of King of the Mountains. Between them, Chiappucci and Banesto neutralised the fine Gatorade rider, who that year was sporting his Italian champion's jersey. All the same, beneath the driving rain and on those 10-per-cent gradients, Miguel suffered badly, as rarely occurred in any of his Tours, except that of 1993, when he was suffering from flu, and the last Tour in 1996. And, as is the way of things, we weren't aware of it.

A couple of routine days and then the final time-trial, which was flat and perfect for Induráin. Although it was nearly 50 kilometres long, the Navarran could only take 27 seconds out of Bugno and 48 out of a re-energised Greg Lemond.

Echávarri used to say that all roads lead to Paris. He was right. Expectation was sky-high for a Miguel triumph. He was as happy as a child with a new toy, only he wanted more out of that same toy. Banesto claimed the team award, a competition that had been fiercely contested throughout the Tour. Everyone was happy and there was a huge party in Villava and in Pamplona. What about the pessimistic voices from elsewhere in Spain? Well, they certainly didn't disappear with their tails between their legs. On the contrary, they were saying they knew well in advance that 'it' was going to happen, and gave the impression they had more or less 'discovered' Miguel. I can imagine the smiles of satisfaction from Echávarri and Unzúe, that pair of wise and tenacious Navarrans who, from the Banesto car, had designed the *coup d'état* strategy for the Tour. Although, as they have always recognised, in reality the protagonist, Induráin, did it more or less off his own bat. As geniuses do.

Paris was beginning to get used to a population of Basque *ikurriña* flags, Spanish flags and banners held aloft by Miguel's fans. Paris endured it in a rather offhand manner, beginning to mutter under its breath a name which might free it from that excessively noisy plague. And that name was 'Bugno'.

Back in Spain people were going crazy. In Miguel's native Villava they went overboard – medals, balcony appearances, official receptions, a symbolic presentation of the jersey to the Virgin of the Rosary, traditional Basque dances and dance groups wearing the traditional *txapela* beret. Songs, folk music and the typical Aragonese *jota* dance were in evidence everywhere, although one particular song, by Patxi Oroz, was to become famous:

In the mountain
Reigns the eagle,
On the plain
It is the partridge;
And a farm-boy
From the valleys
Reigns
In the Champs-Elysées
In Paris.

After a short rest, it was the World Road-Race Championship in Stuttgart. As you would expect, Miguel gave it his best shot, but could only finish in the bronze-medal position. The winner was Bugno, who, to the delight of all of us, thereby managed to save his season. Induráin finished behind Steven Rooks, a man who had virtually no sprint finish, which goes to prove that, when he saw gold was beyond him, Miguel might have let a place slip. To round off the season he comfortably won the Tour of Catalonia.

The following year, 1992, would be Induráin's most complete year, in terms of both his sporting and personal life. It was a year brimming with prizes, awards and ceremonies, but also with triumphs on the road. He was awarded the Prince of Asturias Prize for Sport, and he visited the Pope in Rome, presenting him with a bicycle and several jerseys. As André Gide once wrote: 'What isn't there in the Vatican vaults?'

In the autumn of that year he married Marisa in the church of Oblatas in Pamplona. At the wedding ceremony, several bridesmaids, who were members of the Pamplona Choral Society, performed, amongst other pieces, Schubert's *Ave María*.

But Miguel was proceeding with his own particular Symphony, only this time it didn't start off in yellow but in pink – in the Giro. There was a kind of spell attached to the Giro d'Italia which, although it lacked the tradition of the Tour, was still a very tough event, and one which had become tougher during the preceding two decades. Bahamontes had won a Tour; Ocaña had won a Tour (and how!); Perico had won another Tour. And we had seen other Tours slip through our fingers: Pérez Francés, the brave Cantabrian, could have won, as could Julio Jiménez, and Arroyo, too, if he had really gone for it in his *annus mirabilis* of 1983 when he flew up the Puy-de-Dôme. The Giro, on the other hand, seemed to hold a jinx – for Poblet, for Fuente who had Eddy Merckx on the ropes in '74, and for Paco Galdós, who, the following year, reached the Stelvio together with Fausto Bertoglio on the final stage, separated by just a few seconds. Galdós won out at the summit, but the Italian took the race that was seemingly designed and destined for the *azzurri* riders. More than that, it seemed perfectly natural that many of the Italian winners of the Giro were incapable of making any kind of showing in the Tour, while there were not too many of the great Tour champions who ended up winning the Giro.

The Giro was strange, a mystery to itself, though beautiful. It had forced a number of riders into abandoning in its early stages, due to sunstroke, but it had also had some hellish stages, such as at Gavia, the year Andy Hampsten won. Rarely in the history of cycling had there been such a scene straight from Dante: riders abandoning; riders sobbing at the roadside, not knowing what to do or whom to ask for help; riders urinating into their hands in an attempt to get a little bit of warmth. And others coming to blows amongst the boulders on the roadside, totally oblivious of their bikes and the race, overcome with anger and showing signs of frost-bite. That day, in Hampsten's Giro, the cyclists were ghosts on pedals.

Then there was the legendary episode of the stage up Mount Bondone in the 1956 Giro. At the bottom of the climb it was sunny, halfway up it was zero degrees, a little higher and it was minus five. The temperature dipped as low as minus ten. The cyclists were literally fainting on their machines; they were like zombies without the strength to pedal. And in the middle of that blizzard emerged the agile, gaunt figure of Charly Gaul, who was speeding up the hill. He didn't say a word, even to his handlers when they called him from the car. He was a machine. When he reached the top the *carabinieri* who had to pick him up and carry him away, realised that his jersey was frozen solid, and they had to cut it off him with scissors.

There is an undeniably epic dimension to sport, which has always brought a malicious smile to the face of certain intellectuals, and chronic layabouts, but which also enthrals a huge number of people who are able to appreciate the enormous effort made by these true titans. For these reasons, and because no Spaniard had ever succeeded in winning it, the '92 Giro was a formidable challenge which aroused unusual expectation at all levels.

The schedule included a lot of mountain stages, and Miguel, who made no secret of the fact that he was using the Italian race as preparation for the Tour and wouldn't be going flat out, was only one of a number of favourites. The real favourite was Franco Chioccioli who, the previous year, had given a master class in cycling over every kind of terrain. Marino Lejarreta, who was always up for the Giro, had performed admirably up to the Mortirolo, but that was where Chioccioli made his break, blowing the race apart more dramatically in the Dolomites than anyone had seen for ages.

The prologue of that '92 Giro was won by Thierry Marie, but Miguel was close, just ten seconds behind, and he made what was, for him, a strange comment, which revealed his true intentions: 'It would have been nice to have got the *maglia rossa* today.'

One of the key stages occurred two days later, from Uliveto Terme to Arezzo. Max Sciandri won the stage, but shortly before the finish on the summit of the Foce di Scopetone, and with Chiappucci in no mood to give any quarter, the fuse was lit. There, Induráin and a group of favourites opened a gap on the peloton. The final stretch of that mountain had seen Marie flag, as Miguel had upped the pace, and then we saw the great Induráin in full flow, in command even in a race which was not yet his. It is well known that the Italian TV helicopters have always broken all the rules. In a bid to get spectacular pictures the pilots and cameras come in at near ground level – disconcerting for the riders who need to concentrate very closely on the noise of the brakes of each and every bike. Those unmistakable screeches give a few tenths-of-a-second warning of any sudden braking and, thus, accidents and multiple crashes are avoided in the mountain areas. But the terrible racket produced by the helicopter drowned everything. Induráin then cycled over to the race organisers' car, right there in the middle of the race, and said: 'The helicopter's too low. It's deafening and we won't be able to hear any sudden braking,' and he pointed upwards several times.

Incredible as it might appear, the TV cameras gave hardly any prominence to Miguel taking the *maglia rossa* that day. All their attention seemed focused on Sciandri. No matter. There would be other days to watch Miguel in all kinds of situations and to worship at his feet.

Just to get them used to that idea, there was the time-trial at Sansepolcro where the leader struck hard. The Italian favourites began to fall further behind, in a prelude to the festival that was soon to commence. After a few days devoted to the sprinters and more days in the small mountains, there was a finish at the summit of the famous Terminillo, the first tough climb in the Giro and the favourite mountain of Benito Mussolini. Seventeen kilometres with an average gradient of 7.3 per cent on its western slopes.

The Giro is not like the other two grand tours. The Tour of Spain is quite easy for us Spaniards to get to grips with because we know the places well enough; the Tour de France is yellow and earthy, soporific and with a permanent backdrop of *gendarmes* guaranteeing the efficiency of that romantic race which you learn to love, even if you always doubt whether it really has a soul. But the Giro, by comparison, tends to be the image of spring bursting into flower in every valley, an event in which the predominant visual experience, perhaps even more than the cyclists' multi-coloured jerseys, is the mauve and fuchsia splendour of the bougainvillæa, gladioli and hortensia. As it passes through each village, everything is special and beautiful, like a picture postcard. The people are welcoming, unlike those you might encounter in France. Even if you yourself are warm and personable, the French are normally rather cool and self-controlled, displaying natural courtesy and a studied politeness rather than any generosity of the soul.

That is what the Terminillo was like on that late-spring–early-summer afternoon: lush green, and exultant. First of all, while still at the foot of the climb, came an attack from Ramón González Arrieta (with the Lotus–Festina team at the time but subsequently a team-mate of Miguel's at Banesto). Then Ugrumov attacked. These were just attempts to play on other riders' nerves. The proper break appeared to come from Roberto Conti, a cyclist who would always maintain an excellent personal relationship with Induráin. For a good many kilometres Conti, from the Ariostea team, stayed away on his own, but someone must have warned him of the cyclone that was approaching from behind.

Miguel was accelerating, and the whole of Italy fell silent in amazement. Chioccioli had been dropped miles behind. Fignon had disappeared on a bend, somewhere or other. Even Chiappucci, choking on the hellish pace set by the Navarran, had to give up and lift his foot off the pedal in the final kilometres of the mountain. No one dared take over from Miguel. He was riding with his eyes fixed on the road and gritting his teeth. This was a Miguel we had never seen before, not even at Val-Louron where he shared the work with Chiappucci, nor on Alpe d'Huez where he contented himself with watching rather than attacking Bugno. Behind him, seemingly tugged and dragged along by an invisible rope, were those rivals who were to be with him in the high mountains: Herrera, Giovannetti, Hampsten and a few others. A long way back were the Navarran's splendid *domestiques*, who restricted themselves to keeping watch over the main bunch, and conserving their energy.

I think that was when we in Spain, seeing those pictures of Miguel's prodigious ascent, started to shout: 'Oh, oh, oh!' perhaps because we had no other words to describe or to grasp the enormity of the feat.

At the 'One kilometre' banner, Lucho Herrera kicked strongly. The Little Gardener from Fusagasuga, perhaps one of the best climbers in the history of cycling, saw Miguel looking at him as he passed. 'You can go' those serene eyes told him. That is how it would be with several other riders in other stages. 'You can; you can't.' The *padrone* was a good man.

There were other difficult stages remaining, and some where there was a mixture of sun and rain. The terrifying Passo Giau was another ten-kilometre-long 10-per-cent gradient, like the Joux-Plane in France. That's where the pests started to attack him – Chiappucci, Giovannetti, Chioccioli, and Lelli and Furlan. Miguel would normally follow just two wheels: those of the Devil and of Coppino (Franco Chioccioli's nickname because of his physical resemblance to Coppi). Every time there was a break, Miguel moved calmly up behind, and the sheep went back to the fold. They gazed at him in amazement. 'This guy's so big. How on earth can he climb so easily?' And he just kept on doing it: Forcella Staulanza – nearly 1,800 metres high; and the Valparola Pass – short but winding; the Campolongo Pass, and the Pordoi itself which, a year later, would witness Induráin cracking. That area, known as the Cadore Forest, saw Miguel in more imposing form than anyone could remember. Time after time, as they crossed all these mountains, the Navarran tracked the moves of his two or three main rivals. But there still remained three other serious engagements: the Bondone, the Monviso and the Pila.

That year, 1992, Miguel was once more to suffer a bad day and it was on the Bondone, not unexpectedly, in the rain and cold. But no one realised its significance; we didn't even know. Not content with including one ascent of the Bondone in the route, the Italians had added a second. And no sooner had the riders crossed the summit for the first time, still near the beginning of the stage, than Miguel started showing signs of hunger, and exhaustion. These were danger signals. The Banesto boys tried to hide it as best they could: at moments like that you have to, come what may, otherwise you'll be pounded to pulp. Furlan, an excellent all-round rider, won the stage, but the Italian climbers were so convinced Induráin was invulnerable, they didn't dare wage war. Only Chioccioli escaped in the last few metres to gain a bit of publicity.

On Monviso, just as he had done during the twelfth stage on the climb to Corvara, Miguel exerted regal control with the tried and trusted tactic: 'You can, you can't.' At the finish he allowed Giovannetti, a good and respectful cyclist, to win. Then, the following day, going up the Pila, we saw the Spaniard, Arrieta, who had opened up a substantial gap, crack calamitously and be reeled in by the German, Bolts. Induráin repeated his tactic and forbade anyone to move. Certain sections of the Italian media slated their climbers for not launching fiercer attacks on the leader. It's so easy to hold that opinion when you're an armchair critic writing your little daily article. But the fighter, Chioccioli, took it to heart, and the Giro can hold many snares, more even than the Tour, because its terrain is rough and scheming. Just when we believed things had finally settled down, there was the stage from San Vincent to Verbania which had a whole series of such potential pitfalls. It followed the valley of the Aosta, crossing the Corce Serra and Colma passes, and after that, there was the biggest trap of all – though fortunately some way from the finish – a little-known mountain bedecked in lush vegetation, the Alpe-Segletta. It's a climb of nearly nine kilometres and a gradient of 9.2 per cent, which hadn't entered into anybody's calculations, nor had it deserved a mention among the big and problematic climbs in the Giro. But there it was, lurking menacingly, just as, the following year, no mention would be made of Oropa, nor in the '95 Tour would there be mention of that schizophrenic and terminal climb to Causse Mende, where the ONCE and Jalabert would cause more than a gasp of anguish.

Up till that point Induráin had been the subject of constant, if short-lived, attacks, designed more to test him out than anything else, but on Alpe-Segletta Chioccioli attacked wholeheartedly, just as he had done on the Mortirolo one year earlier when he'd left the peloton for dead. We saw Miguel clasp the dropped part of his handlebars (an unmistakable sign he was preparing to wage war) and he launched himself like an arrow after Coppino. Whatever uncertainty there may have been, it lasted no more than a minute but, even in that short time, Chiappucci suffered the fall-out from the ferocious duel, and had lost time at the summit. Things eventually returned to normal, however, and Chioccioli gained the reward for his perseverance, winning the sprint into Verbania. Everyone was happy. They were good vassals, the other riders, and they had a great Lord.

In the final time-trial, between Vigevano and Milan, Induráin averaged more than 50 kilometres an hour, despite the length of the course – 66 kilometres. To the embarrassment of the Italian *tifosi*, the Navarran caught and passed Claudio Chiappucci in the home stretch, even though the Italian was actually setting a very good time. It was less a case of humiliating him in front of his home crowd than dealing him a psychological blow in the light of the coming Tour. It could be translated as: 'See what's waiting for you in the time-trials next month. So just take it easy, OK?'

But the Devil did not take it easy; on the contrary, he seemed to reserve all his anger for July and would unleash it furiously on a precise day, at a precise moment.

Meanwhile, Miguel continued to think and say that his only real rival for the Tour was himself, and that if he were on form, there would be no problems. But that was only partly correct, because, as he himself often demonstrated, cycling is anything but an exact science, and it is precisely that which makes it so interesting. He probably continued to reflect on Bugno, whose form was an enigma since he hadn't participated in the recently concluded Giro, and his focus on the Tour (for which his preparation was more in keeping with Miguel's) could even have been a cause for real concern. What condition would Gianni be in for the '92 Tour? Induráin must have thought about those legs climbing the Joux-Plane the previous year, and escaping from him at each and every bend, about those strong calf muscles which had been so hard to track up the slopes of Alpe d'Huez.

In 1992 the Tour was scheduled to make scarcely more than a token appearance in the Pyrenees. So, did that mean that the organisers had taken pity on the cyclists, and decided that the race would be gentle that year? Nothing could have been further from the truth. In the Pyrenean section there was only one main obstacle – the Col de Marie Blanque – although this time it was negotiable, since it was a long way from the finish in Pau. The climb was on its tough, French side, however, and Hinault was pointing out to the journalists: 'Have you ever cycled up the Marie Blanque? I strongly advise you to. It won't disappoint you.'

Climbing the slopes of Marie Blanque, which were shrouded in haze of course, we had realised the Tour was going to be a war of nerves. The very first incline saw Chiappucci's initial burst, though he calmed down a little when Miguel came alongside him. The rest of the peloton was shot to pieces, with the exception of Bugno and Charlie Mottet, who, like Leblanc the year before on Alpe d'Huez, seemed to be on a piece of elastic that was on the verge of melting. Bugno was the one Miguel was watching, and Bugno was waiting, holding back. A bad sign. Not once did the Italian rider, resplendent in the World Road-Race Champion's jersey, take the initiative; for a change it was left to Induráin and Chiappucci. Everyone was looking for signs, and the fact that Miguel had triumphed in the short prologue in the city of San Sebastián had to be symbolic. Right now the yellow jersey was on Zülle's back; it was better that way – less pressure for the team. After three kilometres on Marie Blanque, the riders at the front of the main peloton were the very ones who would be on the podium in Paris.

Before the Alps would come Luxembourg, and a long, flat time-trial, 65 kilometres long, where it would be interesting to see who was on form and who wasn't. There we witnessed something of a miracle. Some, such as Bugno, or Induráin's hare, De las Cuevas, rode well, but Induráin himself simply flew once again. It was merely confirmation, as we said, of the warning he had given in Milan a month previously. Induráin, at more than 49 kilometres an hour, wiped the floor with them in the Luxembourg time-trial, which, if you look closely, was not that flat: there were numerous uphill sections – Schrassig, the Côte de Senningerberg – where, if the wind was against you, you could crack. And that day the Tour was blown sky high, in the widest sense of the word. The ease of Induráin's pedal cadence, moving those enormous gears (54 front ring and almost always between 12 and 15 on the rear sprocket, both uphill and on the long downhill sections which really tend to take it out of you) evoked admiration amongst friend and foe alike. It was not so much because of the speed he was moving at, but, and I stress this, the fluidity with which he moved what in Spanish cycling parlance is known as the *paellera* or paella pan – the big ring. He was constantly overtaking other riders and, eventually, two kilometres from the finish, he caught Fignon. That was the famous day of the Parisian's equally famous phrase: 'I saw a missile fly past.'

Nevertheless, the silent lead character in the endearing anecdote of that day was not Fignon, but another man whose idiosyncrasy was similar to Miguel's. He was introverted and serious, spoke little and his pedalling revealed a special gift. He was the legendary Tour and Giro winner, Charly Gaul, who had retired many years before. Charly pedalling uphill had been as splendid a sight as Induráin fighting the stopwatch and the deep, bitter solitude of riding for an hour or more with his heart pounding at almost 190 beats a minute. The fact is that Charly Gaul had not appeared in public for a long time. He had been living as a hermit in a woody region of Luxembourg and wanted no contact with the cycling world. He wore a thick beard and had put on quite a few kilos. But that day, since the Tour was passing not far from where he lived, he decided to go and see it.

And, in Gaul's own words, he saw 'an angel' pass.

Such was the impression made by Induráin flashing past like lightning on his Pinarello 'goat' (specially adapted for the time-trials) that Gaul confessed he had been pierced by a kind of light.

He had been known as the 'Angel of the Mountains' and now he was speaking in similar terms about Miguel. The sight of Miguel's grin of ultra-concentrated pain, elbows resting on the handlebars as he travelled at high speed, would later encourage Gaul to re-integrate into society. That incident was to give a new twist to his life. From then on Charly agreed to be the starter for amateur events, for criteriums and junior races. And when he was asked why, for years after he would repeat: 'I saw an angel pass.'

And the whole world went 'Ohhh...!' just as we had done in the Giro. But the real body blow, that day, was suffered by the legs, and the head – most especially the head – of Gianni Bugno. This was supposed to have been his Tour. There had not been an Italian winner since Gimondi in 1965, and Bugno prepared especially for France, and most specifically for the time-trials. What's more, he had been viewed as a traitor by his Italian fans for not having taken part in the Giro.

But a drama was to erupt between St Gervais and Sestrière, a 254-kilometre stage which could still turn the classification on its head, in spite of the gap Miguel had opened up over his rivals in Luxembourg. Pascal Lino, of the RMO team, was the overall leader, although no one was under any illusions about that. But the earthquake was brewing under the searing sun, for the Tour is constantly throwing up this kind of surprise. One very qualified individual was devoting himself to spreading panic through the peloton: Chiappucci. For him it was all or nothing. There were five mountains, the Col des Saisies, the Cormet de Roselend, the fearsome and gigantic Iseran – at almost 3,000 metres the highest point in the Tour. Then came the ever-awkward Mont-Cenis, with its average gradient of 7 per cent, and, to finish, Sestrière, which had been literally invaded by an army of Italian *tifosi*. Some of those fans were hoping to see what they would, in fact, see – one of the most devastating massacres in the whole history of cycling; others were hoping to see *their* Bugno bounce back. The first group ended up the happier, since the stage proved to be as ground-breaking as the kinds of stages Lapize, Buysse or Coppi had ridden in their heyday.

Chiappucci, the Devil, attacked, incredibly, on the first mountain. No one could credit such stupidity. That's what we thought at first. But he went on, mountain after mountain, building up a bigger and bigger time advantage. He was the virtual leader of the Tour on the road, and the people crowding on Sestrière and the preceding cols were going crazy. And behind him no one seemed to believe it, or to react. Induráin, himself, was only concerned about one man – Bugno. And I must stress that, from Chiappucci's point of view, while the loss of six or seven minutes to Miguel Induráin in the Luxembourg time-trial was important, it was far from conclusive. On the Sestrière stage there were some who lost out completely, and others amongst the big guns who would come in half an hour or more behind. Lemond and Leblanc finished 50 minutes adrift. Once again, however, Miguel rose to the occasion.

That day Bugno had aimed to get even with Induráin, but Chiappucci's daring early attack had scuppered everything: he'd got his move in first, even if it was bordering on madness. And so a war of looks and nerves broke out between Miguel and Bugno. Ably backed by his men, Delgado, Rondón, Gorospe and others, Induráin was able to wait. Mountain after mountain, pedalling calmly alongside Bugno, he knew he was gradually driving him mad. Maybe that day the Italian would have preferred Induráin to attack on the Cormet or Iseran, but even then they were still a very long way from the finish. Time continued to amass in the Devil's favour, and Bugno was close to exploding. Induráin was turning the screw in macabre fashion, in those special circumstances, without even attacking. Just waiting. Waiting. But for what?

Bugno didn't know. Miguel did, although he was beginning to enter the danger zone because of the incredible advantage Chiappucci had built up over them. Miguel climbed Mont-Cenis in the same way, with Gianni Bugno looking at him as if to say: 'What the hell are you waiting for? What are *we* waiting for?' Miguel knew it was more a game of chess than of brute force, and that the chase had to be initiated by the two together. Bugno was ripe now, ripe for picking. Then, as they passed over Mont-Cenis, he reached crisis point. He couldn't stand it any longer; his nerves must have been sapping so much energy he could wait no longer. And he made the furious move which Miguel was waiting for, after 200 kilometres of merely observing him. The Italian's patience was shot to pieces. And, as Gianni's legs swelled, and he panted, and he looked and looked again, Miguel knew his rival was gradually succumbing in that psychological battle which often takes place off camera on certain stages of the Tour. There are times when this can happen even without the technical back-up staff knowing about it.

A series of personal circumstances came together in Bugno, which made him exceedingly vulnerable to particular tense situations. He was a strange character, with a hectic love life, and certain peculiar quirks, some of which he himself admitted to the Press. For example, he was panic-stricken on the descents due to a long-standing problem with his eardrums. He was even 'treating' himself with Mozart on long training sessions, to rectify that defect.

He couldn't stand people calling him 'champion', which they no doubt did out of courtesy or because of his status as World Champion. For him, the only race that mattered was the Tour, and Miguel was the only champion. He also liked reading books on mathematics, and he collected toy trucks.

This was the psychological profile of the man whom Induráin feared for a long time, at least until the '93 Tour, although even afterwards he would continue to include the Italian whenever he made his predictions or listed the race favourites.

Seeing Miguel alongside him all the time, even on Italian soil (and Induráin, remember, had just won the Giro), Bugno felt he was with the Champion, who, what's more, was constantly demonstrating it with his astounding serenity.

So Bugno was scared of high-speed descents, was he? Well, now they were going to descend Mont-Cenis like crazy, ready to claw back as much time as possible from Chiappucci, who was renowned for making headlong descents – 'without a rope', as they say. And there would be no headphones playing Mozart or Vivaldi to relax anyone. In fact, that Tour was the fastest in history, with an average speed of 39.509 kilometres an hour.

When it came to mathematics, no one could outsmart Miguel. He'd been doing his mostly subconscious sums for 200 kilometres, and playing with figures that were so dear to Bugno. In the end it was the Italian who lost his nerve, and made his move. And that gesture betrayed him – like Lemond on the Tourmalet, a year before, and like Rominger on the Galibier, a year later.

And when it came to trucks, Bugno collected them, but Miguel had spent his time as a kid dismantling them. In that memorable stage, he did with Bugno's brain and patience what as a child he had done with trucks: he took them apart. And Bugno must have felt, if not like a truck, at least like a plaything in the hands of the Navarran.

Climbing Sestrière, having cut Chiappucci's lead quite considerably, Bugno just blew up. Judging by his pedalling action this had appeared imminent, and as soon as Induráin accelerated slightly, Bugno cracked. Hampsten stayed with him, having just about held on to them up till then, while Franco Vona followed Miguel for a few metres. But it was a vain chase, since the Villava rider had gone into turbo mode and was climbing Sestrière at the same hellish pace we had seen on the Terminillo a month earlier. He was on his own, now, in pursuit of Chiappucci, who was losing around half a minute a kilometre. He got to within twenty seconds of him. He could see him. I remember that day, when many of us were convinced Miguel was going to catch Claudio – and it seemed inevitable judging by the way he was reducing the time gap. Then, someone amongst the Spaniards shouted: 'No, Miguel, not today... Let him win.' We could still recall how Chiappucci had been humiliated in the Milan time-trial. And also Claudio's vomit-inducing display that same day, when, so they say, he emptied himself completely in his shorts.

Chiappucci was now a sorry sight, destroyed but limping to victory, nevertheless. And Bugno was a sorry sight, broken like a little truck and with no hope of being put back together again. However, we then witnessed one of the mysteries of cycling, one of those things which legend has bequeathed us. Miguel, who was growing stronger all the time and was by now very close to Chiappucci, suddenly cracked, himself. Later he would say he hadn't eaten well, and that must have been true, but I maintain that what Miguel encountered on that memorable ascent of Sestrière was something he had never seen or 'felt' before – a compact mass of people going crazy and touching his back, arms like the tentacles of an invisible octopus. Hands grabbed his saddle, and maybe others were even surreptitiously touching the brakes. But, above all, a faceless wall of people. Chiappucci himself received a compassionate 'beating' as he went through the densest part of the human tide which almost caused him to fall. He was hindered by the motorbikes, too. He kept pleading with people to let him move forward. He even had to brake, and he was just two kilometres from the finish.

And behind him was the legend. We shall never know what happened to Miguel, because in a blink of an eye he went from closing spectacularly on Chiappucci to not being able to see him at all. The human tide suddenly swallowed him up, literally. They slapped him on his back, presumably to encourage him, since the Italians are so ardent and passionate, even with their rivals. There was a period of dead time on the TV screen, and then, when the pictures came back, you could see Miguel, sensibly adopting a more prudent and restrained pedal action, and, a long way in front of him, what appeared to be the back of Franco Vona, already in an area protected by barriers and where the road was therefore a few metres wider, which at least gave the cyclists room to breathe and escape the manhandling. Vona, a fine climber on his best days, must have come from behind and overtaken him (Where? When? How?) and left him practically standing.

Miguel showed signs of exhaustion when he arrived, that is true. All the same, regardless of the fact that he had expended too much energy trying to get on to Chiappucci's wheel, and regardless of the fact that he hadn't eaten and drunk as much as he should when he should, it seemed clear that something in that human sea of enthusiastic *tifosi* had shaken Miguel. Or it had made such an impact on him, that he had reduced his speed. He had decided he wasn't going to risk the Tour by falling or through some other incident, since at that point in the ascent he was assured of the yellow jersey. Sometimes, on a bicycle when you are at the limit of your efforts, you're set in your rhythm and the slightest thing which distracts you, or makes you reduce your rhythm (braking suddenly, or the presence of a threatening car), can make it impossible for you to recover it. A mixture of all these factors must have affected Induráin on Sestrière, although he was supremely generous and never mentioned the dangerous, over-the-top reaction of the enthusiastic Italian fans. Miguel always spoke of his 'sudden dip'. He never mentioned the threatening human tide and his broken rhythm. A true gentleman, just like Jacques Anquetil. Not as cold as ice, nor one to bandy about excuses or explanations, Induráin was polite and introverted, like the Norman rider.

Miguel himself gave me his version of the events. He had asked Bugno and Vona if the mountain was very tough, and they had told him the gradient was variable – tough in places. And so it was, except for a section where Induráin came to a halt. And when I pushed the *tifosi* factor, he smiled his enigmatic smile again, and denied it: 'No, nothing to do with it.'

From having been close to catching the Devil, he came in one minute 45 seconds behind the Italian. And Chiappucci had then moved to being a little less than this behind Miguel in the overall classification. A very slim gap, despite the time-trial to come at the end, because, the following day, they had to climb the Galibier (albeit by its gentler side of the Lauteret), the Croix de Fer and Alpe d'Huez.

The hopes of the Italians were still high, since the stage was one of those where you could gamble everything, a stage which would allow another massive break like the previous day's. But this time the game was up. This time Miguel wouldn't allow Claudio Chiappucci to take a single metre off him. The person they didn't need to take into account was Bugno who, supported by Fignon, the *domestique de luxe* in his team, led him up the first slopes of the Galibier. Induráin didn't bat an eyelid. 'They can go,' he must have thought. Even so, by the summit, they and the other pair of riders in their escape held an advantage of around two minutes, and the chase group wasn't exactly the sort to calm your nerves either – the combative Neil Stephens and Robert Millar, a man with wings in his pedals. Not to worry. A spectator caused Bugno to fall near the summit, which was a sign that he wasn't fully concentrating. At those moments of new and surprising psychological warfare, Miguel surely must have wondered: 'Who is Bugno really riding against? Is it against me, Chiappucci or himself?' The last option seemed the most plausible, but the wounded pride of a champion shouldn't be discounted, a champion who couldn't stand the name 'champion', and who had seen the whole of Italy worshipping Chiappucci, his greatest rival amongst his countrymen. Bugno, too, wanted to go for broke.

But perhaps he didn't take into account what Miguel had already considered – the endless and terrifyingly open descent of the Galibier, with its sinister cliff-faces, once more under the baking sun and with the wind whistling at the exit of every bend. Excruciating for the eardrums, and there was no walkman there playing Mozart. There were only motorbikes which sped past you at over 100 kilometres an hour, and you descending at 90 kilometres an hour, supported on a mere seventeen millimetres of tubular, the equivalent of a finger. It wasn't even necessary for Induráin to order a hell-for-leather chase. Simply not touching the brake levers was enough. In fact, Bugno had been neutralised by the advance units of pursuers commanded by Miguel even before the end of the ride on the breathtaking big wheel of the Galibier. As he passed Bugno, Induráin avoided looking at him. That was more effective. The Italian was fatally wounded. And this time it was for good.

Perhaps Bugno understood that the real Symphony was coming up behind him, dressed in yellow and expressionless. What was expected happened because it was dictated in the score. The *Andante Maestoso* of Miguel's Symphony continued its course, and Bugno fell to pieces as soon as they started climbing the Croix de Fer. And the same thing would happen to him on the Marmolada the following year.

Induráin always wears a small gold cross on his chest, and you hardly ever see it above his jersey. Miguel is a believer, he has faith, although it would never occur to him to ask the Virgin Mary for anything, or at least anything related to his races: that is for men to sort out. Faith and conviction in his own strength was going to be required, because soon afterwards, as soon as the ascent of Alpe d'Huez began, an incident occurred which could have changed the destiny of the Tour, in some measure at least.

It was another of those events that belong to the secret history of the race, and I heard it from Pedro Delgado, who was riding with Miguel at that moment. They had just passed Le Pré des Roches, at the foot of Alpe d'Huez, and the favourites were in a compact group. Induráin, I must stress, had only a minute and a half-advantage over Chiappucci on general classification, and the Devil had been saving himself throughout the stage, lurking behind the Banesto boys, which was a very worrying sign. And now he was looking in every direction to see who was there and who wasn't. He was looking for Miguel. Chiappucci, even though he constantly and vociferously moaned about the time-trials, knew, as anyone who understands cycling knows, that on a climb like Alpe d'Huez you can lose many minutes if you have a bad day. You don't even need to crack completely. Simply a bad day is, I repeat, sufficient for your whole world to cave in on you. That was where Zoetemelk and Van Impe and Hinault and Merckx all lost a considerable amount of time, and the Tour in the process. Those 21 numbered bends amounting to no more than fifteen kilometres eat away at you at each push of the pedal.

We saw aerial shots of the group, who were tackling the initial stretch of the ascent – a very long and straight 12 per cent – at a lively pace. There was still a long way to go till bend number 21, and some riders were already dropping back. The Devil was camouflaging his acceleration, sitting upright, but threatening in his saddle. Suddenly our hearts missed a beat. We realised that the Yellow Jersey wasn't there. Chiappucci also noticed, and he pressed on up the hill on his own.

What Delgado told me was that at the precise moment the climb began, as Miguel shifted on to the little ring, his chain came off. When Perico saw what had happened, he held Miguel's saddle for a moment, because he'd almost come to a standstill. Miguel himself fingered the chain back into place, but the Devil had gone, opening up a gap of maybe 20 metres. Yet, instead of pedalling with conviction, he continued to look over his shoulder, unable to believe that Induráin wasn't there. They were almost at the first of the 21 hairpin bends and as they came out of the corner there was another cliff-face, scorched by the sun.

Suddenly, out of the saddle to make up lost ground, appeared Miguel. At that moment, just like Gaul a few days before, during the Luxembourg time-trial, I really did believe that an angel had appeared. He rode up as calm as you like, relaxed and bareheaded. He caught Chiappucci with amazing ease, blowing away the group which was following behind. He even got ahead of the Italian and led him up for a few kilometres at top speed, forcing the pace. Then he weakened and allowed someone else to take over. With him were Chioccioli, Virenque, Theunisse and a brave Jon Unzaga, who worked with Miguel and, for a while, set the pace for the group. In spite of the fact that Induráin had nicked the Championship of Spain from under his nose in the streets of

Oviedo a month before (in a photo finish at that), there he was now, Unzaga, working together with the best Spanish cyclist of all time. It must have been an honour for him to do so, even though he raced for a rival team.

The stage winner was Andy Hampsten, who arrived a few minutes ahead and had to use his fists to fend off people who were trying to get close to him to slap him on the back, encourage him or throw water over him. But the real punches were delivered back down the road, in Miguel's group, with Chiappucci attempting to up the pace, and Induráin calling him to order again after he'd managed to impose his own tempo. And what a tempo it was, as one by one the riders all dropped off the group, except for those two. It was a fast, majestic, memorable ascent, and they arrived together at the finish. The Devil had had fifteen hellish kilometres in which to destroy that irrepressible giant, who weighed 80 kilos and pedalled with the angels, and in the end he'd had more than enough on his plate just keeping in touch with him. The most he could now hope for was a podium position in Paris, behind Miguel.

In the final time-trial, with the finish in Blois, Miguel was quicker than ever. Over the distance of 64 kilometres he bettered his own Luxembourg record, with an average speed of 52.349 kilometres an hour.

Then, once again it was party time, with loads of chanting and unbridled joy. The Induráin phenomenon had, by then, become uncontrollable. The Navarran was being spoken of in terms that went beyond the sporting arena. Not now as an 'Extraterrestrial' or 'Indurainator', but as the man who had really integrated Spain into the new Europe.

In my own experience, I know that, up till that year, people, and especially children, on the roadsides would shout 'Come on, Perico' whenever they saw a cyclotourist. From '92 onwards the cry was 'Come on, Induráin!' And I also know, although it might sound silly, that every time I heard it I couldn't avoid a slight, but definite, feeling of pride.

Miguel rounded off that year of 1992 by triumphing in the Tour of Catalonia. In his normal impressive style he climbed the Vallter-2000, a ski resort with very tough slopes. And all the while he took with him two men who were to be part of his immediate destiny. One was the Swiss, Rominger, who, now that he was aware of his potential on the climbs in the Tour of Spain, was going to be threatening Miguel in the Tour de France. The other was the quieter Antonio Martín of the Amaya team. He climbed with incredible smoothness and was already being talked of as one of the great young hopes of Spanish cycling. In fact, it was destiny which had *him* in its sights.

But Miguel continued to prepare for the 1993 Tour meticulously, even though many Spaniards were gripped by the 'Rominger syndrome'. Once again, Banesto chose the Giro to prepare for the *Grande Boucle*, and once again controversy broke out in Spain because Miguel was opting for the Italian event ahead of the Spanish Vuelta. In the Giro, he was certainly the big favourite and although he insisted he was only regarding it as a training ride, no one really believed it. They were demanding victory from him. And Induráin, whose commitment was generous, strained his body's engine a little more than was wise. That was evident in the later stages. And in the Tour it would be a similar story.

The Italians had included as many mountain stages as possible. The notorious 'mega-stages' such as Corvara–Alta Badia, the extremely long mountain time-trial at Sestrière, and not to mention the various snares they set for the riders. Miguel started off calmly, and the weather helped. He won the 28-kilometre Senigallia time-trial with a trademark performance that put everyone firmly in their place; he may not have been on the top of his game, but he was still strong. The real terror this time was the blue-ribbon stage, which included the Marmolada and two ascents of the Pordoi, as well as other lesser peaks. It was the ideal stage for Chiappucci or Bugno, who had decided to ride that year. The Pordoi was the greater of the two evils. It had been chosen that year as the 'Coppi summit', the highest point in the race, and is damaging because of its gradients and its length – more than fifteen kilometres. But before starting the final climb of Pordoi they had to cope with the Marmolada, and that meant a sixteen-kilometre ascent at an average gradient of 7 per cent. The first part of the climb is a gentle slope, and then, suddenly, they see a huge 12- or 13-per-cent cliff face rising in front of them with seemingly endless straight sections which really take it out of the cyclists' legs. It is well known that riders are very thankful if there are frequent bends on this type of steep mountain: they provide a rest for the legs, and for the spirits. The Marmolada does not allow this. On the other hand, other monsters such as the Stelvio or the Agnel do have bends.

And Miguel, dominating an intimidated peloton, played with the cream of Italian cycling like a cat plays with a mouse. He was clever enough to seek allies amongst the different local teams and the natural knock-on effect of that was that disagreements broke out amongst them. That was perfect because that way there would be many more eyes watching. A small mountain stage saw Armand de las Cuevas fighting it out with Chiappucci, which didn't go down too well with Banesto. Neither of them were exactly naïve, and it meant that they were capable of taking time out of the Induráin group. But the important thing was the massive Pordoi stage.

What happened there was foreseeable. Bugno, under pressure to attack to his limit, *à la Chiappucci*, which was not part of his make-up, gave in to impulse and went for the jugular on the Pordoi. Behind him was a calm Miguel directing the group of favourites (amongst whom was the inevitable Chiappucci, as well as Ugrumov, Lelli and a promising young Russian, Pavel Tonkov). The gap began to narrow as they hunted Bugno down.

One of the images that has made the greatest personal impression on me in all my time following cycling was that sight of Bugno being overtaken on the slopes of the Marmolada. His face was exhausted, corpse-like in its paleness, as he pedalled so weakly and slowly you thought he was going to stop at any moment. As ever, Miguel didn't even look at him as he passed.

That was the great Induráin, grimacing with effort and sporting his dark glasses even though it poured incessantly for a good part of the stage. It was strange, as if he had decided that day that no one should see his eyes. His hands gripped the top of the handlebars; not once did he lift himself out of the saddle. But he was carrying the gasping pursuers, just as in the previous Giro. Chiappucci did nothing to share the pace (he was pedalling as best he could) and this went on for countless kilometres. It was when they were in sight of the banner marking the second and final climb of the Pordoi (which carried points for the Mountain Prize) that the Devil decided to sprint. Miguel followed suit, and crossed the line first. An angry Chiappucci spat at him: '*Grazie!*'

And they say Induráin didn't bat an eyelid as he answered curtly: *'Prego'* – don't mention it. It was a way of showing him you can't take someone's wheel in a stage like that and then expect to pick up the primes; it just wasn't ethical. Chiappucci got the message and from that day on he collaborated a bit more.

In the Sestrière time-trial Miguel was to achieve another of his landmarks as a cyclist. On a near 50-kilometre climb, relentlessly uphill, and on a drizzly day, Miguel pushed his body to the limit. He earned the lasting admiration of the many ex-cyclists who were following the Giro: Moser, Adorni, Bartali, Saronni, Visentini. He crushed the Devil on his home territory, taking five minutes out of him, although he only took one off Ugrumov. Even so, Miguel, with his body and size, made that ascent at an average of nearly 35 kilometres an hour. Phenomenal.

We uncorked the champagne and in Navarra they prepared the *fiesta*. No one thought that one of the worst moments in Induráin's career was awaiting him, the following day, on Oropa. And, as always, it was in the space of the final four kilometres – those last four kilometres to Sestrière in the '92 Tour, those last four kilometres of Les Arcs in the '96 Tour. Those final kilometres of the Sestrière time-trial the day before, when we witnessed Echávarri leap out of the car, urging Miguel on for a few metres, as he ran alongside him. But it isn't easy to run uphill alongside a man who, with his teeth clenched in rage, is doing over 30 kilometres an hour.

On the lively ascent of Oropa – a climb with a varying gradient which makes it difficult, therefore, to maintain a regular rhythm – Argentin, of the Mecair team, attacked as if the race was a sprint. All the favourites went with him, except Armand de las Cuevas, who had disappeared off the map. It was one of the first times we began to see Induráin on his own in the face of danger. Then Ugrumov was out of the saddle, launching one of his frenzied, blood-curdling attacks, and the group, which had included Roche, Argentin and Chiappucci, broke up. Miguel was forced down on to the hooks to counter the break. Then came the second crushing attack; again Miguel went with him. A few metres further on and Ugrumov, summoning strength from goodness knows where, launched a further devastating attack. Just when we thought Miguel would respond again with ease, we saw this wasn't to be:

Ugrumov was inflicting severe pain on him. But an enraged Induráin got back up to him again.

At no point on that Stairway to Hell, with 14-per-cent cliff faces that suddenly decreased to more accessible gradients, but which were always around 8 or 9 per cent, could the Navarran sit down and get into a rhythm, albeit at his limit. The Latvian's fourth attack was the clincher. Miguel slumped back into his saddle, and Ugrumov sped away up the hill. From the Banesto car they shouted to Induráin to stay calm, to try and find his rhythm, because there wasn't far to go and Ugrumov would never be able to take enough time out of him to snatch the Giro. The Latvian also eased off noticeably, exhausted by his repeated efforts. Miguel was passed by all those men, including Chiappucci, whom he and Ugrumov had left behind. And this scene, with a slight change in the cast, would be repeated a year later at the Valley of Santa Cristina. The Italian saints were unlucky for the Navarran.

He came home more shattered than he had ever felt before. Slumped over his handlebars, breathless. He even had to hold onto the protective barriers to keep his balance. He had fought like a wild beast, and eventually he had withstood the onslaught. We were happy, but from that day on Miguel began to be spoken of as a man who did know what it was to suffer and to be in trouble. It had already happened to him in the Tour of the Mining Valleys and the climb up to the Lakes of Covadonga in the Vuelta, as well as other more discreet places. But the events at Oropa scarred us, especially with the imminent threat posed by Rominger who seemed to be a colossus in the mountains. Furthermore – and this was another worrying fact – the Swiss performed very well in the time-trials. Now the march of time was pointing to a key rendezvous: the Tour de France.

While the '92 event had been timidly presented as a duel between Induráin and Bugno, the following summer the opponents were, without any doubt, Miguel and Rominger. Swords were drawn. The Swiss had gone off to train in distant parts and the Navarran had been getting into shape with some low-key riding in the prelude to the battle. Some riders would go off to picture-postcard places such as Colorado Springs or Puerto de las Letras in Colombia, an approximately 100-kilometre-long stretch at high altitude (and with very few false flats), while others remained in the area around Burguete or Ulzama, climbing the Erro again and again, if possible in exactly twelve minutes. Or better still, a little less.

The Tour was the big one, no doubt about it – the French race which, in the heroic years, covered fully 5,745 kilometres in just seventeen stages. And with the conditions that prevailed in those days. Think about it. Almost 2000 kilometres further than today. A Tour which in 1952 saw a gap between the victor, Fausto Coppi, and the second place, Stan Ockers, of more than 28 minutes. A Tour in which the longest escape was by Albert Bourlon in 1947 – 253 kilometres out on his own. A Tour in which, in its post World War II editions, the greatest gap at a stage-finish had been recorded by a Spaniard, José Luis Viejo, between Montgenèvre and Manosque in the 1976 edition. A Tour which saw its youngest winner in 1904, in the person of twenty-year-old Henri Cornet, and its oldest that of the 36-year-old Firmin Lambot. And that Tour of 1904 also had its youngest participant, Camille Filly, sixteen years of age, and its oldest, Henri Paret, 50 years old. That monstrous, grandiose Tour, with all its legends, was forging Miguel's own legend, year on year.

It is a Tour which has been written about across the generations. In France, many writers were also big cycling addicts: Antoine Blondoin, Jacques Perret, Roland Barthes, Colette, Marcel Aymé, Cocteau, René Fallet, Luc Nacera, Cioran, and Jean Giono, who wrote: 'Cycling enables me to understand the bird and the duck, the snake sliding softly and discreetly over the road, and makes me hear more clearly the roar of the torrent and the whispering of the tall trees, all of which holds so much charm for writers.' And Alfred Jarry: 'The bicycle is a new body part, like a mineral or metal extension of our bone structure.' And Émile Zola: 'What better education for a woman than to ride a bicycle. If I had a daughter, I'd have her ride a bicycle from the age of ten, so that she could learn how to get along in life.' Add in Montherlant, and so many others. In 1993 it was a Tour which Miguel initially took calmly, like every Tour, chatting not only to Rominger, but to many of the favourites. But in the prologue at Le-Puy-de-Fuy he made his first thrust, winning by eight seconds from Zülle.

The early stages, Vannes, Dinard, Avranches, Evreux, Amiens, Chalons-sur-Marne, and so on, were for the sprinters and chancers.

Then, at Lake Madine, in the Meuse region, in a time-trial of nearly 60 kilometres, Induráin once again 'deterred' all those who had ambitions of winning the Tour. For a lot of the early riders, which included Rominger, it rained. Tough luck. Later on, it cleared up a bit, although it was still spitting when Miguel set off. He quickly began to overtake rivals and then removed his helmet, and tossed it aside – an extraordinary gesture which we were never to see again. He had a puncture near the line and lost around twenty seconds – similar to the amount of time by which Pruden miraculously avoided elimination. Two treacherous steep slopes, the Côte d'Apremont and the Côte du Lion, ravaged the time-trial specialists. Miguel, bareheaded, passed them like a meteor. He took two minutes eleven seconds off the second-place man (Bugno, just for a change). And almost three off Rominger.

On the following day the mountains commenced with a *pièce de résistance*: a finish in Serre-Chevalier. But first of all, after leaving Villard-de-Lans, they had to climb the Glandon, then the Col du Télégraphe, then the Galibier and then downhill to the finish on a slope of the Serre-Chevalier. Miguel was fresh in yellow, although that sunny morning he again showed some of the others that the real time advantages are accumulated in the mountains. Already on the Glandon, Bugno was treading water and Chiappucci was showing signs of flagging. Then on the Télégraphe things went ballistic. Only a few riders (the usual names, as ever: Rominger, Jaskula, Hampsten and the Colombian Mejía) were able to stand the hellish pace imposed yet again by Induráin. That climb up the Galibier almost defies belief. There was a stunned and gasping Tony Rominger struggling to keep up, and Juan Fernández speaking to Miguel from the Clas team car. It was a private conversation, but we could all imagine what was said: 'Don't destroy us. You can have the leader's jersey; we'll have the mountains, OK?'

Anyone who knows what the Galibier is like on that northern face, from Valloire via Les Verneys and, most especially, on the road through Plan-Lachat, and who saw the pace Miguel set that day, will understand the astonishment of the great Eddy Merckx when he asserted that the incredible thing was not the way Induráin rode the time-trials but that he could climb mountains in the same way. At the end of the climb, the Navarran moved aside to allow Rominger to take the points. And at the end of the stage he feigned a sprint. Rominger came home first.

The following day, with the Izoard and the Col de Vars to come before the ever-feared and rarely climbed Col de la Bonette-Restefonds, Miguel ended up without his *domestiques:* Perico had vented his anger on Millar in memory of past duels, and both of them had ended up the worse for wear. With Rominger clearly returned to an attacking frame of mind, Induráin suffered more than a moment's confusion. But if Restefonds was a *hors-catégorie* mountain, so too was the final climb to Isola-2000, nearly fifteen kilometres with an average 7-per-cent gradient, though the finish was on a 100-metre downhill section.

Some riders, Chiappucci and Riis among them, attempted to attack at the foot of the climb but they were swallowed up by that locomotive of panting men dragged along the whole time by Induráin. Millar, who had pulled himself together again, had the temerity to change up to the big ring and launch a ferocious attack. It lasted half a kilometre before the rhythm imposed by Miguel devoured him whole, and Induráin had not altered his pedal rate at all in spite of the Scotsman's move. Millar's face when he was quickly overtaken by Miguel and his line of followers seemed to say: 'This sort of thing didn't happen in my time.'

And all the strength Induráin had inside himself on that Tour was demonstrated in the final kilometre of Isola-2000. By then they were all scattered and Zenon Jaskula attempted to pull away. Indeed, he gained an advantage of several metres, but behind him was Rominger. On the big ring now, and ready to finish it off, he flashed past the Pole. Induráin, however, was alert, and he accelerated so violently he overtook not only Jaskula but the intervening motorbikes. Then he fell in behind Rominger and the pictures showed us he had to brake very obviously to avoid passing him with the momentum of his acceleration. They continued like this for 500 metres. Then a change of gradient and the downhill slope. The finish-line. It looked like a sprint, but Miguel made three almost imperceptible movements, which nevertheless remain there, on the videos, for anyone who wants to take the trouble to see them.

He moved to one side, altering his line in the middle of the sprint.

He looked to one side to see if anyone was coming.

He touched the brake levers a few metres from the line.

Even *L'Équipe* took it as a bit of a joke. But that detail (because of the *panache* business) didn't entirely please them: they were adamant that Miguel should have clinched the win. For Miguel, it was not so clear. He denied it, of course. What else could he do?

Take it easy. Antonin Magne, a Tour winner decades before, maintained that the Tour de France was won by resting and sleeping as much as possible. As proof of that, Echávarri is said to have had to wake Miguel up the day of the Lake Madine time-trial, because he was fast asleep in his bed. That is what you call bottle. In *L'Équipe*, caught half-way between respect and admiration, someone let slip how impressive it was to see Induráin ascending Isola-2000 with that impassive face, immortal and oblivious to everything. And I remembered what I had been told years before by a cyclist who had competed with him in one of those events which took place, I think, in Rome. They were all very young and had to spend quite a few days in the city. The Spanish group managed to hold out for the first two days, but by the third they were conspiring to escape and get out into the city. Which was understandable. 'All of us except him,' he said, referring to Miguel. 'Even back then he was as quiet as an Egyptian mummy.' He didn't say it nastily, but with real surprise that someone should have no special interest in going out on the town, or half the town, which would not have been overdoing it. No, he stayed behind to sleep in his room or think things over.

His 'things', in one way or another, meant cultivating Tour de France wins. That was his harvest. Francisco Chico Pérez, one of the veteran Spanish journalists of the French Tour, always stressed to me that the key factor in Miguel's success was not so much his mental and physical strength, as the fact that he was also a permanent student of the Tour. The secret was in knowing every last detail of the *Grande Boucle*. For his part, Benito Urraburu underlined another fact about Induráin that was so obvious it was not pinpointed in descriptions of his career: he always isolated his adversaries in the high mountains. He would go with a small group of carefully selected riders, and in the majority of cases *at the head*. This meant they could never see his face. Preventing himself from being seen, looked at, penetrated by the senses, was an additional bonus for Induráin as it has been for other champions through history.

It was said of Miguel, as was also said of Alfredo Binda when he was winning so many Giros in his time, and of Merckx when he was winning everything, that one day they would end up paying him not to compete in the Tour. That is what they did with the great Binda; they were so tired of his overwhelming domination. And with Eddy, it was just as well for them that Thévenet came along. But the Belgian and Hinault, too, would take a rest from the Tour now and again. Merckx once rode the Vuelta a España instead of the *Grande Boucle*, and Hinault substituted with both the Vuelta and the Giro. Not Miguel; Miguel was only a fixture with the Tour, and around 1993 that began to be a cause for concern in France, of great concern. They admired him, for sure, but they were hoping that the myth of Miguel would shatter. Ever year the organisers put all sorts of convoluted twists and turns into the route to see if they could trip him up. The team time-trial idea, which was never to Hinault's liking by the way, also saw things go awry with the disaster of Delgado and Reynolds in Luxembourg in the '89 Tour. So Banesto, who were no fools, set out to put together an all-round group of riders who, at the very least, would not cede much time in that discipline. In my opinion, Induráin would end up paying the price for that in the mountains. And I am thinking not so much of stages like Les Arcs or Hautacam in '96, but of less mountainous, but none the less difficult, stages such as Mende in '95.

So then, as Pérez used to say, Miguel not only knew the Tour; he was the Tour. Each heartbeat of the Tour was his, and every startled jump was controlled by him. He was its family doctor, its orthopaedic surgeon and even its neurosurgeon. When an executioner was required (according to the law of competitive sport) he acted quickly and it was soon done. No unnecessary complications.

In the Pyrenees in the '93 Tour, however, Miguel was to need all his innate attributes, heart and willingness for sacrifice. And perhaps to speak to the wind again: 'Is this the end for me, is the writing on the wall?' 'No, but it will be very painful for you', the wind may have replied in his dreams.

It was just that no one realised.

The stage to Pal, next door to Andorra, had 'only' nine climbs, some of which, like the Col d'Envalira, seemed to go on for ever. Anquetil suffered terribly there in 1964, and he risked his life in a spectacular descent to get back on with his rivals. There, in '93, Rominger's Clas crew were constantly turning the screw, and the following day, from Andorra to the summit finish at Saint-Lary Soulan, was to be the deciding one. They climbed El Canto, the never-ending Bonaigua, the Portillon, the Peyresourde and finally arrived in Pla d'Adet, known also by the name of its ski resort, Saint-Lary. A climb of ten kilometres at a gradient 8 per cent, but with a killer stretch at its very base – a fairly long 13-per-cent slope which takes everyone by surprise. And on that bend which led to the slope, Rominger rose from his saddle and launched the most ferocious attack in the whole of the 1993 Tour. Even in the Vuelta he had not ridden like this. It was prolonged and devastating, not in fits and starts like Ugrumov's attack on Oropa a few months before. Miguel, once again, was down on the bottom of the handlebars, and he hung on as far as he could. Behind, everyone blew up, except Jaskula, who was on and off, as if tied by a piece of elastic. From that point on, Induráin concentrated on monitoring. He conceded a few seconds to Rominger at the finish. But unlike, say, his meteoric ascent of the Galibier or of Isola-2000, here we saw a leader who was panting excessively. Behind his dark glasses, Miguel suffered indescribably that day.

The following day, the Tourmalet was awaiting them and the more 'humane' Aubisque, via the Soulor, although it was a long way from the finish. Rominger must have seen something, because as soon as they started on the Tourmalet, which was to be climbed via la Mongie, he escaped and took Jaskula with him. He demanded Jaskula take over from him, but the Pole either would not or could not, and a row broke out between them. Rominger was a rider of the Lemond school, great but perhaps somewhat demanding. He had a minute's advantage by the summit, and Miguel asked a tireless Gorospe not to push the pace because there was still a long way to go. But the truth of the matter was that he didn't feel well. There was something wrong with him, physically. We watched a hair-raising descent from Rominger, and then nothing else for a long time. Our anxiety mounted. Was the lead increasing?

Then, down at the bottom, near the village of Luz-Saint-Saveur, Induráin suddenly appeared behind the Swiss, freewheeling and eating. So cool. He had pulled away from everyone and had set off after Rominger, descending in his typical style, risking everything and making use of all his attributes. His 80 kilos had to come in handy sometimes! As soon as Rominger saw Miguel appear, he must have crumbled mentally. The Spanish writer Delibes considers this to be the episode that made the greatest impact on him in the whole of Induráin's career.

But we didn't know that Miguel was human (he was far more human in what he did here than on those famous and feared *pájaras**) and, being human, had just made a huge, schoolboy error. He had been in such a hurry to chase after Rominger that he hadn't bothered to do what the Swiss had done, and pick up a raincoat or a newspaper to protect his chest. He had sweated profusely on the way up the Tourmalet, and the descent had been a veritable gale of almost freezing air. So much so that when the Banesto car finally caught up with him, as he was already monitoring Rominger, Miguel said with a malicious smile: 'What, were you a bit worried?' Terrified, more like, thinking that the Tour could have been lost in a fall. It was so sunny that day they hadn't even thought of taking into account the cold. And Miguel had become a man of the sun. *En route* to Pau and Bordeaux over the next couple of days, the 'bug', or whatever it was inside him, grew. And the night before the time-trial, on the eve of the race finish, a stage which ended in Montlhéry – 50 kilometres as flat as a pancake – Pruden burst into Doctor Sabino Padilla's room to tell him his brother was in a very bad way, bathed in sweat and almost delirious. Alarmed, they went back to the room. He had a temperature of almost 40 centigrade, and no one in those circumstances would have been capable even of getting on a bike, let alone pushing a gear of 54 x 13. Miguel received treatment, but even some of the Banesto team didn't find out about it, because it was so serious. In ten kilometres he could have lost the entire five-minute lead he held over Rominger. Disaster.

---

* *Pájara* – Spanish cycling jargon meaning a sudden, quite unexpected exhaustion; a slang expression equivalent to the 'bonk' in English cycling argot, but with more dramatic overtones.

But Miguel spoke to his ally the wind once more in his dreams (or delirium). Maybe the wind warned him: 'I told you you'd have to suffer as never before.'

And he did. The time-trial saw Rominger sweep the board. Induráin spent all the time drinking, which was very unusual for him, especially at the very start of the stage. In the end, riding at nearly 50 kilometres an hour, he only lost 40 seconds to Rominger. In the presence of the television cameras, Miguel never mentioned his illness, a raging flu, but he was coughing all the time. The reaction was as expected: *L'Équipe*, after what it had seen in Montlhéry, was predicting that the next Tour would be very tight. Indeed, in their pre-race survey the following year they almost dared to make the two rivals, Rominger and Induráin, co-favourites, especially after what had happened in the Vuelta a España and the Giro earlier that year. In Paris, at the end of the '93 Tour, the elated Rominger was confident enough to assert: 'I'm after the next Tour. I know how to win it.' Echávarri was more laconic and wounding: 'We lost a second a degree.'

That was without doubt one of the greatest exploits of Miguel Induráin Larraya, the wind's favourite, who was punished by the wind as he descended the Tourmalet, the mountain which, two years earlier, had granted him his first Tour. And maybe we never duly recognised the feat.

At the end of that year several members of the Amaya team, including Montoya and the young Antonio Martín, signed for Banesto. Along with them came Mínguez, another Spanish cycling expert, who, at the 1987 World Championships in Villach had approached Induráin, and offered him a contract worth over $300,000. To this the Navarran had replied, simply: 'That's an awful lot of money, isn't it?', and continued on his way.

Antonio Martín had been one of the first over the summit of Isola-2000, isolated and with none of his team around. It was his first Tour and he'd held his own. He was destined for great things. Yet, the following winter, while the other riders were climbing the Sierra Nevada in the Tour of Andalusia, he was killed by a lorry when out training. Banesto were certainly not lucky when it came to signings. While men such as Carmelo Miranda and, most especially, Vicente Aparicio and Arrieta did their utmost to help Miguel take the following Tours, the reverse side (as far as the

Grande Boucle was concerned) was that figures like Montoya and Andy Hampsten failed to settle into the team. Another promising young rider who was to have led Miguel to 'half-way up the last mountain', Mikel Zarrabeitia, was seriously injured shortly before the '94 Tour.

But 1993 was going to bring another 'Oh!' of admiration from us, at the World Championships in Oslo, raced off in persistent rain, and on a very gruelling and impracticable circuit. Induráin controlled the event from the very start, but at the end a break from Lance Armstrong succeeded. Gold was now beyond reach. The final lap was raced at 42 kilometres an hour and, after 240 kilometres in the rain, Miguel went into the home straight surrounded by such consummate sprinters as Museeuw, Fondriest and Olaf Ludwig. His team-mates in the Spanish team had worked for him, and he couldn't let them down now. Just as he had worked for Bernard, or Gorospe or De las Cuevas even after he had become a Tour champion, and years before that for Carlos Hernández in a Tour de l'Avenir, so now they'd done the same for him. He went for a long, powerful sprint, full of conviction, and he did not fail them: it was silver.

The following year began with problems in the Banesto setup. People high up in the bank started to stick their oar in again over the Vuelta a España. The pressure on Miguel to ride was enormous: it was a real sword of Damocles hanging over him. What a cross he had to bear.

All winter, apart from the tremendous psychological blow of Antonio Martín's loss, there was a continual exchange of 'messages' between Rominger and Induráin. Then came Paris–Nice, and Milan–San Remo, where they were watching and studying each other. In the Tour of the Basque Country, Miguel did something unexpected: he broke the peloton asunder with a devastating surprise attack. It caused mayhem. But it was raining and the following day he withdrew.

In the Vuelta a España, Rominger took no prisoners. He dominated and overwhelmed the opposition; above all, he impressed with the strength of his climbing. Meanwhile, Induráin hit a raw nerve again. He stated that Spanish Television and the Vuelta organisers had made him a very generous offer, and that if it were money that made him race, then it would be a different story. But he wanted to prepare for the Tour and, for that, the Giro was more attractive because of its higher speeds on the flat stages and its more demanding mountains. More cutting criticism then followed, hurtful whispered comments. How ungrateful they were.

That 1994 Giro held four key days for Miguel, all of which would, at first sight, be essentially negative, but they would provide him with useful lessons. On the fourth stage, Eugeni Berzin made an escape towards Campitello-Mattesse. Nobody reacted. Miguel was the only Banesto rider near enough to go after the Russian, but the blond Gewiss rider snatched a good deal of time off his rivals.

Then came the Navarran's 'bad' day, only this time it occurred in a time-trial that was tailor-made for him. He came out clothed in a strange tracksuit type jersey which covered his head like a hood. It was dubbed the 'Little Red Riding Hood' model, and he never wore it again. Between Grosseto and Follonica, 44 kilometres, Miguel didn't break sweat, 'not at any moment', as he would admit immediately after the stage. He couldn't find his rhythm. He was awful, and he lost two and a half minutes. To make matters worse, he started to be affected again by his allergies. Sensitive to the pollen, grass, and particles in the spring air, they brought his skin out in a rash. And on top of all that, having arrived in Italy with 1,000 fewer kilometres in his legs, he once again found the suffocating pressure of the Press taking its toll. During the previous Giro, Miguel had lost his temper with a joker from an Italian TV programme who let down his tyres every morning, and on one occasion he'd almost smashed the bike frame over his neck. But then he'd been wearing the leader's pink jersey. This time it was a different story and he was forced to attack.

The stage to Aprica was to be decisive. Remembered as one of the great cycling moments of recent decades, it lived up to all expectations. As ever, nerves started to jangle on the Stelvio because they were climbing at a leisurely pace and Induráin was not attacking. He climbed that huge snowy mountain wearing a lot of warm clothing, which he didn't remove until it was too late. And then came the Mortirolo, where, on one of the first bends, Pantani launched a furious attack just as they came out of a pretty village, with the people clapping and looking at them as if to say:

'If you only knew where you were headed.' For an instant Banesto's Santi Crespo showed his face, but he was gobbled up by the group at the front. Once again – and this was something that was becoming all too frequent – Miguel found himself isolated.

Berzin (who is from the Bugno school) let his nerves get the better of him and caught the bald Italian. Armand de las Cuevas made a similar attempt. Then two or three other riders pulled off the front. Pantani was giving an early glimpse of the talent that was make him the *grimpeur* of the decade, and Miguel let him go. And with it, the *maglia rossa*. Whereas in the Tour he had only needed a 21 rear sprocket at most, here he had to change to a 25, and a front ring of 39. That was unheard of. Miguel didn't move during the whole ascent and remained glued to his seat, unlike Pantani, who was climbing in bursts. Álvaro Pino, who'd been an excellent climber, said he'd gone up the Mortirolo at ten kilometres an hour. And Marino Lejarreta as well. Some Spanish cyclists remember having zigzagged their way up it, from one side of the road to the other because of its tough slopes – almost thirteen kilometres with an average gradient of more than 10 per cent and with numerous stretches at 18 per cent, such as Viorca, Bradalba or San Mateo. From Valtellina to Val Camonica it was horrific, despite the trees.

Chioccioli held the record for the ascent, set during the '91 Giro, with an average speed of 15.595 kilometres an hour. Pantani was to raise this to 16.954.

But behind, Miguel, having made up his mind to make his move, was arriving like a whirlwind. With a wince of pain that had hardly ever been heard from him before, he overtook several riders, including De las Cuevas, who had blown up. He went after Berzin, caught him and left him for dead. The whole of Spain raised the roof. We could see the Giro in the bag. By the summit Pantani had taken 52 seconds out of him. But, given that the Italian had attacked at the base of the mountain, and had initially opened up a huge gap of maybe a couple of minutes before Miguel begun to respond – one third of the way up – it is not difficult to calculate that the Navarran must also have ascended the toughest part of the Mortirolo at around 17 kilometres an hour. After a frenetic descent, by the time they reached the area of false flats leading to

Aprica, Miguel had managed to link up with Pantani, who was accompanied by Nelson Rodríguez, another consummate climber. Pantani must have been told to wait for Miguel and for them to 'work together' (presumably there had been contact between the Carrera and Banesto team cars). His contribution was limited to letting Induráin lead him all the way while he waited.

Thus, with a brave Berzin, who was slowly pulling himself together, pushing from behind with Chiappucci, Pantani's teammate and team-leader, glued to his wheel, they went along for kilometre after kilometre. Miguel was leading the trio up, and the Giro was on the line, although not so much for Pantani, who was more concerned about the stage win.

The route maps indicate that the final climb to Aprica is gradual and manageable, but the section around the Valley of Santa Cristina was a mere blip on the map. A 'short little pass' before Aprica, which at first has gradients of 13 per cent, although only for a short stretch. That was another trap: from the bottom up to the summit at Pian Gambro there was a series of hellish cliff faces. As soon as they came in sight of the climb, Pantani launched a furious attack, and Miguel was left for dead. It was a monumental collapse. He was using the 25 rear sprocket and not getting anywhere, although curiously the pictures showed us Rodríguez beside him, apparently going quicker, but not getting anywhere either. On that stupid mountain, including the false flat of Aprica, Miguel lost three and a half minutes. What's more, Berzin had narrowed the gap considerably behind. Personally, I believe that was the day Miguel put Pantani's name in his little black book. He would, to put it politely, stop him winning it.

Once again everyone was talking about him 'cracking'. We touch paradise, and a moment later we plunge into despondency. But it had been a really epic journey. In the end, the great Induráin would simply be identified with specific defeats.

There was a gruelling time-trial climb to go, the Passo del Bocco, 35 kilometres of which only the first few were reasonably flat. Then one of those fierce climbs which forced Miguel out of the saddle all the way up. Berzin triumphed, but the Navarran was twenty seconds behind. As proof that he was recovering and that he had Pantani 'in his sights', it is worth recalling that the bald bomber came home more than a minute behind him.

There were two mountain stages remaining. On one of them, Deux-Alpes, it was almost impossible to attack. Even so, Induráin turned the screw several times. On the other mountain, in a real blizzard, they would ride almost the whole way as a compact peloton. It is said, however, that the previous night Miguel had confided to some of his closest friends: 'Tomorrow I'm going to blow the race apart.' It was not to be. That part of the legend is lost. He was third in that Giro, despite having been quite ill and having arrived there without any warm-up event. Many raised their voices in protest: 'And that's why he kept away from the Vuelta?' They took the view that he was finished, especially after the performances of Rominger in Spain. In France, the odds were 6–4 on Rominger winning the Tour. How disrespectful, stupid and naïve people were.

Now we were into a new phase of preparation. Some went far afield, to high altitude and exotic places. Others put in the kilometres in Navarre, with an excursion or two to neighbouring Guipuzcoa. Miguel put himself through the mill, despite his rather low morale.

And he fired a warning shot in the Spanish Road-Race Championship. He escaped, despite the desperate attempts from the peloton to stop him, and made a break of fully 150 kilometres in which he opened up a gap of six minutes! All of a sudden he decided to relax, and wait for the terrified group. Then he got off his bike. He was preparing for the Bergerac time-trial. *Voilà*...

The 1994 Tour was very important for Induráin, not only for his self-esteem or for the 'weight' that from then on he would be accorded in the peloton, but because he no longer seemed so infallible, having lost a time-trial on the flat (against Berzin and others) and cracked hopelessly in the mountains because he had overstretched his body. The threat from Rominger was also greater than ever. I remember spending a whole early summer arguing with my friends and fellow cyclotourists about Rominger: they were adamant he was stronger than Induráin. 'Ye of little faith,' I repeated endlessly. Very soon, they and everyone in the Tour Press room – including myself, I won't deny it – would be wide-eyed as cockatoos, once again uttering the classic 'Oh!' that marked every July. As Echávarri pointed out, in Spain we could call the month of July 'Miguel'. Many of us would have voted for this proposal.

Induráin began quickly, but not so quickly that he would exhaust himself. He finished three seconds behind Boardman in the prologue stage at Lille. Then came the all too familiar week of sprints and nerves. By then we were already beginning to think that if Miguel won that Tour, distant though it was, and difficult though it was, he would equal the record of Merckx and Anquetil who had each claimed four consecutive wins – the Norman in '61, '62, '63 and '64; the Belgian in '69, '70, '71 and '72. They had also achieved the historic double of Giro and Tour, but not with the kind of run Miguel had put together. He was within striking distance of becoming a Great Legend. Our hearts were in our mouths, and, as well as the usual anxious finishes over the opening days, we saw two significant events. One was the terrible crash at Armentières, where Jalabert split open his mouth but at the same time discovered himself. He would show he could cope with adversity. We also saw the triumph, in classic *rouleur* style of Kelme's Francisco Cabello in Brighton.

So, villas, hotels, Press rooms, finishes, were being left behind. Rennes, Futuroscope, Poitiers, Trelissac. The next day was the time-trial. The eagerly anticipated (and feared, by those suffering from 'Rominger Syndrome') individual time-trial of Perigueux–Bergerac – 64 kilometres largely flat but with the inevitable uphill sections at the beginning between Atur and Vergt. Then a motor-way to Lembras and Bergerac.

The Son of the Sun had still not unveiled all his weapons, not even in the Tour. And the sun, like his other ally the wind, did the rest.

No one could remember such a scorcher in years. The cold drinks ran out in the Press room. The previous days had seen the renewal of the psychological battle between Rominger and Induráin. The Swiss was constantly complaining about everything, including his knee. 'I don't think there's anything wrong with Rominger. We ride together in the peloton, I've been watching him, and I can't see anything unusual. If he says so, it must be true, but I'm not convinced,' said Induráin. Strangely, at the *village-départ* in Rennes, a couple of nuns went up to the Navarran to wish him luck. He would need it. Especially in the time-trial.

Others continued to open their mouths, generally too much. The '94 Tour belonged to the loudmouths, the cycling prototype to which Fignon, Lemond, Virenque and Rominger, himself, belonged. Rominger actually stated that he was not bothered if he lost a minute, or a minute and a half to the Navarran in the time-trials, because he could 'easily take two minutes out of him in the mountain time-trial at Avoriaz'. Easily? Such total naïvety beggars belief. Vicente Iza, Miguel's masseur, had said that the Navarran champion suffered a problem with his thigh muscles in those high-intensity stages, whereas when he was OK all he had to do was focus the massage on his lower back region and his neck muscles. In Bergerac something more than a high-intensity stage was coming to the boil. The Tour itself was coming to the boil, and in the literal sense of the word. The tarmac was bubbling, as were the riders' heads and skin.

The journalists were constantly going to the bathrooms to throw water over themselves. People were wrapping wet T-shirts on their backs and foreheads like cooling, soothing turbans. And that was in the shade. Outside, it was hell for the whole peloton, except Miguel.

He destroyed the Tour; he crushed it. He managed to ride at an average 50.539 kilometres an hour. It was the wildness of the scorching heat. Rominger, who rode the time-trial of his life and overtook numerous other riders, was a full two minutes behind him. The Navarran's pedals powered up and down in a kind of controlled frenzy. That, indeed, was a murderous rhythm – and incredible if you took into account the temperature. The other favourites were left miles behind. The French media thought the Tour was over. In fact, we all did, except Rominger, who was still speaking about attacking in the mountains even though he now considered the situation to be 'more problematic'. So they came to Hautacam, two days later and after 250 kilometres of flat that was not really flat, since there was the gentle ascent up to Lourdes itself. From there, the steep face of Hautacam, where Miguel had Jean-François Bernard go off at a lung-bursting pace; for three kilometres he demanded more, more and still more from him. Rather than climbing, it looked as if they were descending from a summit. It was unbelievable. Miguel was looking over his shoulder. The riders were crawling along. We saw pictures of Rominger who was totally overcome. Saliva, mucus, his kidneys done in. He was a wreck.

Up ahead Virenque 'grassed' to Induráin: 'Rominger... bad.'
And then came the lash of the whip, whose first victim was
Virenque himself – as the old saying has it: 'Rome does not reward traitors'. One by one all those who had gone to the front at
the beginning of the mountain attacked. The first was Pantani,
who was keen to win in the Pyrenees. The gap he opened up was
substantial, and, since he was recognised as the best climber in
the world, he seemed virtually unassailable. Back down the road,
Rominger and the other favourites were in agony, while the yellow jersey was flying uphill, to be joined by Luc Leblanc, although
the Frenchman did not do his share at the front. Amidst the haze
and the cheers of the tens of thousands of Spaniards jumping up
and down on both sides of the winding road, Miguel was nar-
rowing the distance between himself and Marco Pantani. No doubt
because of Pantani's attitude on the stage to Aprica in the Giro –
'I'll wait for you, you can lead me, and then I'll stab you in the
back' – Induráin didn't seem prepared to let him have things his
own way. The Italian was riding fast, but Induráin was a cyclone
unleashed. They were almost under the one-kilometre banner
when the Navarran and Leblanc caught, and then pulled away
from Pantani, who had perhaps been overhasty with his attack.
As was his custom, Induráin ignored the Italian; he contented
himself with passing him and continuing his unstoppable pace,
but that was a piercing thrust into the morale of the bald Carrera
climber.

It is impossible to prove what actually goes on in the heat of
competition, since there has always been 'needle' and always will
be, even if time eventually erases everything. It seems certain,
however, that Miguel was 'gunning' for Pantani, who would come
out of that Tour still yearning for a stage win: he was third at
Hautacam, 18 seconds behind Leblanc who won by two seconds
from Induráin; he was second the following day at Luz-Ardiden,
and at Morzine, and third at Val-Thorens. We should remember,
too, that on the way up Mont Ventoux while the riders at the front
were constantly upping the pace, Miguel remained unperturbed
until Pantani attacked. Then he did jump off the front after his
prey, and he jumped as if he had received an electric shock. Until
José Miguel Echávarri drew up alongside him and shouted at him
several times from the car telling him to slow down and that he

mustn't exhaust himself too soon because there was still a long way to go. But it was clear that Pantani was 'leading' Miguel up, even when the Navarran knew that by following the Italian's wheel he was running the risk of destroying his own rhythm and his lungs. Even when Pantani fell on the Glandon, and was clearly looking to abandon, the leader didn't react as he passed him.

I share the opinion of those who think that if Pantani had done his fair and normal share of work when Induráin went through his bad patch in the valley of Santa Cristina, he would no doubt have taken the stage, and he would have benefited in the long run, even if the '94 Giro would have been Induráin's. But Pantani didn't realise that till it was too late. In fact, the following year he became Miguel's favourite 'hare', and that season the Italian (behaving himself at last) would be allowed to win prestige stages. That is, as long as Miguel 'planned' it first. But even in the tight sprint in the '95 World Road Race Championships in Colombia, when Olano had already won the event, Induráin seemed to be invested with greater energy when he knew he had to take on Marco Pantani. And Pantani's face on the podium in Colombia was a real picture – he couldn't believe it. After all the excellent hard work the Italian squad had put in on his behalf. But he was one of those riders who had been petrified as they had gazed at the face of Miguel, who in turn had looked back at them defiantly as Olano was building up the seconds out in front. Marco will never forget the attitude displayed by Induráin, who turned towards the indecisive group of pursuers, as if to say: 'Go on, go for it and you'll see what happens to you.' Indeed, that day he was like a huge cobra lifting his neck in the face of destiny. He would never win a World Championship, not even that year, when it was a moral triumph for him, but those incredible moments in Colombia, with the Navarran literally paralysing his rivals, and thereby handing the victory to his team-mate, was perhaps the most emotional moment in the career of the five-times winner of the Tour de France. He was as magnificent in his second places and heavy defeats as he was in his most resounding triumphs.

The '94 Tour continued as per the schedule. After the hammer blow of Bergerac and the massacre at Hautacam, it all seemed ready for the final act of judgement. That particular Tour was one which boasted immaculately turned-out hostesses and administrators dressed in white designer polo shirts and blue slacks: with motorbike riders sporting shades reminiscent of the bad guy in *Terminator II* – all black leathers and hard-man looks; with mountains and roadsides packed with people holding out their hands for a free gift from the publicity caravan. A Tour, like all Tours, where the journalists following the event almost always have a worse view than the TV audience: always on the move from one hotel to the next, each day bringing a new town and new problems, as well as thousands of kilometres in the car, getting to the Press room a few minutes before the end of that day's stage, and struggling to follow the pictures on the monitors, between the mounds of accumulated paper or the preparation for the next day, often nodding off from exhaustion. Professional journalists seem to re-emerge from their nebulous world only on days such as Bergerac, as the thick beads of sweat dripped from their brows onto their computer keyboards. Or on days such as Hautacam, where we could scarcely credit the show put on by Induráin. Even leaving that aside, the Tour is still very tiring for the Pressmen. In the *village-départ*, always eager for any snippet of news, any detail, you have to chase riders and coaches, chat to masseurs and mechanics. Everything belongs to a superior and invisible geometric order, which imposes itself on the consciences of everyone who is, one way or another, part of it all. That has always been the case, but especially so over the past few decades, when television has raised the race to the status of a myth, of a timeless epic which we are immensely fortunate to witness today, even with all its potential cruelty and injustice.

The crowds massing around the *village-départ*, are generally hoping to catch sight of their favourite cyclists, the local or national heroes or such-and-such a veteran who has ridden any number of Tours. It is a crowd which wants, more than anything else, to see the leader. But this leader, this great and lordly Navarran, is hardly ever there, unlike some little peacocks who tend to spend a large amount of time being fêted by the masses. All this adds to the aura surrounding his person. We glance at our watches. Right now, *He* must be signing in, because the Control will be closed in a couple of minutes. If he doesn't, he'll be immediately disqualified. The first few times, I have to admit, I was sweating with anxiety. Maybe he hadn't fully recovered from what had happened to Pedro in Luxembourg. It's hard to believe, now, that all that belongs to another age. The new leader is always there, even in his absence. And here he comes, cutting it a bit fine, as usual, in a bid to escape the inevitable throng. I'll never forget the expression on the faces of several very young girls who were standing behind the crash barriers waving their arms asking for autographs from any rider who passed. When a particular French cyclist who was very much in the media spotlight passed, they screamed like fans at a rock concert. It all seemed a bit of a joke or a ritual; after hanging around for so many hours all they could do was to kick up a racket.

Suddenly Induráin came out to make his way through that narrow corridor of people. A motorbike was parked by the barriers, which forced him to move nearer the crowd. One of the girls stretched out her arm and touched him with the palm of her hand. She lightly touched the back of the leader, that's all. She held her hand up above her head and was sweating with excitement and incredulity, as if that hand were an alien object, and she started shouting excitedly to her friends: *'Je l'ai touché, je l'ai touché...!'*, I touched him, I touched him! To be honest, that young French girl looked as if she wouldn't know what to do with that hand over the next few days. The Navarran has an aura about him, which creates an impact on people. Everyone agrees on that. Years ago there was a French rider called Roger Chaussabel who described himself as follows: 'I'm not a road-racer, I'm not a climber, I'm not a sprinter. But I am an all-round *routier*. In other words, I'm a Tour man.' Something similar, raised to the enth degree, could be said of Induráin, at least until 1993. From that moment on he became the essence of the Tour. What was it that made him so? A host of extraordinary factors which quite possibly will never come together again in one and the same cyclist. We have already said he could descend like a bullet, but never as fast as Maassen, Konychev, or Ekimov, that he would never sprint like Abdoujaparov or Cipollini, and that on the mountains he would never possess the devastating *punch* of a Pantani or a Ugrumov at their best, nor on the long, flat strategic stages would he have the ability of Fondriest or Argentin to weave their strategies, but he could sweep the board with all of them, and on any kind of terrain, through the sheer strength of his class.

That was the time when going abroad and saying 'Induráin' was the equivalent of saying 'Spanish' if you wanted to put yourself at a psychological advantage when dealing with someone. And in France the mere mention of his name led to you being treated properly and politely. People admired him, and you felt a kind of pride when you saw that doors opened for you simply because you were of the same nationality as the champion. What a champion, if he had the power to make all that happen and more! Because Miguel became the standard, shield, flag and emblem. I remember climbing a mountain in the Alps on my bike and suddenly being passed by a couple of French cyclotourists. They were all smiles, but muttered a few snide little comments. Even though I was overtaken, I inquired in a loud voice: '*Qu'est-ce que vous dites d'Induráin?*' What are you saying about Induráin? And I swear their faces changed completely. They went all quiet and focused on their own riding. Miguel's name was so important, it had a huge impact on anyone who cycled.

And the '94 Tour continued under the dominance of Induráin, who never turned into a tyrant. The mountains were invaded by the hordes and there was always the fear that he would fall or be hemmed in. Miguel skidded coming out of a bend on the descent from Ventoux, went over to the side of the road and even released his foot from the pedal; the whole episode left us in a state of shock. One journalist from *L'Équipe* who was obsessed with seeing symptoms of what they dreamed about for five long years, said: 'At the finish yesterday we reckoned we could discern a scarcely concealed sign of fatigue, and even panic, in the leader's stunned face.' That went on for five summers. The French are a persevering lot!

Bouvet's gruff voice, on Radio Tour, would get excited whenever the French cyclists attacked on one of the mountain climbs. But over and over again, within ten seconds at most, he would rasp in that guttural, aseptic, resigned voice: 'An immediate response from the yellow jersey. The escape has been neutralised.' Leblanc no longer had a green light to make breaks so easily. He was a bad boy: he hadn't once taken over at the front during the climb up Hautacam, and to make matters worse he'd taken the stage victory. Virenque continued to shout his mouth off. With his King of the Mountains jersey he'd already got his reward. On the other hand, Pantani and Ugrumov, who could see the Tour passing by without them gaining their stage wins, were not inclined to give any unnecessary hassle. They were good boys.

On the climb to Val-Thorens, I could see, just as I'd seen shortly before on Alpe d'Huez and was to see one year later on the cliff faces of Causse Mende, the extent to which there are two Tours within the Tour: there's one for those riders who are fighting for victory in the mountains, or at least to put in a good performance; and there's another for those riders whose aim is limited to getting through the stages in one piece. The race organisers tend to turn a blind eye to the latter. There are loads of riders, Belgian, Dutch, French or other nationalities, who ask people for help in the toughest sections of the mountains. Instinctively, and with their experience in such critical situations, they know the nationality of the fans who offer them water, encouragement or a helpful push. With the crowd hemming the cyclists in, the organisers have difficulty seeing what is going on. In the '95 Tour, the French rider Frédéric Moncassin (a sprinter) was seen to receive 'assistance in the form of pushes' on numerous occasions, and was fined for doing so. But the organisers cannot prove that the cyclist has requested assistance. In theory, it is the spectators themselves who step forward, get hold of your back or saddle and propel you a few metres uphill. Several times on each mountain. There's no doubt it's a relief. But some riders actually ask the fans to do it, and they normally address them in their language. In this way they climb slowly and jerkily, but in a more relaxed fashion. They say 'grazie' or 'merci' or 'danke' if a fan comes up with a bottle of water but, if they don't grab it to cool themselves down, it's because they are grateful for the push that's offered.

That is another Tour, which the cameras never show us. For example, on Alpe d'Huez the time differences can be monumental. As is well known, the record for ascending the mythical summit (43 minutes and 19 seconds) was held by Eric Breukink until 1990, and he'd been in the second group, not in contention for the stage. Jacques Goddet himself had used his personal stopwatch to calculate the time taken by Fausto Coppi in his blistering ascent in 1952: 45 minutes and 22 seconds, but that was almost 40 years before, on roads with a worse surface and on heavier bicycles. When Hampsten won on the Alpe he took longer than Coppi, and yet the American climbed like a meteor: 45 minutes and 15 seconds. While Pantani, who attacked in '94 and '95 at the foot of the climb (the first time with no chance of victory) recorded incredible times: around 38 minutes. You would think there was nothing Induráin could do in the face of such a 'squirrel'. Indeed there wasn't. In truth, Miguel was frightened of 'cracking' if he attempted to react to an initial kick from Marco Pantani, so he would calmly let him make his way up the mountain. The Italian would gain an advantage of a minute or more, and would consolidate his position in the race. From that point on (that is, after several kilometres, almost half-way up the climb) Miguel would begin to press, constantly winding up his pace, as a heavy cyclist must. And he would maintain that pace to the top. Induráin would end up overtaking another bunch of cyclists up ahead, but if the actual time was calculated from the beginning of his effort proper, we would see that Miguel's times were very similar to those of Pantani.

This happened on the Mortirolo in the '94 Giro. A mountain on which Chioccioli held the record, raising it to an average 15.595 kilometres an hour, and which Pantani smashed at an average of 16.954. But we should remember once again that Miguel didn't react until several kilometres had gone by and Pantani never increased his advantage over the Navarran; rather, the gap narrowed. So we are left with the amazing evidence of a rider weighing more than 80 kilos, who was not in top physical condition and who, what's more, had just come through a serious allergic reaction, climbing that fearsome Dolomite cliff face at close to seventeen kilometres an hour without once raising his upper body from the saddle. Although it was shortly to cost him dear, at that moment we could enjoy Miguel displaying the *panache*, which certain 'French' versions of the events denied us. Pantani's ascents on some of these mountains were categorised as '*époustouflantes*', astounding, amazing. On the other hand, Miguel's were quite simply phenomenal. To be specific, Alpe d'Huez was always a mountain with pleasant memories and vibes for Induráin. And yet that was where, at one moment or another, Fignon, Lemond, Delgado, Thévenet, Van Impe and Zoetemelk all cracked. That was where Hinault was symbolically 'crucified' in the '84 Tour, and Merckx himself in the '77 event. Perhaps, despite its horrific gradients, it is the ideal mountain for the Navarran. Not necessarily to win the stage, but to wrap up the Tour, which is what he more or less did on four occasions. That's some record.

And in the evenings or at nightfall, after the tough stages in the Pyrenees and Alps, you would go to the hotels where some of the teams were staying and, if you went to the wrong room and went in without knocking, you would see what you were never supposed to see: prostrate men, with tubes literally sticking out of them, pale and dozing; it was the 'sick-bay' or 'pharmacy', or whatever you want to call it. Terrible and at the same time understandable. Otherwise, how would many of these men stand the hellish pace of the race? That's another side of the Tour. It has always existed and will continue to do so, although fortunately it does not reflect a general picture. That's how it is from the junior ranks upwards, which makes it even harder to accept. In the end, life, the body itself, sport, all put people in their place.

To be specific, it was the extensive use of the famous EPO that was a main talking point. EPO, erythropoietin, is a glycoprotein that is excreted in the peritubular cells of the outer layer of the kidney. It was 'invented' in Italy in the mid '80s and its use leaves no trace.* A large number of the peloton used it. So it is said. A former cyclist from Spain who achieved international honours admitted to me that, after some of the tough stages in the Giro, he personally had seen one of the organisers' employees collecting syringes with a special broom.

Even on grey and rainy days Miguel would still impose his sun, his brilliance. Monitoring and rewarding. Making us happy by giving us victories and by the serene manner in which he achieved them. His calm, relaxed strength was the best part of it, and that caused us to savour every last drop of those triumphs as if they were a precious elixir: he made us into gods, small gods. We knew we were certain to be happy in July, a month when the whole country would be brought to a satisfied standstill by Miguel's exploits. That was what made us supremely happy – just as we had been before through the emotion and uncertainty that Delgado generated – and it allowed us to savour the triumph in advance, with huge delight. Even ecstasy.

---

* This was the official medical view at the time.

That '94 Tour still had a couple of those sprint finishes where the cyclists seem like something out of *Ben-Hur*, with the bikes zigzagging like the demented blades of the racing chariots in the Roman circus in that film. Hair-raising finishes where the speed is so great the wind billows the jerseys of those thunder-men and ostentatiously whips them against their chests. This visual effect can only be appreciated in slow-motion replays. There's no doubt that's another side of the Tour, which could be called 'what the eye doesn't see'. Faces, grimaces, angry shouts, gobs of saliva, mucus and tears, insults and arguments. The cameras get almost everywhere. But note the 'almost'. No shots were ever seen of Gérard Saint urinating on his fingers, frozen solid on Belgian soil, in the heroic years, nor of Nello Lauredi and Christophe Mangin going into a barn and lying down under a cow, half demented in their search for warmth, and oblivious to the stewards' protests. Nor did we see cyclists fainting in the Alpine sun, swallowed up by the apparently liquid asphalt which the altitude turned to lunar swamps where all sense, honour, memory and conscience was lost. The Tour tends to show us the men who are dominating the race. The gods. Their angelic chorus hardly ever heaves into view, and yet the struggle of those men also has merit, and much merit, since they don't enjoy the same conditions as the big favourites. They climb the same mountains, albeit a few minutes behind, and they cover the same number of kilometres. As Induráin himself once said: 'The best thing about arriving with the leading group is that the suffering ends sooner.' A philosophy of life that is not Epicurean or hedonistic, but lucid. The harvest.

That is the profound loneliness of the long-distance cyclist. To ride and ride alone, especially during training, stacking up the kilometres, risking your life at every stretch of the road. Tuning your ear. A noise – a river, or a car perhaps? Be careful. There's no stopping place. Not even a sad little lay-by to pull into. No other sport, not even the 'high risk' sports, holds as much danger as cycling, and none claims as many anonymous victims. That's why there are times when watching someone like Induráin riding reconciles us with this sport which is perhaps rough rather than aggressive; or the other way round. Gary Kasparov asserted, with some justification, that chess was the most violent sport in the world. But cycling involves a three-way chess game: it is you against yourself; you against your main rivals, who you are expecting to attack or whom you ought to attack; and lastly it is you against the others, the rest of the riders and circumstances which may change the course of the race. Therefore, every cyclist, even if he's unaware of it, has within himself a potentially infinite game of chess, and is constantly moving the pieces around, even when he remains passive. You need to know all this, but you also need to have the intuition to anticipate it, with all the tension that's involved in being forced to take decisions.

Induráin was a master of those 'moves' and in the '94 Tour he tired of playing with some of his rivals. That is what happened at the top of the cols they were passing: the Croix-Fry, the Colombière. 'You can, you can't.' He battered Virenque and Leblanc, subjecting them to vice-like marking. Leblanc had already had more than enough with the Hautacam stage – if there's no working together and doing your share at the front, there are no more stages. Virenque also had his big Pyrenean stage, but he kept on shouting his mouth off. And Miguel doesn't take kindly to loudmouths. The last straw was the evening before the time-trial climb to Morzine-Avoriaz. It was raining and Induráin was not prepared to risk his career in a fall: others could push the pace. But Virenque just had to make his threat: 'Tomorrow, when Induráin and I are alone in the face of the mountain, I'll show my mettle. The mountain will decide.' Wow. That's really scary talk. Virenque stretched himself to the very limits of his capabilities and almost crashed on a bend. In fact, he literally went off the road. Miguel was behind, reducing the gap with each kilometre, and he wasn't even forcing the pace. Pantani and Ugrumov, on the other hand, did press, and that's why they gained time. But Leblanc and Virenque, the Frenchmen who were aiming for a podium position on the Champs-Elysées, missed out on a chance they would possibly never be within touching distance of again in their lives. It's best to be on good terms with the Lord of the Tour, who on that very same rainy morning in Morzine (so they say) picked up the maps and asked for a car to go for a long drive around the area. Those lonely spots, presided over by a distant Mont Blanc, bore witness to his meditation. Indeed, he had cruised through that fourth consecutive Tour as though it were a garden in Olatz. During the days of the race the sun hardly showed its face, but everything seemed to be flooded, none the less, by the warm yellow light of his powerful and dominant jersey, the colour of a fresh sunflower. And his eyes constantly hidden behind dark glasses, which made him more fantastic, more mysterious.

His first two Tours de France had been garnered without us really believing our eyes. He'd overcome the difficult and magical barrier of the third without us suffering unduly. His raging temperature in the Montlhéry time-trial remains a secret, part of the legend, and discreetly silhouettes his grandeur as a man and a champion. And the fourth, the Tour that put him on the threshold of the gods of the Mount Olympus of cycling, had perhaps been the most straightforward of the lot. It was emotional to have been there, with the rest of the members of the specialised Press. I was lucky enough to be a close witness of that marvellous five-year run. My daily articles in *El Mundo* were an excuse; in reality, as with millions of Spaniards, no matter where I was my heart would always have been on the French roads, because, as my journalist colleague, Benito Muñoz, says: 'The real passion is in France'. Though without Miguel it won't be the same. The handful of fellow media professionals who also witnessed that incredible period knew it too (and some of them had many, many Tours behind them). The beautiful nightmare of 'not knowing what the hell to say now about Induráin's latest exhibition' is something we will miss in the future.

You could taste glory everywhere at the end of that '94 Tour. As preparations were continuing for the presentations in Paris, as Francis Lafargue was sprucing Induráin up to try and make him look as dapper as possible, we saw a sad Pantani whom the Navarran champion didn't even glance at, just as he hadn't on Hautacam when he'd passed him in the fog, and just as he wouldn't after the sprint in Colombia. I must stress this point again: although the Italian was there because Miguel had allowed him to be there, the wound from the day on the Mortirolo remained open. The peoples of the North of Spain are good. Goliath is good. But those people have a keen memory and do not easily forget. Anyone who is ungentlemanly is treated accordingly and must earn their status. That's what happened to Pantani. Those who act in a gentlemanly fashion (such as Zülle, Giovannetti, Herrera, Roberto Conti and many others) will see themselves quickly rewarded. That Tour concluded with the appearance of T-shirts with the following slogan in English: '*Endurance = In-'d(y)uren(t)sn. The ability to withstand hardship adversity or stress. e.g. New York City Marathon.*' Induráin. The legends, the mystery. There is surely no better definition of Miguel's character.

In the '94 Tour I was moved to see the large number of children with disabilities or various difficulties who would go up to the leader so that he could ruffle their hair and sign an autograph. On one occasion he cut off an interview with a journalist from *L'Équipe* to go and give his signature to a lad.

And so, on to the fulfilment of the dream, the '95 Tour. The mere possibility of achieving five straight Tours seemed unprecedented to us, despite the fact that no one doubted Miguel's ability to manage it easily enough. That year, the main bunch of reporters were backing the Navarran, although the route chosen for the *Grande Boucle* held countless possibilities for ambushes. One was Mende; another, Guzet-Neige; and yet another was l'Alpe d'Huez, as well as the blue-ribbon stage of the Pyrenees. It was to be the most satisfying of all his Tours. The Great Harvest. It was dominated so comprehensively by Miguel from beginning to end that it lacked vibrancy. Journalists were seen complaining (and yet happily so) about the obvious tyranny to which Induráin, the Sun King of the Tour, subjected his rivals. That was in the very first week of the race. There were yawns all round. In the second week, some were nodding off at the stage finishes. So was the foreign Press. In the third week I saw people sleeping out in the open near the Press room. The problem was not that the race lacked real excitement, because there was more of that than ever, it was simply that fate had clearly decreed that this definitive and historic fifth Tour should belong to Induráin. In my opinion, it was his most complete Tour and the one in which his greatness shone brightest. This was because he attacked and dominated where no one had expected – on every imaginable kind of terrain, even where it was unimaginable.

The season had produced a rich crop of victories, and Banesto 'pre-registered' Induráin for the Vuelta, anticipating what would actually happen in the Tour. Meanwhile, the Navarran had triumphed in the Tour of La Rioja, in stages of both the Tour of the Mining Valleys (where, years before he had cracked horribly) and in the Tour of Asturias, in the Midi-Libre, in the Tour of Galicia and even in the 'Rominger Classic'.* What psychological torture that must have been (and at the same time what an honour for the Swiss rider) to see Miguel winning in *his* Open for cyclotourists. Even there he'd been beaten.

Yet, there were still the usual dissonant voices, which resulted in Induráin commenting to *Miroir du Ciclisme*: 'I know a champion said in your pages that he didn't like the way I won. That's his right. But it's also my right to believe that winning is the only thing that counts, and that in ten or twenty years' time they'll only be speaking about my palmarés and not about the manner of the victories.' A Lord and gentleman. As though wanting to prove his superiority and brilliance to the entire world, that 1995 Tour was perhaps to see his greatest display of shrewdness, class and power. He attacked on all fronts: on the flat, descending, and climbing; when everyone, including his rivals, were expecting it, and when no one thought it possible. It didn't matter. That unforgettable '95 Tour was the true challenge in Miguel's life: to put himself alongside the greats on Mount Olympus. He was a giant. And for a change we were lost for words. But seeing him in France under a baking sun with fans from different countries, including the host country, paying tribute at his feet, that was a moving moment in history.

The only time it rained (though it did so by the bucketload) was the afternoon of the prologue in Saint-Brieuc. For a change, Miguel was not taking any risks. Several riders came off, and Boardman ended up in hospital. Then, on to Lannion, and Vitre, with electrifying and dangerous finishes. Miguel's peaked cap was watching over everything from privileged positions. He never launched the sprint (there were expert sprinters to do that) but instead concentrated on avoiding any falls. And Rominger was nervous: 'I don't know what Induráin thinks he's playing at getting involved in the sprints.' He should have been reminded of three things: Induráin didn't get involved in the sprints, but was simply being careful to avoid being taken by surprise; secondly, he would intimidate his closest rivals by showing his strength in those final minutes when the peloton, guided by the Italian beacons, reached

---

* The Rominger Classic actually came after the Tour de France.

dizzying speeds; and, thirdly, he would avoid the sort of thing that happened to Jalabert at the finish in Le Havre, where a fall cost him the *maillot jaune*.

It was in the team time-trial between Mayenne and Alençon, almost 70 kilometres, where Banesto first really put the hammer down, especially those brave lads like Monchi González Arrieta and Aparicio who were riding in hostile territory. The way Miguel took over at the front, constantly encouraging his team-mates, was staggering. And Pruden was the 'victim' chosen to respond there and then to each and very crack of the whip. That was a crucial time-trial, to be sure, and Induráin congratulated them at the end, in a simple but moving gesture which made such an impact on Thomas Davy, Banesto's young French rider, who would say: 'When I saw Miguel for the first time in ordinary everyday clothes he made a bigger impression on me than when he was on his bike. He was so big and with such a deep voice. "He's the champion," I said to myself. Alongside to him, I feel smaller in every sense.' The same big, good, down-to-earth and deep-voiced man who, after that damned Follonica time-trial (where he really lost any remaining chance in the '94 Giro), apologised to his men for having 'failed' them, when the truth is he had no need to do so. A genius and a great figure. After that gesture in Italy, and despite the fact that everything was lost, they continued battling their hearts out for him. I remember the young Santi Crespo at the bottom of the Mortirolo and Rué in the snow and ice along the roadside, on the way to Sestrière.

In the Tour of '95, D-day was now approaching. Or at least, the day when he was going to destroy the race psychologically – the seventh stage, from Charleroi to Liège. Before that, there had been nerves, looks and sideways glances among the favourites. That and Induráin upping the pace close to the finishes. There were nervous scares. Extremely long and apparently flat stages to Dunkirk and to Charleroi, but riddled with speed-bumps that forced you to be constantly changing gear. Miguel had watched every clue with his owl-like eyes that peered out from the shadows. His conception of time was different, as if he belonged to a superior dimension. He didn't wear a watch; he was governed by a kind of water clock. He was entangling his rivals in a dizzying dance of active and passive movement. Like the anemone before it attacks. They watched and saw the same vision they always did: an imperial eagle among little dazzled tawny owls.

Sometimes he would pedal with a certain degree of tiredness. But that was a mirage; he was watching too. As he'd watched Bugno and Chiappucci in his first Tours, as he'd watched Rominger in the following Tours, until on Hautacam he had seen him open his mouth a millimetre wider to breathe, ponderous and with his eyes glazed, his shoulders swaying a little bit more. Then he raised the guillotine. Now Induráin was watching, too. But what he saw surprised him more than he'd expected. The ONCE boys were nervously shuttling back and forth, Zülle especially; there were too many journeys back to the team car. Rominger was too far off the pace by the time they got to the slopes in the final part of the stage, in Durbuy, Stavelot and Haute-Levée, on the Côte de Ferrières. The specialist climbers didn't worry him. The pace was too high for them. A hellish pace and constant ups and downs, which forced them to scale the short, steep cliff faces on the big ring. Either that, or they'd lose touch. Ten of those slopes are enough to finish anyone off, especially in the blazing sun. The regulations of the Belgian Cycling Federation decreed that the riders had to wear a helmet, the Navarran as well, of course. Just like in his early junior events. Or like the stage to Jaca in '91.

On the way to Liège no one thought anything untoward could occur. And yet it did. Once again, the typical 'bad moment' that Miguel had in each of his Tours. In '91, his strength failed on the way to Gap and he had felt weak climbing the Joux-Plane in the rain. In the '92 event it was his chain, which jumped at the beginning of the climb up Alpe d'Huez, and with Chiappucci attacking. And his mysterious and claustrophobic last three kilometres on Sestrière. In the '93 Tour, his soaring temperature, concealed behind the autographs and the smiles. In the '94 race, his partial 'loss of motivation' on the time-trial climb at Morzine-Avoriaz, where, basically, he was just being careful. Also, in '94, his skid on Mont Ventoux, which made our blood freeze in alarm. We saw, simply and terrifyingly, how easy it was to lose a Tour through a skid, a fall: Rivière, on the Col du Perjuret; Ocaña, on the Menté; Wim van Est on the Aubisque; Bruyneel, a year later, on the Cormet.

In 1995, on the road to Liège, Induráin knocked into the arm of a woman who had leaned forward too far to see the riders pass. For several kilometres the Navarran was opening and closing his hand. Anyone who has ridden a bike knows that you can't ride with an injury to your forearm, which receives all the pressure of your body. It happened near the end of the stage. There are no photos of that moment (just as there are none of the key or critical moments in Miguel's career, which thereby almost deliberately serve to make the legend greater) but we did see it on the TV monitors, in the Press room. With my proverbial pessimism, I remember I exclaimed '*Adiós, Tour!*' But Miguel raced through the pain, and what he saw continued to encourage him, and that reduced the pain in his arm.

By default, the pace of the race was quickening. The ONCE team was scattered. Some riders who had no chance of winning had taken up positions at the front, but they were still in sight. The imperial eagle drew out his claws. In fact, on the Côte du Rosier the silhouette that Miguel was looking for most of all, that of Rominger, had disappeared; he hadn't been dropped, in the literal sense, but he was just not fully concentrating and was losing a few metres on each slope. Berzin, on the other hand, was younger and more of a fighter. He'd been Miguel's executioner in the '94 Giro and was always glued tightly to his wheel. Miguel made up his mind. He told his men to up the pace. A whistle. Without looking back. A codeword. Especially to Monchu González Arrieta. The road was getting steeper, the sun was shining hotter than at any time in the last five years. This is how he reached Mont Theux, a mere three kilometres with a 5.7 per cent gradient. Miguel gave the order to Monchu: 'Faster, faster.' Berzin panted, opened his mouth, puffed, his tyre separated a few metres further back from Miguel's white Pinarello. The Navarran was using a gear ratio of 53 x 19 (or at times, 20 or 21). It was time to blow the race apart. He shifted on to the 17-tooth sprocket, lifted his upper body, and put down the hammer, pulling away and passing the several riders up ahead. He went like a rocket.

The last we saw of him was when he had to dodge one of the race motorbikes. An incredulous peloton was unable to respond to that all-guns-blazing attack. The miracle took place between Mont Theux and the Côte des Forges, another two kilometres at

5.8 per cent. He was gone in a flash. Back down the road, no one had the presence of mind to organise the counter-attack, the chase. Miguel did not raise his eyes; his chin rested on his handlebars. He didn't once look back. He left Eric Boyer trailing, caught Bruyneel, who was at the front, and who started to pedal like a man possessed. One again, he was riding the stage of his life against the clock. Behind him came the pack of hounds.

No one could understand it. How could the race favourite have the temerity to try such a thing? In the Press room, French faces dropped. Bruyneel, who was almost gasping, turned to the Navarran and whispered: 'Look, I can't push the pace, I've got my bosses back down the road.' Later he would admit that it had been an experience without parallel in his cycling life: 'I felt I was riding behind a motorbike for 25 kilometres, at 50 an hour.' Of course, Miguel didn't even look at him. Of course, he never re-proached him for not taking his turn at the front. Of course, the other big favourites, once they had decided to join forces with their chosen *domestiques*, must still have had their doubts: 'What the hell has that madman done?' On the following day there'd be the demanding time-trial at Huy, and two days later the Alps.

What was Induráin trying to do when he went for the jugular on the flat in Belgium? No one knew that months before Miguel had reconnoitred the same stretch during the Liège–Bastogne–Liège race. The *coup de grâce* was premeditated. A masterful, un-repeatable chess move. By the time everyone had clicked, the man from Navarra was almost a minute ahead. The very thing none of the others had wanted (Induráin starting the following day's time-trial in yellow) was going to happen. It panicked and horrified (and above all deflated) each and every one of them. However, those 30 kilometres to Liège, with Induráin chased by the cream of the international peloton, who not only couldn't catch him, but in fact saw the gap widen with each revolution of the pedal, be-long to the annals of cycling history. That was something which, until then, only the great champions had dared to do: Coppi, Merckx, Hinault. Not even Anquetil, who was more cerebral, had tried it. Didn't the French want *panache*? Didn't they want a show of genius, improvisation, risk and rage? There they had it, and it was a farewell call. Because Induráin was sealing his fifth Tour win even before the first time-trial stage, even before the first mountain. It was unprecedented. Let us stick our necks out and proudly say that neither Coppi, nor Merckx, nor Hinault, nor Anquetil had dared to do this after having previously won four Tours, and when they were up there for everyone to shoot at.

But Liège meant much more than Induráin closing in on another yellow jersey. In spite of the fact that Bruyneel won the sprint at the end of the stage, the Navarran was dealing an unexpected hammer blow to his rivals' morale. Miguel has always sprung surprises. He won his first Tour by surprising everyone on a suicidal descent. The second, by producing an unreal time-trial performance. The third, by striking ruthlessly on several different terrains. The fourth, by repeating the feat, but more spectacularly and convincingly, at Bergerac and Hautacam. So, what could he come up with to take the longed-for fifth Tour? Everyone thought it would be in the mountains: 'When he reaches Cauterets, the emblematic summit that will be thronging with Spaniards, that's when he'll strike.' Others were more cautious and said to themselves: 'No. It'll be in the time-trial in Belgium, and after that he'll use the minutes he has in hand.' No one imagined it would be before all that, on an undulating road stage. It was an attack that defied the natural order of things, an assault that was rationally psychopathic. Which is what defines the great champions. But there was something else, something which was closely linked to pain, to the capacity to accept it, to endure it and to recycle it. And perhaps that day in Liège, the day Miguel went for his fifth Tour, we saw in his mouth something unprecedented, something that had never been seen before either in his great exploits or in his less great failures. We saw white saliva.

When white saliva appears in the mouth of a top professional cyclist, it means something has happened inside him. He has gone beyond his own rational limits. Loss of salts and sugar, a complete collapse of the system, a savage bursting over the threshold of the permissible. There was white saliva in Bobet's mouth after Izoard. And in Gaul's on Luitel. And in Ocaña's on Orcières-Merlette and after the fantastic cavalcade of Les Orées. There was white saliva on the lips of Merckx going towards Mourenx, with the Aubisque as the judge. And in Anquetil's on the Gavia and the Envalira. And in Kubler's and Malléjac's on the Ventoux, where they thought they were going to die. And in Simpson's, who did die on those slopes. The Ventoux, that Sahara suspended in the ether – there Merckx passed through agony as he did on Pra-Loup, and so did so many others.

That white saliva was in Delgado's mouth on La Plagne, and in Riis's in the final time-trial of the '96 Tour. That white saliva in Jalabert's mouth on Mende, and in José Manuel Fuente's on the Three Summits of the Lavaredo. That white saliva which Miguel himself concealed during his amazing ascent of the Mortirolo, and which caught up with him later. The white saliva on the Ventoux (always that sinister peak, the Giant of Provence, which in days of yore was praised by Petrarch) in the twisted mouth of Jean-François Bernard. We saw white saliva in Koblet's face, despite his composure and his neat and tidy haircut, after his crazy dash to Agen in the stage that started from Brive. And in Bahamontes' on the Puy-de-Dôme, and in Bottechia's on the Tourmalet. And on Lucien Buysse's in Luchon. And in Pélissier's and Magne's between Nice and Gap as they chased determinedly after the Italian Pesenti. And on Vietto's, after he offered his wheel to Magne himself on the Col d'Ares, weeping with anger and exhaustion from the effort on the side of the road. It is the same white saliva as in Hinault's mouth, so many times, and in Zoetemelk's and Thévenet's, in their duels amongst the snowy mountain caps. And in Agostinho's and Kuiper's, Breu's and Winnen's, who were so determined to be kings of the Alps. It is the white saliva in the mouth of a sprinter like Angel Edo, going beyond the limit for just a few seconds on Alpe d'Huez, lying broken over his bicycle. And in Félix García Casas' mouth, at the finish at Le Puy-en-Velay in '96, after a stage that had departed from Valence. That same morning, in the start village, I had been encouraging Félix who was exhausted and complaining, telling him that the Tour rewards those who stretch themselves and persevere. He took it as a joke, but minutes later he was part of the successful breakaway of the day. He came within a whisker of a stage win, which went to Pascal Richard. And I saw him cross the line, his knees and hands trembling so much he was unable to hold the bottle of water he was offered. It spilled down his jersey. There was white saliva in his mouth.

After the Liège adventure, when white saliva appeared on Miguel's lips, the Tour was as good as over, psychologically. In

the time-trial the following day, Riis was recording better intermediate times than the Navarran, who in that blazing Caribbean-
like sun could have done with a higher gear. He hadn't taken
into account the long descents on the route, and should have had
an 11-tooth sprocket fitted. At the end, he stepped up the pace to
a crescendo, bettering the Dane, who was wearing his national
champion's jersey. Induráin was already in yellow. After a rest
day came the first Alpine stage, to La Plagne, via the Col des
Saissies, the Cormet de Roselend before the final ascent to the
colossus which years before had witnessed the tremendous fight
between Stephen Roche and Perico Delgado.

La Plagne is one of the toughest mountains in the Tour, because
of its length of almost eighteen kilometres and because of its
average gradient of 7.3 per cent. In Spain there are no climbs like
it. A fierce sun beat down once more, forcing Eugeni Berzin to
gradually drop back through the field, after his breathless attack
had lasted just three minutes and twenty seconds. The Tour was
blowing apart. Miguel saw all this, once again, and at the very
foot of the Cormet he asked his men to push the pace. Up ahead
was Zülle, who for a few moments would be the race leader on
the road. But the Navarran once again had gathered interesting
information about his closest rivals' faces. They reached La Plagne,
where Rué and Aparicio exhausted themselves assisting their
leader on the first five kilometres, between Aimé-Macot and
Villard de Haut, as Miranda and Arieta had done on earlier
mountains. Then, out of the blue, another miracle occurred. With
an initial acceleration from the leader at Prariond, several of the
favourites were dropped, including those closest in the overall
classification – among them, Riis, Jalabert, Rominger and
Virenque. Induráin's pedals worked with the criminal fluidity we
had seen on the Galibier, at Luz-Ardiden or on Hautacam. The
hurricane was starting, and, with it, a witch's brew of heavy
panting. There was the usual backdrop of pale-faced men, their
eyes coagulated and convulsing from the effort and pain, jerseys
opened to the navel and their tongues hanging out. Bodies nailed
to the road like broken dolls.

With Miguel's second acceleration, between Les Charmettes
and La Roche, Pantani, Gotti and one or two others lost touch.
Only Paolo Lanfranchi was able to hold on to the Navarran's wheel

for a few metres. Apart from Alex Zülle, who was as brave as any, but who was losing time irredeemably to Induráin, there was only Pavel Tonkov up ahead. Induráin caught and passed him. The Russian was literally sprinting uphill, while Miguel was sitting on his saddle, riding with a steely yet graceful pedal action. Zülle was turning the pedals with a weak, jerky rhythm while the rest of the riders had that unfathomably surly cadence, pressing the pedals slowly – like a weightlifter, as was said of Hinault on one occasion. Induráin was an angel going to the summit; it seemed as if he were riding on the flat, his face impenetrable, his hands and back motionless. After a long hairpin bend he looked back down below and there was no one there. They had all been blown away. The Tour was his! Another acceleration took him a few metres away from Tonkov. The Russian was destroyed.

On the La Plagne, a mountain with a gradient like that of the Tourmalet, that glorious Tuesday 11 July 1995, Miguel gave what was perhaps his greatest exhibition in the mountains. He showed that when the chips were down, and he truly went for it, there was no one to challenge him, not even the climbers. The rest was simply a matter of control. Two kilometres more and he would have caught Zülle. *'Quel Champion!'* wrote the French sporting press. 'Oh!' journalists from all over the world drooled once again in the Press room. That was phenomenal. Miguel crossed the finish and a few minutes later, like a divine punishment for the stragglers, it started absolutely teeming with rain. Berzin arrived in pieces, almost 17 minutes down. The others were floundering in an ocean of frustration and choking. Gérard Rué, the brave lieutenant, came home slumped over his machine, more than 26 minutes behind Miguel. But a little bit of the Tour belonged to him too!

That evening in La Plagne, in a pizzeria at the foot of the mountain, I ate with a group of Spanish journalists. I remember hardly anyone was hungry. We were all laughs and smiles, simply oozing success. On the following day, with La Madeleine and the Croix de Fer to come before Alpe d'Huez, it was another party. Pantani pulled away at the base of the Alpe and Miguel decided not to make a move until he thought the time was right. That is, when the Danish rider Riis, in a clear foretaste of what was to happen the following year, began to show signs of overconfidence. He was called to order. Only Riis and Zülle, who was totally honourable, would manage to endure the gut-wrenching pace set by the Navarran. Once again climbers such as Tonkov, Gotti and Virenque were swept aside by the avalanche from Miguel, who seemed to be the only cyclist in the world able to maintain that pace on the slopes of the Alpe without getting out of the saddle. The voice of Daniel Mangeas, Radio Tour's normal anchorman, was going berserk over the PA system: 'There he is, the great Miguel sealing the destiny of the Tour which is his and his alone. He is the greatest, King Miguel!' And the crowd had no option but to watch in shell-shocked admiration and applaud. But – and I swear this is true because I saw it with my own eyes and heard it with my own ears – they did it more out of some religious respect than out of pure sporting enthusiasm. So huge, so yellow, so elegant, so lordly. And without getting out of the saddle!

In the ever-feared stages of the Massif Central, which used to be as crucial in deciding the outcome of the Tour as the Pyrenees and the Alps, nothing happened. At least not on the stages to Revel and Saint-Étienne. But in an awkward finish at Causse Mende, a beautiful spot, the colour of dry mud, we had a fright. It was a long stage, full of lower-category climbs. There was no wind, and the final climb to Mende, around three and a half kilometres, had an average gradient of 9.7 per cent. Rather similar to the Mortirolo. No one was expecting anything awkward, and yet it proved to be uncomfortable, especially because there were stretches of almost a kilometre at 12.5 per cent, followed by other, shorter ones, at 14 per cent. An hour and a half before the cyclists passed, as we began the ascent by car, I remember thinking anxiously, 'Oh, no, it's Oropa all over again!' But since I was the doom-monger amongst the journalists, they paid no attention to me. What no member of the Spanish group could imagine was that an error by the whole Banesto squad, and a more than commendable performance from the ONCE team, would have us all on tenterhooks.

ONCE put Jalabert, Neil Stephens and Melchor Mauri in a smallish breakaway group, which began to gain minutes and minutes. Stephens rode his heart out and Mauri was tremendous, while Jalabert was holding himself back for the finish. He was within a hair's breadth of the lead at certain moments during the stage, and his compatriots were going wild. To cap it all, it was Bastille Day! Things were going horribly wrong. The time deficit grew to many, too many, minutes, and when Banesto, with a little help from other teams, decided to up the pace, Mauri, produced the performance of his life: he was able to cope with anything they threw at him. At the beginning of the almost vertical slope of Mende, Jalabert gleefully jumped off the front. I remember noting the time Miguel was losing, and I went through torture as never before. Fortunately, *he* didn't.

That was Miguel, and that's why we stacked up five Tours without ever really emerging from our daydream. He weighed things up. Everyone else found their nerves had gone to pieces – Echávarri and Unzúe, his Banesto team-mates and Manolo Saiz, the Director of ONCE. A possible knock-on effect of that was that Jalabert himself was panicked as he started to receive the news from the ecstatic crowd which seemed to be going wild. '*Nouveau leader, nouveau leader!*' they chanted, giving a V-for-victory sign with their fingers.

Jaja was pedalling with sunken eyes. White saliva was sticking to his chin. It was his day. It was now or never. But Induráin stirred. He had already sliced a chunk off the lead, and was riding calmly until Riis made a move, and then Pantani jumped off the front – it was the perfect climb for him. But not this time. After him went Induráin, at the same time blowing away Riis and Zülle who normally stuck to him like limpets. I was in the middle of the throng of people, about 500 metres from the summit, although the finish was almost a kilometre away, on the flat. I think that was the most nerve-racking half-hour of my life as a cycling fan. The French had their watches in their hands calculating the times, and they were euphoric. The Spaniards reacted in all sorts of ways. Some, like myself, were on the verge of a nervous breakdown while others maintained a blind faith that Miguel, on his own against the field, would recover enough time to retain the leadership. Never in all the stages I was fortunate enough to witness was I ever so frantic. The suffocating heat was all-encompassing. Our skin was burning. A few of the French made ironic gestures at us, as the latest news became ever more alarming.

But in a prudent and controlled time *He* appeared, once again, filling us with such joy that, as I recall, our screams of encouragement choked in our mouths. That afternoon, on the ghostly and torrid slopes of Mende, the Spanish fans present were almost hoarse, and yet we hadn't been able to shout. Miguel looked tense and gritted his teeth as he shot past like a bullet after Pantani. He remained in the saddle and rode at speed even on those stretches that were like cliffs. He was more imposing than ever. He had managed to climb the whole of the Mortirolo in his saddle, so of course he could do it on the Mende which didn't hold the same fears for us! But the fright, I tell you again, was pretty real.

In the Pyrenees, on the road to Guzet-Neige, in the rain and on a dangerous surface where it was easy to crash, Riis put the cat amongst the pigeons. First at the Port de Lers: but Miguel went after him. And then later, shortly after going over the Col d'Agnes, Miguel hit him again and even dropped him for a few metres on the dangerous descent. Pantani had escaped. The Lord had given him his tacit consent: 'Since this year has been a bad one for you, no Giro, no podium at Paris, at least you'll have your stage wins in the Alps and the Pyrenees.' On the climb up to Guzet, Bjarne Riis had another go, but Miguel, fed up with him by now, accelerated, and it was only with great difficulty that the Dane managed to keep more or less in touch with him.

I remember Pantani passing, surrounded by motorbikes, dancing on his pedals and panting for breath. We had an aerial-shot of the wet road, and I remember, on the bend where I was standing, the moment when the inevitable group of three came past – Induráin, with Zülle and Riis hanging on to him like fraying fringes. They were drawn and haggard, except the Navarran, who was slightly ahead of them and was throwing them rapid glances out of the corner of his eye. I won't forget Zülle's bony and bluish face, nor the mucus hanging from Riis's nose, and his mouth wide open, a clear sign of breathlessness. A little way ahead was Miguel, imperious, calm, dominating. With his aristocratic pedal action and attitude. The spectacle was priceless. We had deserved this for more than a century.

I remember the following day's ascent by car of the Tourmalet (before the news of Casartelli) which would be my most fulfilling moment as a cycling fan. Kilometre after kilometre there were Spaniards showing us the palms of their hands: 'Five'. Five Tours; it seemed incredible. I think I must have returned the greeting from the window thousands of times: 'Five'. Those hand-signs continued for many joyful kilometres.

The following day was the rest day at Saint-Girons. We didn't give too much credence to Induráin's statements that he felt drained. Demotivated. 'I'm 31. People like Hinault or Merckx retired at 32. At the moment I feel strong, but next year could be a different story. I know one day it's got to end.' He was warning us. Miguel was no longer feeling so enthusiastic about the harvest.

They'd reached the Pyrenees, with its magical and fearful aura, with its haze, as in Ariège, which enveloped Guzet-Neige or the fearful mountain sides that imprison the Tourmalet. Moss merges with flowers, earth with grass, there are treacherous micro-climates with unbearable sun or rain, often all these mixtures within a few kilometres. Cycling is one of the few sports where you encounter this. Or where, as you descend from a summit at 80 kilometres an hour you might swallow a fly the size of a walnut, and simply have to scrunch it up. Or have to contend with a gob of saliva from a team-mate in front of you, who, through lack of concentration or inexperience, hasn't thought about his position or the wind direction. Or where an error of judgement can kill you at any bend in the road, or where fine calculation can be scuppered by skidding on a patch of oil or a hole in the road, or by a puncture or a stone. That was how Fabio Casartelli was to meet his death that day when the Lord of the Pyrenees arrived in his territory – Portet d'Aspet, which would see the fatal blow to the young Italian. Peyresourde, the Aspin, the Tourmalet via Sainte-Marie-de-Campan (the legendary spot where Christophe had to have his bike repaired in the smithy's when he was out in front on his own, a job which took hours and lost him any chance of winning the Tour in the dim and distant year of 1913) and last of all, Cauterets.

But it was not in the Pont-d'Espagne nor in the area called Le Cambasque, which was where Miguel triumphed in the blue-ribbon stage in '89, but in a high and shady spot known as Crêtes-du-Lys. Hollows and valleys, abysses and rocky outcrops, mountains like needles. An icy climate there, which can weaken the lungs, flood them like sponges and soon afterwards shrivel them up through lack of air. Places teeming with legends, which saw Buysse weep, Bottechia faint and others cheat and take short-cuts. Woods and precipices, which inspired artists and writers, Kings and princesses, queens and nobles. Possibly Charlemagne, and the Spanish philosopher Ortega y Gasset, who felt so nervous looking at those harmonious hills of numbing savagery, where the wind scorches and the light deceives. And Hugo, who wrote, 'Here sensitive realities stand before us, at certain times of the day, in unusual guise.' And he didn't say that after pedalling 200 kilometres up six imposing mountains, pummelled by a blazing sun, and knowing that his 'workmate', as Induráin referred to Casartelli, had just bathed the asphalt with his blood. His cruel fate awaited him just after he had entered the Haute-Garonne.

The following day there was mourning and consternation. They rode gently up the Soudet, but even then many cyclists dropped back pleading with their colleagues: '*Piano, piano*', slower. Only Riis protested, insinuating that he wanted to be able to attack the leader on that stage. That day, I suspect, he earned the enmity of the whole peloton. The Italians would never forgive him. In fact, he left Gewiss for Telekom, the squad which, like a sized-down but equally efficient version of the Wermacht, would sweep the board the following Tour. At Cauterets Virenque claimed his inevitable victory, but Induráin smothered all attempted attacks. He was the emperor and wrote his own particular *Chanson de Roland*. From that day on, his name would be forever linked to the fleur-de-lis, the flower of the kings.

The rest of that magical fifth Tour was little more than a permanent remembrance of Casartelli. The arrival of the Motorolas en bloc, the emotional victory of Armstrong in Limoges as he pointed to the heavens: '*Fabio, c'est pour toi!*' The time-trial around the beautiful Lake Vassivière. Miguel pressed just enough to produce a new and final thrust, like Lancelot of the Lake. It merely remained to watch the compact peloton cruise at almost 50 kilometres an hour over the cobbles of the Champs-Elysées, with wheels licking each other, to end the grandiose spectacle. Another podium, with Miguel again at the top. Riis and Zülle were on either side of him. Many of us had tears in our eyes when the anthem was played and the crowd went quiet. But we would have to wait until the following year for certain feelings really to surface.

At the ceremony, among the other dignitaries, was the Spanish princess Elena and her husband. Induráin had a bouquet of flowers in his hands and the rumour went round, based on protocol: 'He's going to give the flowers to the princess.' But the Navarran continued seeking someone out in the crowd, and eventually he found her: Marisa. Under her dress, Marisa could not hide the fact that there was another Miguel waiting to come into the world. Her smile was wide and radiant. The flowers were for her, and cordiality for the rest. The dream, the great dream, had been fulfilled. Miguel now figured amongst the four greatest cyclists of all time. Only he had achieved it in a way no one else had: by winning five consecutive Tours. Let someone else take up the gauntlet.

The French reacted in their customary fashion: on the one hand they worshipped at his feet, and on the other hand there was Marc Madiot writing things like: 'Up till this point, Induráin won the big races because the others lost them.'

Weeks later, we engaged in the yearly trawl through the dozens of photos of that great event we had just witnessed. And it was then, in the inert fidelity of the photographs, that we could grasp the tremendous effort put in by the cyclists, including Miguel, indeed especially Miguel, because he was the one who was mostly at the front. His dislocated grin as he climbed the Causse Mende, his face bathed in sweat and mud on Guzet-Neige, his cheeks puffed out on the Tourmalet, those white teeth seemingly discharging electricity on l'Alpe d'Huez. I was moved, and remembered one of those Luz Casal's songs he likes so much: 'Every time I see your photo, I discover something new I hadn't seen before.' And those pictures were mingled with those of the calm ritual on the podium, each time they put the yellow jersey over his head: 'Give me your inner world, give me your smile and your warmth.' But over all those other scenes from that July which will rise like a monument in defiance of oblivion, the voice of Luz could be heard as he accelerated once, twice, three times on La Plagne: 'Give me your cold and your heat.' When Miguel crowned his marvellous five-year run with his solo break to Liège, followed in vain by a peloton of disconcerted, frightened and defeated men: 'Give me your calm, give me your fury.'

Because it was from that mixture of calm and fury, of tempered passion, that his glory and our happiness were born. In France we would never again be so happy. We still got excited in Colombia when Olano triumphed in the World Championships, and Miguel protected him like a wounded animal guards her favourite cub. Then Olano would say: 'I'll always remember how Induráin hugged me moments before we went up onto the podium in Diutama. I suddenly found myself there with him and he hugged me. It sends a shiver up my spine whenever I speak about it.' The same will happen to us when we see pictures of Miguel in the sprint raising his right hand as he bites his lower lip. Because he was second.

Perhaps being second would have ended up being his habitual destiny, as it became for Merckx, Hinault, and Anquetil. And Coppi, who was as great as any of them but, who in his last Giro had pleaded with the other riders: '*Per favore, per favore*' whenever they upped the pace on a climb. It was very sad. Induráin had already put in too many superhuman efforts. The glorious day in Bordeaux, to take the hour record. And all the big stages in each and every Tour. And the Giros, even those he didn't win. So many races, although the Vuelta a España was still missing from his palmarés. Confirming, on one occasion, that Miguel would again be missing from the event, the president of Unipublic – the organisers of the Vuelta – commented: 'Spain grows oranges and exports them to France, and here in Spain we have to make do with mandarins.' Perhaps nothing is said in vain, but I continue to count myself among those who, like Benito Muñoz of *El Mundo*, believe and will continue to believe that the passion is in France. The Tour is today's *Iliad*.

Second place. Miguel didn't like that possibility. As in Larrau or the Lakes of Covadonga. And it was now impossible for him to contemplate it. After the intoxication of the fifth Tour, the author Manolo Vázquez Montalbán again so perceptibly noted: 'What is going to happen the day he doesn't win? And above all, what is going to happen to us? For the last five years Spaniards have depended, for balance of body and soul, on the Tour. The Tour has emerged as a single stage with Induráin always out in front. He has assumed everything which our collective hope has lost. He has been the motor towards modernity, the lever for change. Anyone who says otherwise is talking nonsense.' It would be little more than a year later that we would learn that Induráin was retiring, and then the dazzling pen of Jorge Valdano, Real Madrid's Director, would give the following explanation: 'From now on our summers are going to be disastrous.' In a certain sense they were.

A year was ending which strangely had been Induráin's best, but we couldn't have imagined what was going to happen next. Miguel belonged, as Nietzsche wrote, to the kindest and most serene class of men: 'They dominate, not because they want to, but because they exist. It is not lawful for them to come second.'

Grand Finale

(The Rain)

NOTHING WILL EVER BE THE SAME AGAIN

Miguel's failure to win the sixth Tour no doubt accelerated his decision to retire. As the Luz Casal song goes: 'And even if there is an end, nothing will ever be the same again.'

Indeed, after that disastrous Tour which did bring an end to his glorious reign, nothing would be the same again, not for us or for Miguel. He himself said as much, in what was like a terse epitaph, after that prologue against the clock in the Dutch town of 's-Hertogenbosch. It had rained during the preceding days; it rained during the prologue; and on the first day there was yet more rain. Induráin was getting out of the Banesto bus and a group of journalists, with the French TV cameras at the front, asked him how he thought the Tour would go. Miguel didn't want to talk, and he carried on walking with his bag slung over his shoulder. Someone asked him why he didn't speak a bit more French. Although he carried on walking, Induráin turned to the questioner, pointed upwards and declared curtly: '*La pluie.*' The rain.

He smiled again, but it had been deliberate, a fateful judgement as to what the coming days were to bring. Just *la pluie*. That was all. What more was there to say?

I know that every afternoon, in my article for *El Mundo*, before the disaster of Les Arcs, I was seeing what perhaps wasn't there, and I didn't want to see the huge storm that was looming over us every day. I thought that the skies, which now and again showed a timid patch of blue sky in the midst of that solid curtain of water, had something of Vermeer about them, with their violet, burgundy, and yellowish tones. They were magical skies in a land of friendly people, no doubt friendlier than the French were in general, but every time you breathed, steam came out of your mouth. The rain formed pools. That invisible, off-white mass was everywhere. You could taste it, though you couldn't grasp it with your bare hands. It would be the opponent that would destroy Miguel. Just as Echávarri had poetically suggested, an opponent twice as dangerous because it didn't have a number on its back – *La pluie*.

When Induráin was a boy he struggled to come to terms with riding in sunny conditions and, contrary to what might have been expected, it was in difficult conditions where he shone. As time passed, this was completely reversed. Because of the muscle mass he had acquired, the rain and damp became his worst enemies. It is worth recalling an interview published in France shortly after his fifth and final Tour win: he was asked by a journalist when was the last time he had got angry. 'Angry? Well, just before the Guzet-Neige stage, with that terrible weather we had. I didn't want to get out of bed.' That day it had been raining and there'd been thick fog in the Pyrenees. 'You mean you got angry because of the weather?' the journalist pressed. But Induráin quickly put the record straight: 'Oh, only for five minutes or so. Then I calmed down. Anyway, I didn't have any choice, I had to get up.'

Strange though this was, it was really more symptomatic. Miguel had had rainy days in every one of his victorious Tours, but the memory of that morning in Guzet-Neige still bugged him, in the cold light of day. His obsession and his worry were clear.

In the '91 Tour he almost fell off his saddle during a terrific downpour going up Joux-Plane. In '92, it only rained a little, on and off, during one small mountain stage. In '93, there was rain on the day of the Lake Madine stage, but he was lucky enough to avoid it. In '94 it poured during the time-trial up Morzine-Avoriaz, although the Navarran had such a big advantage over his rivals by then that he could afford not to go flat out. In '95 it was Guzet-Neige. There were always specific days, negotiable hurdles. On the day it would be a case of suffering in the wet, but then he'd have a good massage and a rest, and the next day, if the weather changed, it would be a different story. Until the '96 Tour.

In 1996 the race organisers had given him two 'gifts', one more poisoned than the other. Firstly, breaking with a long-standing tradition, they were going to arrive in the mountains – Les Arcs to be precise – before the first long individual time-trial. It was a way of preventing Miguel blowing the Tour away again before they faced the first climbs. Secondly, the race organisers, always very conscious of that kind of thing, had arranged a stage to Pamplona. A 'double-edged' stage, as Eusebio Unzúe described it before the event. A good few kilometres, plenty of mountains, but the finish was almost directly in front of Induráin's house and a fair way from the last climb. It was, indeed, a gift, but an ambiguous one, a poisoned chalice. No one doubted at the time that the stage had been designed with the best of intentions, but it was also clear that, if Miguel didn't have the Tour as totally under control as on previous occasions, the proximity of Pamplona could well exert enormous added psychological pressure on him. Perhaps that was the only way to bring things to a head, to force him into the kind of risky manoeuvre he would normally shun. For example, it might encourage him to go for the stage when it finished so close to his village and his house. The Tour people knew full well what could happen when Miguel vented his anger: the Mortirolo in the 1994 Giro, or the pursuit of Chiappucci towards Sestrière in the '92 Tour.

In the end, it was to make little odds, since Miguel would arrive in Pamplona in very bad shape, anyway. He did well even to finish the stage. But, if the organisers had kept things as normal, putting a long, flat time-trial of 40 or 50 kilometres before the mountain stages, I think it might have made some difference. But only *some* difference, because what happened would have happened anyway. It was written in the runes. It was a complex accumulation of circumstances which, one by one, came together and mounted up around one fact: Miguel was not well. That was something nobody and nothing could alter. What has, perhaps, never been clarified was Miguel's fitness coming into the Tour. Hardly anyone has any real doubts about his condition, although there are some who feel he was suffering from having ridden too many races, and was not in as good a physical shape as he usually was in the summer: his thighs were certainly broad enough, but the rest of his body was too thin. The fact is that Induráin cracked owing to the weather conditions of the first hellish week of the Tour. *La pluie.*

Months after the French Tour I happened across a few photos of the race, taken on one of those rainy days, and I was stunned.

In one of them you could see, in the foreground, the whole group of favourites, clustered together in the driving rain. Some wore raincoats, others didn't. Miguel was in the middle, well wrapped up in his raincoat and helmet (which he'd never previously worn in France, nor in such weather conditions), but the expression on his face was unforgettable. His face was contracted in a grin which could well have meant: 'What the hell am I doing here?' The expressions of his rivals were totally different. These were men who were focusing their effort, literally devouring the road with their glazed eyes. Induráin's face, on the other hand, seemed to belong to someone who had been forced, against his will, to go on one of those pointless, stomach-wrenching fairground roundabouts. Even then, before the big mountains, there was Miguel, riding as if he'd been plunged into the dizzying circles of a big wheel, which gripped his senses and was gradually crushing his muscles. That happened during the Tour but, as ever, he muffled his complaints. He didn't want to let the cat out of the bag.

Another of those photos shows a general shot of the peloton. There is Induráin, in amongst many other cyclists with their helmets, caps and raincoats. You can see in the photo that they're all struggling, but with him it's more than that: his helmet is skewed completely to the left. He looks like one of those fresh-faced leisure cyclists who buy themselves a top-quality helmet, and then don't know how to put it on. You see them, sometimes, with hugely expensive helmets which they've put on back to front. That image of Miguel, enduring the pouring rain, with his helmet awry, is something which, with hindsight, could only lead to one conclusion: even then, before the drama, Miguel was *out* of the Tour. He had still not really got into it. In fact, he was floundering around. He could see his fate coming; he was trying to study the gestures and movements, but in those conditions it was difficult and risky. You don't see him at the front, and that, too, is symptomatic.

But we need to backtrack a few months, to the beginning of the season. Or further back in time, exactly one year, to that rest day in the department of Ariège, in the village of Saint-Girons, when the Banesto team had gone through their customary drill: they'd ridden an easy 80 kilometres and then gone for a walk around the area. A lot of relatives of the Banesto team members were there. At the entrance to their hotel, dozens of young fans were hysterically shouting Miguel's name, over and over again. In the garden of the hotel, he gave a pool-side Press conference in which he said pretty much the same as he had said in similar circumstances during each of his victorious Tours. I remember I was standing just behind him, and I noticed that he had a grey hair, and that made a deep impression on me, because it was a single grey hair, on the side of his head at the back. Miguel had said just as much as he had to, to the inevitable despair of half the world's journalists gathered there, and especially the Spanish reporters, and later in the Press room, we would, as usual, have to put all the pieces together to work out exactly what it meant. But suddenly, for no reason at all, Induráin said: 'I'm tired.' I think someone also mentioned something about his physical condition. 'No, tired of all this,' declared the Navarran. I stared again at that single grey hair, which was like a cliché in the middle of his uniformly short, thick black hair. But perhaps that was more than just one grey hair and a cliché. For the first time in all those years Miguel admitted he was tired, and it seemed clear he was referring to his state of mind, that he was also feeling the heavy burden of pressure. Having to go through with Press conferences like that one, for example, which were quite superfluous since we all knew what was going to be said, and what would be left unsaid.

However, nobody knew then that the following day, at that very hour, Fabio Casartelli would be killed descending the Portet d'Aspet, which in the distant past had seen unforgettable triumphs for our legendary climbers – Bahamontes, Julio Jiménez and Fuente. I can imagine Miguel's thoughts after what happened to Casartelli and his conversations on the phone to Marisa and his family. I can think of that 'I'm tired,' and that other, unspoken 'I'm risking my life every time I go out training and in every race.' And: 'If I've already won everything, why should I force the machine more? Why should I take a risk?'

That was a year earlier, but it had undoubtedly left its trace. Then, in 1996, there were to be some new surprises, in some cases just minor concerns, mostly little internal 'domestic' matters which never became public. Yet, they were pulsing away inside the Banesto team. To start with, after one or two 'differences of opinion' following Miguel's trip to Colombia and the failed attempt on the hour record, his personal doctor, Sabino Padilla, announced he was leaving his post with the team to work with Athletic Bilbao football club.* He would still look after Miguel Induráin (and the marathon runner Martín Fiz, as well as other athletes of his choosing) but he was leaving Banesto. The new team doctor was Iñaki Arratíbel, who had previously looked after Olano. The situation, perhaps, seemed rather confusing, and a likely source of conflict. Two doctors for the same champion – the official team doctor and his own personal doctor. Apparently Induráin took Padilla along to some races, paying his hotel expenses and even a whole month's stay in France out of his own pocket. Bizarre. And Arratíbel gave everyone a scare in mid May when he said that Induráin was still 'around four kilos overweight'. Just as well that Eusebio Unzúe promptly played his usual mediator's role and gave a more upbeat and kindlier spin to the situation: 'Miguel is 85-per-cent fit.' It was a matter of how you looked at it, and at the figures. In the end, they were more or less the same as every year. So there were certain doubts, uncertainties, fuzzy areas. Sometimes he looked heavier. At other times he seemed lighter, and less powerful. Nerves were fraying before the Tour, despite him already having five in the bag.

For Miguel the Tour was still his garden. That is how he once described it. The first was magical, and the second and third were bagged because he just kept on winning. That was what he was there for. But the fourth brought the following strange comment: 'The '94 Tour came down to experience. I arrived there, knowing it like the back of my hand – the rhythm of the event, the Press conferences, the race organisation, the other riders, everything. It was like being in the garden at home.'

Deep down, part of his heart had remained there, in Villava, amongst the geraniums and the other flowers at number 2, San Andrés Street. Nor had he left his comfortable house in Olatz. The flowers speak, and sometimes they say more than people do. Whatever the case, the flowers do not lie, and neither do the crops.

---

* Induráin had stayed on in Colombia after the World Championships to make an attempt to regain the hour record. The attempt failed when, after 31 kilometres, Induráin found himself behind schedule.

If you take care of them, and the heavens don't ruin them for you, you can reap that harvest. That is your reward. But the heavens would ruin it in '96.

On one occasion Miguel told me that stages like Sestrière in '92 were way too far: 'There comes a moment when you don't take things in any more; you don't know where you're going, or who you are. People are touching you and shoving you, and you carry on; you scarcely know what you're doing.'

On the road, Induráin rarely lost his identity in that way, fortunately, although the times he did do so were all crazily unique and gave rise to a lot of debate. Around ten million Spaniards would hold their breath as they saw him on the point of cracking, say, but that collective gesture was always performed with boundless admiration. The fact that it happened so rarely meant we were spoilt, which is why, when it really did happen, we were stunned. Whenever we saw Miguel dip into that inexhaustible source of calm strength, it was difficult to imagine that he knew how to suffer better than anyone. His subtle and modest language would unerringly give a more neutral and reserved view of the situation – it didn't seem any big deal. It was just part of his private life, even though chapters from that private life were witnessed by ten million people. 'You go not knowing who you are, but you go.'

Every year he would sow for the harvest of the Tour. And that's how 1996 began. He started with a gentle Tour of Majorca and then the Almeria Classic. Flu caused him to retire from the Ruta del Sol and he couldn't go to the Luis Puig Trophy, either. The following weeks saw the Tour of Murcia, the Catalan Week and the Milan–San Remo, the Estella Trophy and the Amorebieta Grand Prix. In the Tour of Aragon he started to take the reins of the peloton for a while.

At the same time, another 'war' was breaking out in certain sections of the French media, which saw Laurent Jalabert wiping the board in the events he took part in, including the Paris–Nice. Meanwhile the Spanish media seemed to be focusing on the ridiculous quarrel between the Banesto team (that is, Induráin) and ONCE, without doubt the most powerful squad in the world at the time. Everybody remembered all too well the stage to Mende in the previous Tour, where, for a few moments, they had Miguel on the ropes for some time. In France, Laurent was not only being pushed as the alternative number-one rival to Miguel, he was even being talked up as a possible overall winner of the Tour. Incredible. We could recycle old Obelix's words about the Romans to describe the French: 'These French are mad.' Anyway, the whole thing had to be taken in good humour, as Miguel did. None the less, it is true that, as the weeks passed with the ONCE machine sweeping everything before it, and Laurent Jalabert their main dagger, concern did suddenly spread among many in Spain. It was instinctive, but we were making a huge mistake in letting ourselves get worked up in this way.

Induráin went to the Amstel Gold Race. He was not content just to cruise along (which in the Classics is impossible, anyway, since you have to ride at such breath-taking speed), and he made something of a showing a few times. In the Tour of Alentejo, in Portugal, he began to press the pedals. He won two stages and the overall classification, but that event would be remembered by the Portuguese as the 'Race of the two Induráins', since Pruden won another two stages and was second overall. In an article about him in *El Mundo* I called him affectionately 'Van der Pruden': it was a tribute to a great rider, of huge potential and class, who always managed to be where he was needed. He put that role above his own interests and, of course, above the opportunities he would have had to win a whole string of races, if he'd decided to go for them.

In the Tour of Asturias Induráin seemed to be back to his old self, with his historic climbs of the Acebo, as tough a mountain as any. He obliterated everybody in the time-trial up the Naranco, and had hardly any problems in the high mountains. Strange that the Asturian mountains, which had been so cruel to him in each and every one of the Tours of Spain he'd participated in, should have surrendered to him in the local race. Meanwhile, Olano was winning in the Tour of Romandy, and he almost caused a stir in the Giro, where he went through a similar torture to the one Miguel suffered in '94. The Mortirolo did for him, together with that long drag up to the finish at Aprica. In the meantime, in Spain, the Induráin–ONCE battle was developing. In the Bicicleta Vasca, things got out of hand. In fact, that vibrant event came down to a spectacular duel between the yellow ONCE riders and Miguel, who decided to go on the attack in the third stage and really turn the screw on the rest of the field. Still surrounded by the yellow hornets, he blew the race apart, and the fifth stage on the tough slopes of the Arrate, with Zülle stuck to his wheel, saw one of those moments when cycling becomes the cream of sports. A majestic Miguel Induráin left the Swiss for dead, as he sped to victory in fine style.

Although we all breathed more calmly after the Bicicleta Vasca, having seen the Navarran's body getting back to its normal condition, the Classique des Alpes was to give us a new scare on the road to Chambéry. Successive and persistent attacks from all ONCE's heavy artillery tested not only Miguel, who was physically unable to respond to such constant pressure, but also the Banesto team as a whole. And that seemed more serious. As a group they could not compete with their rivals, not by a long chalk. Despite the great individuals they possessed, man for man there was nothing they could do. In the Banesto team, everything rested on the legs and heart of Miguel. Eventually, around Aix-les-Bains, he let Jalabert go and the crowd went wild. They forgave him everything except that he was in a Spanish team, spoke Spanish fluently and had only praise for Spain. The impression we were left with when we saw a resigned Induráin facing the fifth or sixth attack from the hornets, and Jalabert going clear so easily, was not exactly pleasant. In all probability, since the Tour was his objective, the calendar of events was progressing satisfactorily enough, despite the slight modifications there had been compared to previous years.

But Miguel was ready once again to put things right, to put each rival in his place, and to show the watching crowd he was still in charge of the international peloton. That was how he arrived at the Dauphiné Libéré, which has always been considered the last and most important warm-up event before the Tour.

As far as his rivals were concerned, Rominger didn't seem to be in his best shape, although he was slowly getting into form. No one knew much about Riis, except that he was obsessed with the Tour, and convinced he could win it. Apparently, on a very steep slope in the Tour of Switzerland, the Dane had got off his bike and walked the last few metres to the line, to the laughter and jeering of the crowd. No one knows for sure if that was because he didn't have the right gear ratio or because he had simply decided not to overstrain his body's engine. Cycling moves in mysterious ways. Ugrumov (already a late-starter in the professional ranks) was now getting on a bit, and although Leblanc, Dufaux and Virenque seemed to be showing their normal fire, in truth it was really no more than a harmless firework display: they were all good *grimpeurs* but not one of them had the ability to do damage in a Tour, and certainly not to hurt Miguel, who for years had led them up the slopes like little lap-dogs. At the moment of truth they weren't going to make things happen. All the same, the Dauphiné was an event of crucial importance: above all, it would test the strength of Jalabert and his ONCE praetorian guard.

Right at the start, Miguel triumphed in the time-trial, but the French were still exultant, especially when, on Mont Ventoux, they saw Jalabert, supported by Virenque's attacks, again dropping Induráin. Although Miguel didn't, at any point, lose his composure, he was almost a minute behind at the summit, and once more concern spread amongst certain elements in the specialist Press. The stage to the Izoard, on the way to Briançon, had a knee-quaking summit finish like a cliff face – although not very long it has slopes of up to 20 per cent. It was going to be, perhaps, Induráin's final demonstration of power on a bicycle. Much more so, without a shadow of a doubt, than the Atlanta time-trial.

He attacked relentlessly on the Izoard and passed the Casse Déserte in the manner demanded by the moral code of the great champions – out on his own. Then, on the descent, it was a tug of war with the strung-out line of other riders. It wasn't in his interest to solo the whole way. Halfway up the Izoard, the French idol Jalabert cracked, which really put the whole nation's noses out of joint. He cracked so badly he had to climb off his bike and retire into the team car – they had to 'keep him back' for the Tour. This was something Manolo Saiz had not counted on. Although cannier than most when it came to cycling strategy, Manolo must have half forgotten what it meant to have Induráin away up the road and in an attacking frame of mind. On the slopes of the Bastille, the Navarran flew past Laurent Madouas, the fine climber who could already see the trophy within his grasp.

It is said that Miguel decided to use a triple chainset that day, with a 36 inside ring. A similar tactic had been adopted years before by a group of Italian cyclists, including Giovanni Battaglin, to get through the worst of the Dolomites; bearing in mind the final hurdle on the way to Briançon, Miguel opted a 53/41/36 triple, apparently. But that 'apparently' is all part of the legend, too. His mechanic, Carlos Vidales, would know for sure, just as there are so many things that only his long-term masseurs would know. As far as *Le Parisien* was concerned, after the Dauphiné Libéré the Navarran continued to be the undoubted boss of the international peloton, and *L'Équipe*, who were normally so sparing with their praise, declared: 'Still God and Master.' As you can see, eventually even the French took on board the religious symbolism of Induráin's divine aura. Better late than never.

Nevertheless, more with an eye on the publicity benefits than because they really believed it, they kept hyping the Tour as the great duel between Induráin and Jalabert. They even dared to publish surveys putting the two rivals neck and neck. 'Who do you think will win the next Tour?' was the question.

In interviews shortly before the start of the Tour de France, Induráin mentioned a long list of possible close rivals and, out of decency and respect he tried not to leave anyone out; even Gianni Bugno's name slipped in once or twice. He was showing what a gentleman he was, which is rare enough these days. As the Tour approached he seemed more enthusiastic, although still not as eager for the start of the race as he appeared to have been the previous year. Months earlier he'd made some comments which, reading between the lines, had provided food for thought. 'I haven't decided whether I'll put away the bike at the end of the season,' he'd said. 'It depends on how the campaign goes. If I think I'm not riding well and things aren't going as planned, then I'll quit.' But few people paid attention to those words.

He who gives forewarning is no traitor, so the saying goes, and Miguel rarely went back on anything he'd previously said in public, or on any firm decision once he'd taken it. It was not a question of money, just as I don't think it was when he did make up his mind to retire, because he has a very clear philosophy about money: 'The amount you need depends on the kind of life you lead. For the life I lead, I've already got more than enough.'

There were high expectations in the days before the Tour set off from the unpronounceable town of 's-Hertogenbosch. In training, the Banesto team had done a more or less complete dummy run of the whole route of the Pamplona stage. And on one particular day, little more than a week before the Tour, Miguel and several of his team-mates had put in another marathon stint, but when the rest of the team finished training for the day, Induráin decided to continue on his own and cycle back to Pamplona. A total of almost 280 kilometres. The question remains: weren't these distances excessive in the run-up to the Tour? Was Miguel concerned that, in spite of his marvellous performances in the recent Dauphiné Libéré, he still hadn't done enough preparation, that his legs still needed more kilometres? Perhaps.

The routes he followed, accompanied by Pruden, in the days before the Tour were through all the usual places he knew and loved so much: Campanas, Cizur, Ororbia, Zunzarren, Esparza, the inevitable Erro mountain pass, which Miguel must have climbed hundreds of times.

Seeing the magazine photos of the champion's final marathon training session, riding the whole of that last section on his own, you couldn't help asking yourself whether, in fact, he had actually done it *alone*. In the photos, taken from various different angles, there didn't seem to be any support car behind him. Furthermore, in the same photos you could see Miguel with his tyre pump and a spare tub on his bike, just like a cyclotourist – why would he have had to carry more weight than necessary if he had been accompanied by a support car? Yet, it's unbelievable, if that is really what happened, and I confess I nearly fell off my seat when I saw those photos. I still think that a five-times winner of the Tour de France shouldn't be left to train on his own for a single kilometre on those roads.

It's just as well that good people have a good angel guarding them. But the angel sometimes gets distracted and closes its eyes for a moment, and then a tragedy occurs, as happened to Antonio Martín.

Induráin didn't seem happy in the run-up to the Tour, but he didn't appear worried either, although maybe less talkative than in the two previous Tours. What could have been the reason? It is impossible to be sure. But, seeing him prowling about, dodging the throng swirling around him in a fierce maelstrom on the eve of the prologue near 's-Hertogenbosch, I recalled his 'I'm tired' comment of a year before in the hotel at Saint-Girons. I admit I felt a degree of apprehension. Something was missing. I remembered that sunny day in the '95 Tour beside the pool, but on the other side from the dozens of cameras of the world's media, when I witnessed another scene that made an impression on me: in fact, it was a two-part scene, and both starred French Banesto riders. In one corner was Gérard Rué, who had worked phenomenally hard helping Miguel down from the dangerous Cormet de Roselend to reduce Zülle's advantage. And then he had led him up some five kilometres of La Plagne. He was speaking to a French journalist, who must have been trying to get a solid (and preferably controversial) story out of the loyal Rué. The Banesto cyclist simply repeated, in his own language, naturally: 'He's a great guy, you know? Really great. A good, down-to-earth guy who's grateful for what you do.'

I then recalled an anecdote from Induráin's second Giro win where Rué was chief *domestique*. He hadn't been in the first Giro, although another generous French battler, Fabrice Philipot, had. It was getting towards the end of the race and that night Rué was apparently a bit down. He'd started thinking how hard it was to be the *domestique* of a top rider who was always under attack, who always remained silent, who hardly ever spoke to his own team-mates, but for whom you sacrificed everything.

At that very moment there was a knock at the door of his room. It was late at night. Who on earth could it be? He was flabbergasted to find it was Miguel with a *maglia rossa* in his hand. He looked serious as he stood outside the door. Rué asked if there was anything wrong. 'I don't say much, you know that,' Induráin said to him, 'but this is for you, because you deserve it more than anyone. Here, it's yours.' Rué accepted it. He was so moved he found it hard to hide his emotion. However discreet or sparing with words of thanks Induráin might be, with that gesture he had won the confidence and affection of that great rider, for ever. Even Aitor David and the other founder members of the Induráin supporters club in Villava, in the packed 'Jaizki' bar, complained light-heartedly that Miguel never bothered to mention them in public! But he did show his appreciation, as when he gave away his jerseys or attended the annual meeting with the members or the club's young riders. Ultimately, things like that really matter.

Speaking of the clear and obvious differences between two leaders such as Pedro Delgado and Miguel Induráin, Jean-François Bernard said that Perico would always be the last to arrive at the dinner table in the evening (during the day cyclists eat on the road) and there would often be a lot of banter. 'With Miguel, on the other hand, he could be sitting right next to you for quite a while, eating away, and you still wouldn't have noticed he was there.'

The other detail that made an impression on me in that hotel in Saint-Girons, in July '95, was when I saw the Banesto rider Thomas Davy, along with his girlfriend and his parents, sitting a few seats away from where the leader was talking to the Press. Davy was considered to be one of the most promising young cyclists in France. He was the man, riding then for Castorama, who'd refused to allow Tony Rominger to get past him in the Bergerac time-trial during the '94 Tour. And he was the man who, though some way down the leader-board in the overall classification, fought out a stage place on Val-Thorens in a titanic elbow-to-elbow struggle with Bortolami. That was the other face of cycling, which the cameras never show. Younger or veteran cyclists trying to earn their crust and straining to the absolute limit to come home before their rivals, who are generally men of similar calibre. Davy had refused offers from other French teams and had come to Banesto to be close to the Lord of the Tour. His mission was to accompany him on the flat and the small mountains. I shall never forget the captivated look on the faces of a track-suited Thomas Davy, and his girlfriend, as they watched Miguel. It was as if they had just seen a ghost. Both had a blissful smile on their lips and were speechless. For a man like Davy, it was an honour to defend Induráin, even though he was in a Spanish team. Thomas Davy also made a coded remark about that 'special' feeling which sometimes came over him when he was with Miguel: 'Something emanates from his presence, something you can't put your finger on but which relaxes you and makes you feel happy with yourself.' Davy recalled excitedly how, immediately after the team time-trial between Mayenne and Alençon, when the members of the Banesto team least expected it, Miguel went round shaking his men's hands one by one, thanking them for their efforts. That day men such as Rué, Aparicio and Arrieta had found it tough to live with the pace, while others such as Pruden, Alonso and Davy, himself, had had to give it their all. Davy recalled that, whenever Induráin went to the front, he cracked the whip hard and they struggled to hold on to his wheel as he shouted encouragement at them. That gesture of going up to each of his men in Alençon was a particularly special moment for Thomas Davy.

A year later, however, it would be a very different story. The 's-Hertogenbosch prologue started in the rain, and that would set the tone for the race. The riders set off with the memory still fresh of the crashes that had occurred in the same stage the previous year. Zülle, who almost smacked into the barriers a couple of times, rode those nine waterlogged kilometres at almost 52 kilometres an hour. Induráin was more conservative on the corners, as was to be expected, and came home with the seventh-best time, twelve seconds behind the Swiss. Zülle dedicated his triumph to the late Mariano Rojas, who'd had an excellent Tour the previous year but who had recently died in a car accident. That day some claimed Miguel's pedal rate looked extremely slow – twelve seconds was a big gap – but you needed to know what the circuit was like to have an idea of how dangerous it was. Chris Boardman had bid goodbye to the previous Tour when he was scarcely out of the blocks on a similarly filthy day in Saint-Brieuc.

An incident which will stay with me for ever took place that afternoon, when we took a wrong turning and had to make our way to the Press room along the actual stage circuit, just a few minutes before the first rider set off. By then the road was blocked to vehicles, including official cars, but the three of us in El Mundo's official Fiat still drove through, and the Dutch police didn't know what to do with us. By that point it was useless, and dangerous even, to tell us to turn back. Where were we to go anyway? Their only option was to gesture animatedly at us to get to the finish line as quickly as possible. It's a very different story with the French gendarmes, because they normally stick to their strict and inflexible orders and they don't care what kind of mess might ensue. It was exciting and unforgettable to travel through that narrow corridor of thousands of people watching us and expecting to see a car accompanying the riders. The impression made by that vociferous crowd, gesticulating and putting their hands out in front of you, was unreal. 'This is exactly what the cyclists must see in a time-trial on a narrow urban circuit,' I thought excitedly. Thousands of hands and arms were touching the bodywork of the car, and the shouting was incessant. The cyclists set off from a gaudy sports hall called Brabanthalen, and they had only a few straights in which to accelerate to top speed safely. On the tightest bends on the circuit, before the Grobbendonklaan, which led to Van Veldekekade Avenue, and especially at the bend between a roundabout and the Koningsweg, the people seemed to be even more on top of you. We reached the Press room, in the Kempenhal, an annexe to the main hall. Just for a change it was cold. We were getting heartily fed up with the wet – journalists, too, have to work against the clock. Eventually (after a lot of difficulty) we managed to complete our reports, but the worrying feeling we had in our bones was that it was too cold and too wet.

The same scenario would be repeated the next day on a route which passed through the 's-Hertogenbosch area: 120 roundabouts where you had to slow the pace (which, despite the rain, was always quick), as well as 500 points termed 'difficult' by the race organisers, meant that it was a tough day. Carmelo Miranda crashed on several occasions. The next day, on the way to Wasquehal, the same thing happened. Then, *en route* to Nogent-sur-Noise, it was the same story. Belgium was left behind, but the wet weather continued unabated. There were areas that seemed flat on the route map but which were full of horrible speed-bumps on the road. At the finish, the riders offered their usual bland comments. The favourites were watching each other, but the 170 men who weren't favourites had the chance of their lives. That's why, whatever the conditions, they seemed hell-bent on stirring the race up. That's what makes the Tour the Tour, because a single victory in one of its stages means your name will be recorded in capital letters in the Golden Book of Cycling History.

But *something* was going awry in all the riders' bodies. The photos of Induráin with his raincoat and his twisted helmet prove it. While some could cope with the permanent mud and cold-water bath, something else was happening to others, including Miguel, and it was clearly something bad. The arrival at Lake Madine saw a crash involving several riders. Photos show how Bjarne Riis avoided Jan Svorada, who had fallen just in front of him, by millimetres. Riis even had to unclip his foot from the pedal, and wobbled as he tried to hold his balance. Fate ...

There was just one stage to go before the Alps. Just one. Everybody was on edge, all due to the weather – some of the Press rooms had turned into virtual water-ski runs. But between Arc-et-Senans and Aix-les-Bains things became really unbearable, and at the end of the stage no one was hiding their concern. 'The rain and cold are the same for everyone,' was the general comment among all the Spanish journalists. Wrong. The rain and cold don't have the same effect on all bodies, and we all knew that Induráin's was especially vulnerable to such elements. The words of Echávarri, the Banesto *directeur sportif*, at the end of that day were prophetic and revealing: 'It was like something out of Dante. It's been prejudicial to all the riders, but has been especially damaging to those who have the most to lose, obviously.' That was clear. Never, in several Tour victories and in the many other races in which he'd taken part with various degrees of success, had Echávarri been heard to say anything like that. And at the finish in Aix-les-Bains he would add: 'Let's hope our boys recuperate. First they'll have a shower, then a quick massage and after that they'll wrap up warm. Even then, we'll have to see if we've got more than one left standing after a day like today.'

The following stage was to be Les Arcs, a graveyard for our hopes. And what is there to add which hasn't already been said about that day, what with all the speculation that went on at the time, sometimes in good faith and sometimes malicious? That day changed many people's lives, and really it all happened far too quickly, and bizarrely. But above all – and this is also part of the legend that will be forever tied to the myth of Induráin – it was inexplicable. Just as, in a positive sense, the way he exploded into the '91 Tour in the Pyrenees was inexplicable. Yes, Miguel had been warning us for years. Yes, you could see it coming. But no one, not even his own trainers, could have imagined the kind of performances he produced that year *en route* to Val-Louron, or on Alpe d'Huez, or in the time-trial to Mâcon. They, too, were essentially incomprehensible: they simply happened. Something similar, but unfortunate, was going to happen on Les Arcs. It has been widely stated that this was one of the most brutal, inhumane and illogical stages in Tour history. It was only a stage like that which was capable of causing Induráin to crack. If, up until then, he had been the Lord of the French Tour, it was precisely because he had controlled everything, because each of his Tour wins had been an ode to logic, tinged with unexpected strokes of genius. He still controlled everything, as he always did, except for what was inexplicably happening inside his body. The cold, the damp and the wet, which had brought him life and glory, were now to turn against him and betray him in a single moment and in the space of no more than a 100 metres.

It was especially painful not just because of how it happened, but also because of when: the eve of the famous San Fermín fiesta in Pamplona, with the whole of Navarre decked out, and Spain glued to the television. A Saturday at peak viewing time. And on everyone's lips: 'When will Induráin attack?'

The stage started strongly. I remember we were already at Les Arcs, along with the majority of the accredited journalists, and the riders were climbing the Col de la Madeleine. Suddenly, in a bar where I had gone to get some sandwiches, there was a rather angry murmur: Jalabert was feeling the pressure building up, and was about to crack. Induráin and his men, particularly José María Jiménez, were controlling the front of the race. They had already seen the Frenchman drop off the back, and they upped the pace. One big rival less to worry about. Jalabert's agony, which lasted the whole stage, would have made all the headlines and would have been a talking point for several years, but for the events that were about to unfold. The favourites were preparing to tackle the Col de Méraillet, which, after a short, flattish stretch, led into the Cormet de Roselend, where years before Iñaki Gastón had suffered his dramatic fall. Riis had sent Udo Bolts, the 'climber' in the Telekom team, on ahead just to see what would happen, and he himself made a move to jump off the front, to see how the favourites would respond. And they reacted as expected, leaping on him like a pack of hungry wolves. For the moment they would remain as a group.

Further back, there was another dramatic scene: the abandonment of the current leader of the Tour, Gan's Stéphane Heulot, a Frenchman who years before had been a Banesto rider. He dismounted amid sobs and tears. Ankle problems were mentioned, but it seemed clear that Heulot had reached his limit in a bid to hold on to the *maillot jaune*. The merciless and cannibalistic Tour continued to decimate the field, paying no heed to nationality, status or name. What with the fate of Heulot and Jalabert, France seemed to be plunged into an early state of mourning.

By the time they went over the top of the Cormet de Roselend, Induráin had been left with no support. Rominger had Olano and Ginés; Riis had Ullrich and Bolts; Zülle had Aitor Garmendia. This was the Banesto team's huge tactical error, and the same thing would happen on Hautacam, Larrau and all the other mountains in that race, even on the crazy, short, 50-kilometre stage to Sestrière. Ugrumov, Leblanc, Escartín, Virenque and Luttenberger were without their lieutenants, just as Miguel was, but the role played by Ullrich, Olano and Garmendia, those three *domestiques de luxe* would turn the Tour on its head. They would change the course of history by forcing an unrelenting pace. Banesto, however, had no support near Miguel. It's not going to change anything, now, but we're talking about a top-flight team with a huge budget, the team with the best cyclist in the world, who, they hoped, would win the event that year. But was he supposed to win it on his own? Even more on his own than ever before? That was a massive blunder. It could be argued that when a leader cracks, there's nothing that can be done about it, and in part that's true, but only in part. Sometimes the difference can be between cracking desperately and irretrievably and losing huge chunks of time, or getting on to a friendly wheel which gradually leads you back up. That's an enormous difference, which any rational person can understand. If there's any doubt about it, look at what Aitor Garmendia did for Zülle who, up till then, had seemed to be going backwards: he carried and almost dragged him up, enabling the Swiss rider to come from behind Induráin – who by then had really cracked – to take a minute off him by the finish. The finish which was right there, within sight, but at the same time so unreachable.

It is strange that in the '95 Tour it was one of Induráin's former *domestiques*, Mauri, who put him on the ropes on Mende. Now it was going to be another former *domestique*, Garmendia.

It is very difficult to know if Banesto's failure was in the preparation, or in their choice of men. Either way, the circumstances were as they were, and now that time has passed and we can make a frank and constructive assessment. At the very least, something should have been done differently to mitigate possible damage. I will repeat what I have said before: even taking into account the way Induráin cracked, trying to recover one and a half, or two minutes with half the Tour still remaining is a very different proposition from practically throwing in the towel at the first sign of trouble by haemorrhaging four minutes to each and every one of the favourites. That was the most painful thing.

Things started to go haywire on the summit of the Cormet de Roselend itself. The descent, with a slippery road surface and the riders showing clear signs of being a bit punch-drunk, had everyone's hearts in their mouths. We saw cyclists risking their lives at each curve: we saw Rominger coming off, and recovering with some difficulty, thanks to Olano who was there to help him, and also Fernández Ginés, who would do exceptional work on the false flat up to the bottom of Les Arcs; we saw Bruyneel crash on a bend and fly off into a gorge out of view of the cameras; we saw Alex Zülle, with his eternal sight problems, and presumably with his glasses steamed up, rolling over and over on the ground and ending up in thickets, from which he emerged like a startled ferret. He looked as if he had no idea where he was, but there was Aitor Garmendia patiently waiting for him, and ready to lead him back to a group that had taken more than a minute out of him. And this was how they reached the foot of Les Arcs, a cursed mountain in the history of Spanish cycling, with the Spaniard Fernández Ginés forcing the pace.

They were together and going at a reasonable pace. It was not even a special-category climb, unlike the Madeleine. Induráin had said of this pass: 'It's fifteen not particularly tough kilometres, except you've gone through hell to get there. The first time differences will appear here, and we'll see who's going well and who's not.' The average slope was 5.8 per cent and the whole climb was pretty standard, with a rise of 880 metres. Only on a couple of stretches, at kilometres 11 and 14, did the gradient reach 7 per cent. At other points, right at the foot, and at the point where the Navarran would crack worst, the gradient was no more than four per cent. A few weeks before Induráin himself had commented to the sports daily, *Marca*: 'I really don't like the Alps and the Pyrenees. They really get under your skin when you think about them. You know you're going to suffer, and how badly they'll put you through the mill.' A premonition. Although immediately afterwards he confessed to being fascinated by them: 'The scenery is spectacular, especially in the Alps,' he said.

That was the key moment, with around four kilometres to go to the top, and the pace of the stage had still not really hotted up. When the sun came out, unusually fierce it seemed that day, Miguel Induráin Larraya was watching his rivals out of the corner of his eye, ready to increase the pace and blow the race apart. Up till then his presence at the front had terrified them. The group passed La Ville, La Millerette and Le Chenal. Miguel was up there.

On a left-hand bend, you could see a TV shot taken from the *Antenne–2* helicopter: the lead group had spread out a bit, but Miguel wasn't there. He wasn't there!

Earlier, Virenque had attempted to push the pace, and Luttenberger, too, but without success. Luc Leblanc took advantage of the ultra-tight marking amongst the favourites and shot off like a bullet, changing up through the gears and not wasting any time looking over his shoulder.

They say it was the Mapei men, that Rominger saw something strange in Miguel's face and pedal rhythm, and asked Olano to accelerate.

They say Ullrich did the same when he realised Induráin seemed to be struggling for breath. In the photos taken just before that moment, Riis can be seen at the back of the leading group, in pretty bad shape. The only sure thing is that, suddenly, Miguel wasn't there any more.

They told me that, at first, Spanish TV played down the significance of what was happening in an effort to keep everyone's spirits up. Pedro González, during those bitter moments when French TV was still showing general shots from the air rather than close-ups, was no doubt hoping this was the Miguel of Oropa, voluntarily deciding against tracking any madcap wheel that tried to break clear. Perhaps he didn't notice that the pedal action we were beginning to see in other distressing pictures was identical to what we had seen in the Valley of Santa Cristina, on the way to Aprica after he had ridden his legs off on the Mortirolo. But many people did recall that pedal action, which was volatile, staccato, slow and circular, but lacking conviction.

And there was a knot in many people's throats. The *pájara*. It was a rumour that began to spread round the different channels. The French TV presenter would be the worst of the lot, at least for those of us who were in the Press room, stunned, gutted and slumped in our seats, speechless. Unable to control his excitement, he was shouting for a camera to film Induráin's face. And he carried on bellowing: '*On laisse Induráin, on laisse Induráin!*' Induráin is being dropped!

Indeed, Miguel had never been in such a state in the Tour. And, as far as you could gather from the pictures, his rivals didn't even seem to have put him under excessive pressure. He'd cracked on his own; he was sinking his lonely way into the asphalt, hemmed in by the crowd. One of the motorbike cameras managed to focus on him, and then the euphoric French television presenter went to town, because his face left no room for doubt. He was drifting on the lowest gear, as any middling cyclotourist might, and was asking for water from the other team cars which were alongside and overtaking him. Someone from the Gewiss team car handed him a small bottle. If we were to stick strictly to the religious parallel, then that ascent of Les Arcs would be the Passion, and that hand which gave the drink from the Gewiss car would be the woman who takes pity on Christ on his way to Calvary.

Our hearts sank. The French, conversely, were falling over themselves on TV to put their oar in, and the journalists were beginning to run around the Press room in desperation, seeking more information on what was happening. The Spanish, on the other hand, were like statues. The sun was shining bright. In the far distance, Mont Blanc dominated the horizon.

There was one ray of hope: Zülle, led by that locomotive, Garmendia, caught Miguel, whose head was going from side to side as he moved his upper body pitifully on the bike. The Swiss must have been affected by his two falls on the Cormet de Roselend which had happened one on top of the other. But, after tracking Zülle's wheel for a few metres, Miguel cracked again. That was it, there was no way back. It was a terrible picture, seeing Garmendia forcing the pace to stop the Navarran following his wheel, which would have reduced the damage a bit.

The French TV commentator, who wasn't much interested in what was going on up ahead, even though a Frenchman, Luc

Leblanc, was on his way to the stage win, continued to ask the motorbike cameraman to stay with the broken Miguel and to carry on filming his face. 'An historic moment,' he roared making no attempt to conceal his satisfaction. And he was right: it was an historic moment. But, while it might have been a juicy story for the journalists, the merciless focus on the Navarran champion's agony seemed very unethical, all the more so in view of the excited tone in which it was delivered. On La Millerette his agony became ours, and between Le Mont and Les Lauzeres, that way of the cross reached its climax. It was then that Miguel suffered his calvary.

At that point, which was painfully prolonged over several interminable minutes, many of us felt our blood curdle. And Induráin himself, when he reached the finish at Les Arcs, would confess, 'I had a cloud in front of my eyes.' He couldn't see anything. He didn't know who had given him the bottle of water. Everything happened – and this is the strangest point in the whole story – at the very moment Induráin was preparing to attack, to turn the screw, to thresh the harvest. Just like every year.

But the cloud appeared. Perhaps a silent emissary of the fog on Marie Blanque, which he had reached so often as the Caesar of the peloton and of the Tour, and which now, burned off by the sudden, scorching rays of the Alpine sun, spoke to Miguel: 'I'm going to cover your eyes for a while, the time has come for you to rest. Don't worry, it won't even hurt. Relax.'

It was during those never-ending moments that I was seized by two recollections. One was the way my *El Mundo* colleagues and I had yelled on the way to Besançon as we looked for somewhere to buy something to eat. It was pouring so hard the bodywork of the car had seemed as if it were about to crack open at any moment. It wasn't rain, it was hail, huge hail-stones. Although the windscreen wipers were working, it was impossible to see what was happening on the road just a few metres in front of the car. The hailstorm became more intense, and that was when we shouted: 'Oh my God, Induráin!'

It was three in the afternoon of a routine stage and the peloton was already on the road, 100 kilometres behind us. All this hail was falling on the Navarran, and had been doing so for hours on end. We had been going for a week, and you could count on the fingers of one hand the moments it had stopped raining. By expressing that thought we were giving free rein to all our worries. Something had to happen. And it did. His dreadful agony towards the finish at Les Arcs, when he, more than anyone, knew that with each clumsy movement of his legs the Tour was slipping away from him, was interminable. He even crossed the line with his foot off the pedals, a gesture of resignation.

The cloud.

Then the other recollection came to me – words Miguel had uttered to the French Press corps a while back. It's strange that the Navarran champion has expressed himself most directly to the French. The journalist asked him if it was true that he had once said: 'What's the point of climbing mountains if you then have to race down them?' There was a huge contradiction between this and his own life as a cyclist where he was constantly being forced to go up and down mountains. 'Yes,' Induráin replied gravely, 'maybe there is a philosophy of life in that strength which takes you beyond your own limits for the entertainment of others. But deep down, if you think about it, you push yourself beyond the bounds of what is reasonable in pursuit of something that is completely intangible.' The disconcerted French journalist protested: 'Intangible? But, what about winning?' 'It's symbolic,' replied Induráin, adding: 'You've given people and the fans a great spectacle, you've ridden a good stage, you've performed brilliantly, but in the evening when you're on your own, or in the morning, when you get up and think about it and say to yourself: "What have you really done?" You've climbed a mountain and then you've descended. First you climbed, and then you descended. That's all.'

That journalist, as we might imagine, couldn't credit those words. His disappointment was evident. 'But, you've won,' he suggested, in what was not just a different language from the champion's, but almost a different way of speaking, a different code. Miguel reaffirmed his impressions: 'That's true, at the end of the day you've won. You've got your bouquet of flowers, but you haven't actually achieved anything concrete. You haven't, for instance, made anything with your own hands, like a piece of furniture or something.'

Was Miguel Induráin playing down the value of obsessively

climbing and descending mountains, of winning mythical and inhuman stages, of being or ceasing to be an idol, of pedalling in what, ultimately, is a sincere attempt to offer other people a great spectacle? No, he wasn't. But he was playing down its overwhelming importance. And when I saw him crack on Les Arcs, I thought: 'Deep down, very deep down, despite the passion we feel for cycling, the question basically comes down to little more than this: now you climb a mountain, now you descend – over and over again.'

There was something senseless in it all and, yet, I told myself, Miguel's basic thoughts remained the same: to work and sow with a specific end in mind, whether it was repairing the tractor, or watching over the crops, or collecting bottles for Nekane, or longed-for triumphs for Spanish sport. Induráin, in his meditations from his Mount Olympus, had arrived at the pure essence of the matter by the route of simplicity. He had got there through the humble road of his country spirit, while his noble theory of pain was based on the pendular motion: 'First you climb a mountain and then you descend, that's true, but what lasting, tangible thing have you made with your own hands?'

Nevertheless, he was involved in the fascinating, if at times nauseating, circus of top-flight competition. The only way he could stop was suddenly, and that would cause a collective spasm and then a chain reaction. And even then he would have to continue the cover-up: 'I've had a bad day, but there's still a long way to go in the Tour.' It wasn't true. The only truth is that a string had broken in his heart; something had splintered in his soul. And the best way of putting an end to that fresh pain of letting down the millions of people who still hoped to see him at his best was to finish as quickly as possible. But he could not retire from the Tour, not from *that* Tour, whose route passed through his home region in his honour. The Lord of the Tour couldn't simply get off his bike, as for example Jalabert and others did, and get into his team car with a remark like 'It'll have to be another year.' For Miguel, there would be no other year.

He'd made a beautiful piece of furniture with his triumphs. Anyone could see that. But he didn't feel he had the strength to embark on the task of constructing another. Anyway, we had his Symphony.

The end of the world came on Les Arcs. The Spanish journalists were dejected, the foreign reporters jubilant. I saw Raymond Poulidor, with a broad smile from ear to ear, spitting out the words *'Induráin c'est fini … Foutou!'* at several Spanish former cyclists who were there as radio commentators. Induráin's finished. And the words were accompanied by obscene hand gestures: destroyed, got it? Sometimes you have to put yourself in the difficult position of the French, who had experienced many years of total domination by Miguel. Finally, after those five years of humiliating neurosis, they saw a chink of light, that *their* Tour might acquire a new dimension in the future, that there might be something new to talk about in the coming years. I saw Roche happier than I had ever seen him on any day of a Tour. He was rubbing his hands together anxiously before writing his daily piece on the stage for the Press release distributed by the *Coeur de Lion*, which gave a prize to the most combative cyclist of the day. I also saw one high-ranking individual in the Spanish sporting world who did not seem altogether depressed. It pains me to admit it, but I would swear I was not mistaken,

The town councils of the localities which host Tour finishes generally present the journalists with a red and grey striped top. It is a kind of polo shirt, and on this occasion on the front, at the level of the heart, was written 'Les Arcs.' Never in my life will I be able to put on that shirt, I admit that much. On the other hand I have been unable to give it away, or throw it away. Till now it has been deposited with some friends of mine who understand the situation. Who knows if one day I will be able to break the spell, forget my weaknesses or fanaticism, exorcise my own ghosts, and put it on if only as some kind of macabre fetish. But not to-day. Nor have I been able to watch the film of the ascent of Les Arcs, even though someone video-recorded it for me.

On that day, and at that time I was convulsed and shaking. *L'Équipe* had a headline on an inside page: '*Sire, c'est une révolution*' – the words spoken to Louis XVI when the people rose up. The idol had fallen. Although there was still a glimmer of hope, the gap that had been opened was very big. It was a gaping chasm. And every day it got wider and wider, like an infected wound which isn't given time to heal. But we stuck our heads in the sand. 'A bad day.' 'He could recover and turn the Tour on its head. Even if it isn't enough to win it, he'll give them a real shock.' It was our way of keeping going mentally.

On the time-trial climb to Val d'Isère, where Induráin might have lost another huge chunk of time, since it was clear that something was wrong with him, he only dropped a minute to the best riders. And the following day, on the blue-ribbon stage of the Tour, where they had to climb the Col de l'Iseran, the Télégraphe, the Galibier, the Montgènevre and, finally, up to Sestrière, the race organisers decided to cancel most of the route. They would only ride 40-odd kilometres, climbing straight up the Montgènevre and Sestrière: it was going to be a weird and lengthy sprint. Although most of the race cars were not allowed to pass, we were lucky enough to be able to see the Iseran and the Galibier which were lashed by snow and fearsome blizzards which buffeted the *gendarmes* like scarecrows on the different summits. That really was hell. A desolate, white hell. It is impossible to know what would have happened if the whole stage had been run. Another nightmare, perhaps. The view of many is that Induráin would possibly just have lost more time. But I don't agree; that is simply one of the possibilities. Since he knew these mountains better than anyone and had slowly begun to get to grips with the adverse weather conditions, the other possibility is that one of the favourites, who were not separated by much in the overall classification, might have cracked, as happened in the time-trial to Val d'Isère. Anything can happen over the longer distances. Miguel was well acquainted with the pulse of certain hell-or-high-water stages.

What actually happened was that Riis took everyone by surprise and started to pull away uphill. They let him go, and that was an error. Berzin, the leader at the time, flagged and within a few kilometres, as is the way of things, several of the favourites had lost time. Arriving at Sestrière we saw Induráin move to the head of the chasing group and string them out. The Navarran, driven by pride, was baring his teeth again. He turned the screw brutally. Hardly anyone was able to stay with him, and he considerably reduced the distance separating him from Riis. In the Press room we pounded the floor with our feet, and entertained some illusory hopes, which is why I shall always believe, in spite of everything, that *that* was the day when great things might have happened. I am convinced that riders like Ullrich, Luttenberger, Leblanc, maybe Olano, Rominger and even Riis himself, no matter what he did later, would have been blown away. Maybe Miguel as well – maybe. They were all ready to give it everything, and yet, in view of what subsequently happened, would it really have made much difference if the whole stage had gone ahead? The others were also running out of strength and, just like Induráin, the cold was right down into their bones, but they didn't have his experience. If that stage had been run, I think we would have known moments of anxiety or joy, but, whichever, it would have been unforgettable. We would surely have seen Miguel attack on the treacherous descent of the Iseran or the Galibier, which towards the Lauteret even had patches of ice on it. Something would have happened.

But the most reasonable course of action, from both the human and organisational point of view, was to cut the stage short, and this is what they did. Yet in view of what we did actually see, that was the one day when things might have happened. But because they didn't, from that moment onwards, something occurred which never had before: absolutely nothing. The days went by and everyone was expecting the Navarran to make a move, but he became less and less convinced of his chances and surely feared he might crack again as he had done on Les Arcs. So he rode a more conservative race. 'Others can make the moves.' His confidence was taking a dive. He was putting all his eggs in the basket of the Hautacam stage, or the stage to Pamplona. The pieces of the poisoned chalice provided by the Tour organisers began to come together, and even make coherent sense. Very coherent, in fact. They were going to get the situation they had always desired: Miguel would not only be up against it, and obliged to attack, but in dire straits – due to the time he'd lost and the rivals ahead of him – and, furthermore, forced to attempt heroics on his home patch in front of his countrymen, whose cries of encouragement would surely push him time and time again beyond the limits of his already seriously drained strength.

The following days, to Gap, Valence and Le Puy-en-Velay, were nerve-racking and full of questioning looks, and still nothing happened. Riis was still leader and appeared sure of himself and surrounded by a very strong team. There were two big questions, and both always related to Miguel: 'What's happened to Induráin?' and 'When will he attack?' No one else seemed to matter. They were playing a dramatic and contained waiting game. As far as the second question went, no one was able to make any predictions. But I recall the faces of two people who, for different reasons, had been closest to Induráin in the final years, closest to his doubts and dreams – Miguel's doctor, Sabino Padilla, and his masseur, Vicente Iza. Their faces were always worth a thousand words: they bore a distorted, and even furtive look, full of concern, indicating, perhaps, their lack of confidence in Miguel's chances of pulling that godforsaken Tour out of the fire.

As far as what might have happened to him on Les Arcs was concerned, we can only speculate. Was it dehydration, or lack of food? Everyone asserts this was not the case. Miguel himself couldn't come up with a logical explanation. He knew his own body, and remembered full well the symptoms he had experienced when he had cracked climbing Sestrière in '92, or on Aprica during the '94 Giro. Although he hadn't been in perfect shape and had to risk everything because of the time he'd lost in the Follonica time-trial and in the climb up Campitello Matesse, the fate of the entire race had been at stake on that occasion. He'd been wearing too many clothes when he climbed the Stelvio (which might have been the case on Les Arcs) and he overstrained his body on the deadly Mortirolo. Then, suddenly, when he saw Santa Cristina, he'd cracked.

This time, though, it was different. He'd climbed the Madeleine well and the Cormet de Roselend even better. He was about to attack on Les Arcs when the world went from under his feet. Why? Because of his state of mind and because of an accumulation of different factors. One interesting technical analysis is provided by Dr José Calabuig, a cardiologist from the University Hospital of Pamplona, and chief medical officer of the Banesto team. He knew Induráin and his body like the back of his hand:

Miguel has gone several years without experiencing much cold or rain in a stage. His pre-Tour training has always been in a warm climate, and his muscles, which are strong yet delicate, have grown accustomed to high temperatures, which suggests that the constant cold and rain (to which the body reacts by closing the capillaries and by reducing perspiration) contributed to severe dehydration. In addition, and because of the freeing of certain hormones from the adrenal gland, there might have been a case of glucogenolysis. This would have led to a sudden loss of strength, intracellular dehydration and an increase in lactic acid since his body would not have been able to use the sugar in his blood. This then causes even greater fatigue. The changes in the calcium and potassium levels disrupted the permeability of the cellular membranes and their ability to contract. We should not forget that Miguel had scarcely any subcutaneous cellular tissue. All this meant he produced an amazingly strong performance in the worst possible conditions for him, which led to a drop in a contractile protein ...

Dr Calabuig goes on to assert that in his opinion this did not look at all like a typical case of *pájara* (a momentary loss of energy due to a lack of food or sugar) since, if that had been the case, he would have recovered by the next day. Solving the problem, he says, would have required a whole team of sports doctors (such as Eddy Merckx used to take with him) who would have had to perform tests there and then, on the same day as Les Arcs. A urine analysis, for example, and even a biopsy in order to examine the problem in depth and to find solutions to the doubts raised by such an obvious collapse of the system. Despite that, most of the doubts persist and will always persist: why did it happen on that specific day and at that specific time? That question must always remain – and it enhances the legend.

A cloud in front of his eyes. In his racing career, Miguel was always a bit like those gods in classical literature who chatter and make pacts amongst themselves. He was like Virgil's Aeneas, protected by the forces of Good. That 'cloud' was surely the god of the Tour de France telling him that the time for rest and peace had come. Only anger and courage made him continue, as it had done for Homeric heroes. And Pamplona.

The evening of Les Arcs still had an especially moving climax, but one which I will mention later, because, to some extent, I think it states the measure of the champion. It occurred in the Press conference he gave at the Hôtel Mercure, in Les Arcs itself, which is a ski station like many others in the area. It was an emotional moment and it made me understand a few things about life, such as why the sky is blue, why the wind blows as it does, and why the cold can bloat and even kill you on a bike, while, just like the sun, it stimulates other men. I now know that that sad evening in Les Arcs enabled me to see, even in its distance and vagueness, what the 'cloud' was made of. But earlier, just three hours earlier, all of us, together with half the world and the entire Tour, had fallen from the cloud, a different cloud. And there was no way back.

Although it might seem paradoxical, the sporting world, and especially the world of top-flight cycling, is based on speculation and illusory hope: you mustn't throw in the towel, even if it is wringing with blood. So, the Hautacam stage was eagerly awaited. There would be loads of Spanish fans present on that steep and beautiful Pyrenean summit. But before that, a couple of things had happened during one stage in the Massif Central: there'd been a break with all the favourites at the front, and the Navarran wasn't part of it. It took several minutes before his Banesto men got back on. And then, as if Induráin was resigned to his fate (or rather, was under pressure from all sides), he once more displayed some of his aggression. Maybe he feared Hautacam. Maybe. This was *en route* to Superbesse-Sancy, a summit finish after a leg-busting stage with several lumpy sections in the final stretch. Putting in a roller-coaster route like this is tantamount to treachery by the Tour organisers, comparable only to the Italians in the Giro. There was a moment, quite a few kilometres from the finish, when it seemed as if Riis was relaxing a bit. He wasn't at the front of the peloton. And Miguel could be seen to be looking for something, and he told Orlando Rodrígues to give it all he had. Induráin, out of the saddle, forced a tremendous pace. There was a roar in the Press room, but it all came to nothing, since the Telekom team soon took control of the situation.

As they reached Superbesse, Miguel could see that some of the favourites, most conspicuously Berzin and Rominger, were flagging, just as they had been on each of the previous climbs – the Côte de Saint-Anastasie, the mountain pass through the village of Besse and the Côte de Faux. On the climb up to Superbesse, he ordered his men to press. That afternoon we did see Marino Alonso leading the group up in decisive fashion. The atmosphere was electric. Riis was still there, but hunched over his bike. The road had narrowed, making it very difficult for the Telekom riders to get on the front and control the attack. Then, suddenly, there was another fright: Miguel had disappeared. He'd punctured at the worst possible moment! Fate, the cloud, the air in his tyre, the air and wind of the mountain. Oh, cursed Tour!

How they managed to get him back to the front of the group again was amazing and, of course, praiseworthy, but the huge effort involved had the peculiar result – like everything that happened in this Tour – of the Banesto riders again disappearing *en masse* as if magicked away. All except José María Jiménez, who was riding like crazy. So crazy, in fact, that he went clear on his own, carried along by his momentum, and after just a few metres he ground to almost a complete halt. Once more Miguel had to go it alone against all the climbers. Yet he came through that difficult situation well enough.

The next two days, with finishes at Tulle and Villeneuve-sur-Lot, were tense but uneventful. Everyone was waiting, and the Pyrenees were waiting, behind the grey valleys. There were 180 kilometres from Agen to Lourdes and another ten from there to the foot of Hautacam. Then, 13.5 kilometres at an 8 per cent gradient. A winding mountain pass where apparently unmanageable inclines are followed by even steeper ones, one of those *hors-catégorie* mountains which terrify the riders but excite the crowds. There, on the slopes of the pass, were crowds of spectators who had been waiting for hours. Whole families had been there for days.

The group of favourites arrived, each of them with one or two key *domestiques*. So, Riis was with Ullrich – just 22 and the revelation of the Tour – and Bolts. Rominger was with Olano. Virenque, with Dufaux and Laurent Brochard. Zülle, over-stretching himself, went clear but flagged after a kilometre, just like José María Jiménez on the way up to Superbesse. Treacherous Tour. Soon the usual group of riders were out on their own, all seeming to be struggling on the climb. Miguel was looking for a good position, as if he wanted to turn the screw again, as he had done on the ascent to Sestrière. Once again our hearts were in our mouths, especially as, still full of hope, we saw Riis falling further and further back. Suspiciously, though, Ullrich was still forcing the pace like mad. Riis slipped back to the last rider in the group, Luc Leblanc, the man whom the Dane feared might deprive him of the stage. And he must have seen that Leblanc was in trouble, however, because he suddenly and dramatically accelerated, out of the saddle and changing up through the gears, with no great pedal cadence but with such strength he quickly powered away from the frightened, limping group. The surprising thing was Induráin's response: for the second time in his life we saw him lock on to a wheel that he ought not to have followed – Riis's. The Navarran was so valiant, but perhaps it was a mistake. He withstood a first monumental crack of the whip, and then a second, but on the third, with Riis shooting uphill, Miguel cracked.

The previous time had been when he'd tracked Ugrumov on the way to the Sanctuary of Our Lady of Oropa in the '93 Giro, when he'd withstood a fourth devastating kick from Ugrumov before cracking. Then the Giro had been at stake and he had been defending the *maglia rossa*. On that occasion he had moderated his pedal speed, listened to the advice he was given and continued climbing as best he could. However, at the end of that stage in Oropa we'd seen something we had never previously seen: a completely exhausted Miguel, his head hanging down between his elbows and the handlebars, gasping for breath as never before. Now, on Hautacam, he had gone for the bait, again.

In all likelihood, his only chance in the Tour was to keep on Riis's wheel for those first kilometres on Hautacam, but when he saw the incredible gear the Dane was pushing, he would have done better to ease off, and drop back to the chasing group that contained all the favourites, and come home with the same time as them, at 40-odd seconds. By going with Riis at the outset, and with real determination, Miguel had left Olano and Rominger behind. But he quickly saw the whole lot of them come past him, and leave him for dead. For a moment, it looked as if Tony Rominger was going to offer Induráin his wheel to help him up the rest of the climb, but the Swiss quickly switched line to stop that from happening. That is the law of cycling, as Ángel Arroyo commented to me one day: 'Whenever the opportunity arises, they finish you off, so you can't turn the tables on them.'

Miguel, demoralised and completely resigned to his fate (the Tour was really beyond him now), lost two and a half minutes to the leader. The wound continued to open. And yet, the question remains: what would have happened if Miguel had adopted a different approach on that climb, gradually quickening the pace, say, as he'd always done? What would have happened if he'd had a Banesto climber at his side, especially in the first part of the ascent? We'll never know the answers. But on Hautacam there was no 'cloud', rather something much more prosaic and sad, something less poetic and soul-destroying: a simple lack of strength. The events of Les Arcs had not been a mere 'coincidence', nor an 'isolated circumstance'. Hautacam, the climb on which he'd taken control of the '94 Tour so resoundingly, was now his grave. Whatever had accumulated in his body, and there was certainly something there, was catching up with him at the crucial moments, when his heart had to pound at 190 beats or more a minute, and maintain that rate for a considerable time.

In my opinion, Induráin would have ridden differently if it had not been Hautacam. But precisely because it was that mountain, which he knew like the back of his hand, and which will forever bear his name inscribed in gold letters since, before Riis, he'd been the first rider to reach the top in yellow, he perhaps forced his mental, emotional and physical machinery beyond what was reasonable. There were too many Spanish fans urging him relentlessly on. Too much pressure. He couldn't let those people down. He had to go for it. And he did. But he tore himself apart even more. And the error was twofold. If, that day, he had not responded personally to the wave of attacks from Riis (which says much about his pride and fighting spirit), if he had not once more cracked as violently, if slightly less obviously, than he had on Les Arcs, perhaps he would have retained enough strength for the following day between Argéles-Gazost and Pamplona. But it was not to be.

The Pamplona stage had a lively start. By the summit of the Aubisque several members of the German Telekom team were prominent. That was rather unusual, as was the behaviour of the young Ullrich. Near the summit of the Aubisque even the accepted *rouleurs* of the team had come to the front. Then the Marie Blanque loomed, although it was its gentler, more varied, side from Bielle.

And then the drama began, inaugurating what was going to be the final act: the Soudet, with a climb of almost 20 kilometres at an average gradient of 6.5 per cent, was just too much. I still don't understand how the Tour organisers make it a first-category climb instead of giving it the status of a special or *hors* category. The Soudet is an unmanageable equilateral triangle, tough on both sides. It is one of those Pyrenean mountains which, like the little-known Pailheres, or the Portillon on the French side, could cause a lot of damage if they were situated at the end of a hard-fought stage, like Restefond or the Granon in the Alps. Even though it was placed before the half-way mark of that Pamplona stage, the Soudet turned into another torment for the Navarran, because once again he tried to prevent Riis from dropping him.

It must have been a matter of pride, rather than strategy since, soon afterwards, while ascending to Larrau, with its infernally steep central section, there were to be more dramatic moments. There were times when he seemed to be all on his own, and other times when, together with Rominger, Olano and Fernandez Ginés, he almost got back on. If he failed to manage that by the summit, then tackling the long road to Pamplona, alone, would have been the most unpleasant and moving sight in the Tour.

The road to the heights of Larrau was, of course, teeming with Spanish fans, especially from the Basque Country and Navarre. They gave him so much encouragement it was incredible, almost unbelievable. It was a demonstration of love and respect, which many found extremely touching. Miguel was crawling up the slopes of Larrau, a mountain which, as I've said, neither he nor Pruden were partial to, but he, together with the Mapei men, had to get back on, if he was to avoid shedding a huge chunk of time on the road to Pamplona. There were terrible moments. One woman couldn't stop herself rushing out of the crowd and pushing him, even shoving him out of his saddle. Her gesture was made with the best of intentions, but she shouldn't have done it: you never push kings. The gods, even at the sublime moment of their fall, walk alone with their heads held high.

On the false flat of the Col de Erroymendi the agony was partially relieved. Now and again Induráin was passed by another rider, who was shocked to see him suffering so much. Massimiliano Lelli went by, a man whom Miguel had carried in his wake so many times on the toughest stages of the Giro. Lelli hesitated and then, commendably, offered Miguel his wheel. Up to the top of the pass, from where you could see the peak of Ohri, there was still a 13 per cent ascent. It was a tough, but moving, sight, bitter and endearing, like life itself. It was a Wagnerian twilight. Induráin and the Mapei men fought to cut the advantage of the lead group, which contained all the favourites. It proved to be in vain, and the gap grew ever wider. But at least Induráin would reach his homeland amongst a select group which had battled strongly throughout the day.

They passed in front of his house in Villava. There were his parents, sisters, all his friends; Marisa and his son, little Miguel, too. Induráin threw them a kiss, to the applause of the people gathered there. They were riding on automatic, now, under a blazing sun. Much later, Pruden passed by and the whole of Villava joined in the chant of *'Pruden, Pruden, Pruden es cojonudo ... Como Pruden no hay ninguno!'* – 'Pruden, Pruden, Pruden is awesome ... There's only one Pruden!' The Tour was lost, but that wasn't going to stop the Navarran folk having a fiesta. It wasn't, I must stress, a triumphal fiesta, but a fiesta of love.

Everywhere there were Induráin T-shirts with their 'Sixth Tour' slogans, posters, pictures, caps, traditional handheld fans and stickers. For over 100 kilometres along the roadsides, Miguel must have seen frenzied crowds waving cardboard cut-outs of him in yellow. He must have seen them and he must have been moved, especially when he climbed Beloso, which they once said he would never manage because of his size. That was, in fact, 1,100 metres at a gradient of 3.6 per cent. A piffling little incline. It was his last climb up Beloso; the very last.

Personally, I must make a confession: that day, because of the tension and, I suppose, after having had to control my nerves and emotions for so many days on end, I went completely to pieces. I'm not ashamed to admit it; in fact, I feel it an honour to have the chance to explain it. I simply and totally went to pieces. It was the time when I suffered my own personal *pájara* after all those Tours following Miguel along the French roads. We'd known for some time that Induráin had been dropped by the group containing the leader. Some had dreamed of seeing him gain an 'honorary' win at the finish in Pamplona, in front of his own people. What would have happened if they'd all arrived together in one group? Whatever the case, those of us who had dreamed of Miguel being the first past that very special kilometre 256.5 of the stage – his own house, with its balcony of ever-present geraniums – had to accept the bitter truth. For me there were two choices: to remain in the large Press room and watch the finish on the multiple TV screens that are installed by the organisers, or go to the finish-line and melt in with the crowds chanting non-stop the name of their idol, who had still not come in. My head told me to stay in the Press room, but I took the tougher option, which was what my heart pleaded for, even though I knew I wasn't mentally prepared for it. Fighting as ever with the race stewards who set up filters at the finishes, I managed to position myself exactly ten metres from the line, behind the photographers, who, naturally, are given priority so that they can carry out their job. Dufaux crossed as stage winner. Then Riis leading in the group of favourites. Thousands of faces and shoulders lifted up because people were standing on tiptoe to see when Induráin arrived. The streets and balconies were packed. I began to get more emotional than I should have when I saw that everyone was smiling, and seemed happy. Yet, deep down, they must all have been so dejected. They concealed it by encouraging their idol. 'They're just like him,' I thought. 'If there's a crop, you harvest it; if there isn't, it doesn't matter.'

But the minutes passed by, slapping us in the face. Induráin hadn't appeared. It began to be terribly mortifying. Several times, a brass band strategically situated near the finish had struck up the famous 'hymn' to the Navarran, with their whistles and drums at the ready, so happy to be able to play that popular song again. But they would quickly stop. Then someone would give the order, perhaps spurred by a rumour, since many people, including some of the brass band, had transistors glued to their ears, and they played with renewed vigour. Here he comes!

Miguel didn't appear, however, and I had a knot in my throat. Standing on tiptoe and trying to see something over the shoulder of a giant Dutch cameraman, my nerves were fraying. 'Please, put an end to this soon,' I begged.

The brass band launched once more into the refrain: 'Induráin, Induráin, Induráin!' They were beaming with pride. I gulped.

But Miguel had still not come in.

From the platform where they were sitting and where they must have been waiting for hours in the fierce July sun, they were gazing down to the end of the long Pio XII Avenue along which, after going round a small square, the riders would approach the finish. The last kilometre, the last. I knew that was the end, the farewell. The music faded languidly, painfully, the beat creaked. Only the drum managed to keep time. The whole of the Pathetic Symphony of that unattained sixth Tour, with its epic and terrible moments, with its feelings of emptiness and emotional fragments, now acquired, for a few moments, the musical character of a grande finale, with hints of a Requiem. It was all dragging on far too long. Once again we heard: 'Here he is, here he is!' And yet again the music started up with gusto. But, no. There was a moment's confusion. The big stopwatch over the finish-line showed that nearly nine minutes had passed since Riis's arrival. The Great Symphony of an entire racing career was reaching its conclusion. There was a long pregnant silence, with all the faces turned once more to the end of the avenue. A few motorbikes appeared and several official cars going round the square. Sirens. And suddenly, first a rumour, and then a roar of jubilation. The music boomed out again, stronger and more sincere than ever: 'Induráin, Induráin, Induráin!'

Miguel was coming! The roar was incredible. The buildings seemed to be shaking, and the tar on the road, baked by the oven of the sun, vibrated for a few seconds. The air filled with light. There was a clamouring the like of which I had never heard, not even on the Champs Elysées. A clamouring which was more out of respect and homage than joy. Or, perhaps, it was also out of delight and pride, since they could see how great a champion he was, especially in adversity, and they were thanking him for it, screaming his name to the rooftops over and over again.

That was when, right on the finish-line and surrounded by journalists, I burst into tears like a child.

I know I wanted to stay and see the ceremony, but I presumed that Induráin was going to appear on the podium, as indeed he did, and I couldn't take it. I remembered those picture of his first victorious Giro, where the Italian TV gave us close-ups each evening of Miguel in his *maglia rossa*, while, as background music, you could hear Pavarotti singing *Nessum Dorma*. Miguel flying in a time-trial, Miguel levitating up a mountain, as if a friendly wind were pushing him, and him alone, up the Terminillo. The noise at the finish was deafening. And my ears resounded to those lines: '*Ma il mio misterio è chiuso in me, il nome mio nessum saprà! No, no sulla tua bocca lo dirò, quando la luce splenderà!*' 'For my mystery is enclosed within me, no one shall know my name! No, only on your lips shall I say it when the light shines forth!'

It was with great difficulty, and hidden behind my dark glasses, that I managed to disguise what was happening to me. What's more, on the way back to the Press room I bumped into several journalists I knew. How was I to explain to them that the pressure of Induráin's five Tour wins, and, above all, the pressure of the failed sixth Tour had got to me, a mere spectator? How was I to explain to them that, while in theory we were professionals who were there to give an objective view of events, my emotions had got the better of me, and that my heart was broken, too?

Because I knew then that nothing would ever be the same again. Maybe champions *should* solo up the Casse Déserte of the Izoard. Maybe. But a voice was telling me that there are sportsmen whose place is among the stars, as the lover in *Nessum Dorma* sings. Miguel's place was among the stars; he was unreachable. And suddenly, in a matter of weeks, he had become reachable, and vulnerable, to all his rivals. While they may not have lost their respect for him, they had lost a good part of the reverential fear he used to instil in them even before they had put their feet on the pedals. From that moment onwards – and this was something I realised with absolute certainty – he would have to produce an effort of unprecedented power. And often even this would be useless. If he were to continue in cycling, he would have to triple or quadruple his performances to put things back to where they were before the ill-omened Tour of '96. And that wasn't just a challenge, it was madness. For that reason, at the finish in Pamplona I knew it was all over, even though Induráin's name would continue to fill stacks of newsprint. What's more, he had dragged himself through more Tours than most other riders – twelve – and had managed what no one else had achieved – five consecutive wins. After that, everything would be leftovers from a banquet of also-rans. The murmur of the Irati River, and the *laminak* of his beloved homeland, those mysterious goddesses which protect the country folk, would tell Miguel that the passion would still be in France. And that France was over.

It didn't much matter that the following stages were routine, including the flat Bordeaux–Saint-Émilion individual time-trial after which, apparently, Induráin decided to go to Atlanta.

Atlanta was nice, certainly. Seeing him once again on the podium, and smiling. It was a challenge, certainly. The last one, for an Induráin who didn't want to retire without trying for Olympic gold.

Some got emotional (we all did actually), but deep down we knew that the passion was really in France. Riis was nowhere in that Atlanta time-trial, the same Riis who was seen on the road between Bordeaux and Saint-Émilion with his eyes bulging and with his mouth foaming. A very tall, powerful man who finished the *Grande Boucle* weighing 66 kilos, far below his normal weight, and who could well have lost the Tour if his team-mate Ullrich had been given free rein to win it, since in truth the German was but a whisker away. I've said before that some cyclists who aspire to glory are pathological creatures. That's why Induráin's calmness and good deportment are so striking. He cracked as a cyclist, and as a man, but no one can recall him foaming at the mouth. White saliva, yes, after Sestrière, Oropa and Liège, but not foam.

The end of his career need not detain us. He was forced to race the Tour of Spain even though he didn't want to, and was very upset that he was made to do so when he had no motivation and was in poor form. That was very sad. An insult to all who love cycling. But when we remember Induráin in a few years' time, or even after many years, it will not be for those tepid misfortunes of his *adiós*, nor for his retirement in the Spanish Tour, which had always mistreated Miguel so badly whenever he had taken part in it. That was just how it happened to be. In that ongoing joust with those who made him race the Vuelta, Miguel delivered a technical knock-out when he did not allow the ONCE rider Herminio Díaz Zabala even to accompany him on the descent of the Fito. So, the Spanish public also had a right to see their champion on Spanish roads, did they? Well, for years, Spanish roads had seen him ride, and seen him succumb or triumph in events covering the length and breadth of the country. That was how things were. And Eusebio Unzúe had predicted as much years before: 'Induráin may well never win the Vuelta, but he will win the Tour.'

The mist of the Marie Blanque had told the Navarran, perhaps a long time before that epic cavalcade to Cauterets in '89, that passion, the real passion, would always be in France. And the rest – that was just mandarins.

The details surrounding the protracted process of his retirement from cycling are not really of great importance. No one will ever know for sure what caused the Navarran to take his decision, despite the fact that the experts, supported by clinical analysis, were adamant that his body was still in perfect shape to attempt a sixth Tour de France victory. In his short message which he read to the Press to announce his farewell, Miguel Induráin himself hinted at a challenge he was throwing down to the future, to his own immense legend: 'Although I feel I'm capable of achieving that sixth Tour win ...' No one doubts it.

L'Équipe published a special Induráin supplement when he retired. And, despite the fact that both Guy Roger and Philippe Bouvet continued to refer to him as the 'Great Lord of the Tour', they still mentioned his one 'defect': *'Le manque de panache.'* A lack of panache. Incredible.

There was speculation about financial matters, and all kinds of stuff that had nothing to do with sport, but Miguel kept a dignified silence. So much so that it drove some of those who simply wanted a few titbits of news to despair. 'He's having us on.' Not a bit of it, he had been doing what he'd always done. He'd been reflecting upon an important decision, one which affected him and his direct family. He was alone with his silence.

There was a kind of collective consternation when he finally announced his decision, which, though not totally unexpected, still came as a surprise. At the time I wrote an article for *El Mundo* entitled: 'He's not leaving us.' Basically, I said that, despite what appearances might suggest, Miguel Induráin was not leaving cycling, or us, for three basic and obvious reasons:

A. He had always been there.

B. He is always there.

C. He will always be there.

Spanish cycling fans had been waiting almost a century for an Induráin. They didn't know who it would be, nor when he would come, but in the end he appeared. I don't want to return to the mystic or religious metaphor but, as with the history of mankind, so, too, with the history of Spanish cycling and with the sport as a whole (and quite a few other things, as well, I suspect), time will be divided into the before Him and the after Him. He was our Promised Messiah of cycling.

Apart from that, we will retain our memories, films, photos, cuttings and affection, too.

According to the meticulous calculations of *L'Équipe*, Miguel achieved 99 victories as a professional. I don't think they understood that last great victory which escaped them. Number 100 was a victory of *panache*.

Earlier, I alluded to something that happened on that fateful day of Les Arcs which made a deep impression on me. What we saw on the way to Pamplona showed us how a great cycling champion should behave, but the lesson in humanity and courage Induráin gave in the Alps has, with the passage of time, come to acquire for me a value that is comparable to all his sporting successes. It was in the Hôtel Mercure at Les Arcs where the cloud lifted from me, and I saw his standing as a human being.

Like a funeral ceremony for the day's racing that had just ended, a rumour went round amongst the journalists that Induráin was going to give a Press conference. 'He won't dare,' some suggested. No one was forcing him to do it, referring to the team's management. 'Of course he will. If he's done it at happier moments, he'll do it today as well,' added others. But the final decision, obviously, had to be Miguel's.

In that cold twilight of Les Arcs, with its blood-red, magenta hues, no one yet seemed to be able to come to terms with what had happened. His Banesto team-mates had already eaten and there were long faces everywhere.

And then Induráin appeared, looking dejected as well, but showing his even-tempered and youthful smile. For half an hour he replied to all kinds of questions – some of which were rather impertinent – without getting at all ruffled. He didn't know what had happened to him. He'd carry on giving it his best shot over the coming days, he said, although he was up against it now.

I thought: 'Those legs of his have been through nearly 70,000 kilometres of racing, and more than 400,000 in all. That's more than one and a half times round the Earth. Over the past five years he's done an average of a thousand interviews a year and he's never lost his composure. And there he is, the last of his team to sit down and eat.' The interview ended in that very tense atmosphere and Induráin got up slowly. He simply wanted to get to the dining room, which was no more than twenty metres away. He wanted to be on his own, and to reflect on things.

He walked past me. Two or three people asked him for an autograph. He signed without a murmur. That encouraged more people to approach. At every step, another member of the public, not a journalist, would stop him and ask him a question or say a few words to him. I was thinking: 'I don't believe this.' It seemed as if all those people, even with the best of intentions, were paying their condolences to him. And he endured this stoically and with a smile. Handshake after handshake, metre by metre, he got closer to the door of the dining room. Suddenly, an elderly Frenchman, accompanied by a young lad, grabbed him by the arm. His eyes were red, but he managed to say: *'Toujours vous serez le plus grand des grands.'* 'You'll always be the greatest of the greats.' And his voice faltered with emotion. Miguel surely understood what that emotional man was saying to him as he grasped his hand. And with a broad smile, Miguel gave a short but friendly reply: 'We did our best.'

It made a deep impression on the man and he let go of his hand. He then carried on gazing into space for a good while.

On his way to the dining-room, in that other daily Tour, never seen by cameras and photographers, but which Induráin had to endure in every hotel he stayed in, in every street he walked down, in every place he went to, he was stopped no fewer than fifteen times. And I counted fifteen minutes on the clock until he was finally able to make it through the door into the dining-room. There were hardly any stragglers among his team-mates left there to tell him what the dessert was like. The doors closed behind him.

I saw similar scenes over several years in various hotels in France, Italy, Belgium and Holland. He would always stop. He was never able to walk straight from the lift to the dining-room without being stopped. Nor from there to his room. They say the police officer deployed for his personal protection in the World

Championships in Colombia, who never left his side and who, as a basic security measure, asked him to stop as little as possible to speak to strangers, was driven to distraction when he saw him take half an hour every time he walked from one part of the hotel to another. Without losing his composure or his elegance. That police officer ended up on the verge of several nervous breakdowns. Every now and again Miguel would say to him: 'Tranquilo.' 'Relax.'

As we watch him pedal in film footage which will gradually date, we will no doubt recall those words from Puccini's *Turandot*: '*Tramontate, stelle! Tramontate, stelle! All'alba vincerò! Vincerò! Vincerò!*' 'Set, you stars, set! At dawn I shall be victorious! Victorious!'

It was that character, as much if not even more so, than his formidable qualities as a cyclist, which carried him to glory. That and the connivance of the wind, along with the certainty of the night stars, at the expense of which he even once allowed himself an ironic remark when a French journalist asked him if he knew and loved the stars: 'Not especially,' retorted Induráin, leaving the reporter rather flummoxed. 'But you have a telescope at home,' he said. 'Yes, though it's not much use to me,' replied Miguel.

I don't know whether Miguel looks at the stars from time to time, but he must certainly have done so as a boy, on the quiet, with eyes as big as saucers. He was born partly with stars inside him. Maybe they had been carried by the wind, on the breath of the breeze from the slopes of the Marie Blanque.

And also, in a way, he managed to take us some way to the stars. That is why it was worth waiting for him. That is why, in conclusion, we could slightly alter the words of Luz Casal's song and remind Miguel, when he yearns for his time as a cyclist, that we never minded how long it took him to get there, that if what he gave us was a dream – and it *was* a dream – he knew how to savour every last drop of it. And then we really did know it was Him.

Now, finally, he will be able to travel to distant places and to exotic islands.

And to spend more time with his family, teaching his son how to strip trucks and put them back together again.

And to watch the crops grow.

And to gaze at the mountains, which you climb and then descend, just like that.

And to make furniture with his huge hands.

And to play games of cards.

And to hunt the winged dove.

And to hear the song of the wind.

And to live life. Or, rather, to begin to live it.

I love the bicycle because it has given
me a soul capable of understanding it.
In the History of Humanity isn't the first
achievement of an intelligent being to
free itself from the laws of gravity?
Look, I have wings!

HENRI DESGRANGE, 1911

No matter how long
I have taken to get here,
If this is a dream
Rush me right to the end,
It is you, it is you...

LUZ CASAL

Miguel Induráin's Palmarés

Compiling Miguel Induráin's comprehensive palmarés has been difficult because he had such a long and successful professional career. As in the main text of this book, races in Spain are often referred to in four different languages (Spanish, Catalan, Basque and, occasionally, Gallego), so inconsistencies can arise. We have tried, wherever possible, to use the race names that might be most familiar to English readers. So 'Ruta del Sol' rather than 'Tour of Andalucia', but 'Tour of Catalonia' rather than 'Volta a Catalunya'.

We have included Induráin's positions lower than third in stage-races in the years before he started winning the major Tours, but these have been ignored in later years. This was done to help the reader gauge the progress of his career. Also, although there are many reference books and magazines which contain his palmarés none are better than about 80% correct. So with hard work and cross-referencing, we have tried to give you as concise and yet accurate a picture as possible.

If readers have any corrections or additions to make to the palmarés we would be happy for you to contact us.

1983

1st	Amateur Road-Race Championship of Spain

1984
(Team – Reynolds)

1st	Stage 10 (tt), Tour de l'Avenir
2nd	Stage 11, Tour de l'Avenir
3rd	Criterium de Pamplona

1985
(Team – Reynolds)

1st	Stage 6A, Tour de l'Avenir
1st	Stage 11 (tt), Tour de l'Avenir
2nd	Ruta del Sol
	2nd prologue
	2nd stage 5B (tt)
	3rd stage 4
2nd	Prologue, Midi Pyrénées
2nd	Prologue, Tour of Burgos

84th	**Vuelta a España**
	2nd prologue
Retd	**Tour de France** (Stage 7)

1986
(Team – Reynolds)

1st	**Tour de l'Avenir/EEC**
	1st prologue
	1st stage 9 (tt)
	2nd stage 4
	2nd stage 6
1st	**Tour of Murcia**
	1st prologue
	3rd stage 5
1st	Criterium de Leitza
3rd	Stage 5B (tt), Tour of the Basque Country
3rd	Prologue, Tour de l'Oise
3rd	Grand Prix Zizurkil
5th	Ruta del Sol
	2nd prologue

6th	Midi Libre		**1988**
	2nd stage 1		(Team – Reynolds)
	3rd stage 3	1st	**Tour of Catalonia**
6th	**Spanish Road-Race**		1st stage 6A (tt)
	Championship		2nd stage 4
41st	Tour of Burgos	1st	Stage 4, Tour of Cantabria
	1st Meta Volante	2nd	Stage 2B, Catalan Week
	2nd prologue	3rd	Tour of Galicia
	2nd stage 2B		1st Points Competition
92nd	**Vuelta a España**		1st stage 2
	3rd prologue		2nd stage 1
	8th stage 11 (tt)		3rd prologue
Retd	**Tour de France** (Stage 12)	6th	**San Sebastian Classic**
	3rd stage 7	8th	Catalan Week
	4th stage 5		3rd stage 4B (tt)
		12th	Tour of Burgos
			2nd stage 2
	1987	13th	Ruta del Sol
	(Team – Reynolds-Seur)		2nd prologue
1st	**Tour of the Mining**	40th	**Flèche Wallonne**
	Valleys	47th	**Tour de France**
	1st stage 2		
	1st stage 3		**1989**
	1st stage 4A		(Team – Reynolds)
	1st Points Competition	1st	**Paris–Nice**
	2nd prologue		2nd prologue
1st	Prologue Tour of Murcia		2nd stage 4
1st	Grand Prix Navarra		2nd stage 5
1st	Txitxarro Igoera		2nd stage 7B (tt)
	1st time-trial stage	1st	**Stage 9, Tour de France**
2nd	Grand Prix Bilbao	1st	Criterium International
3rd	Catalan Week		1st stage 3 (tt)
	1st Points Competition	1st	Criterium de Alquerias
	1st stage 5 (tt)	1st	Criterium de Pamplona
	4th prologue	1st	Criterium de Manlieu
5th	Tour of La Rioja	2nd	Subida de Naranco
	2nd stage 1	3rd	**Stage 15 (tt), Tour de**
8th	Tour of Galicia		**France**
	1st stage 1	4th	Bol d'Or de Chaumeil
	3rd prologue	5th	Tour of Valencia
27th	Tour of Catalonia	5th	Grand Prix Navarra
	2nd stage 5	7th	**Flèche Wallonne**
	2nd stage 8A (tt)	7th	Tour of Galicia
64th	**World Road-Race**	7th	Criterium des As
	Championship	7th	Txitxarro Igoera
97th	**Tour de France**	10th	**Liège–Bastogne–Liège**

10th	Tour of Switzerland
	2nd stage 6
10th	Tour of Catalonia
17th	**Tour de France**
42nd	**Milan–San Remo**

1990
(Team – Banesto)

1st	**Paris–Nice**
	1st stage 6
	2nd stage 1
1st	**San Sebastian Classic**
3rd	Tour of the Basque Country
	1st stage 5A
	3rd stage 3
	3rd stage 5B (tt)
3rd	Tour of Asturias
	3rd stage 3
3rd	**Spanish Road-Race Championship**
3rd	Tour of Burgos
	1st Points Competition
	1st stage 6 (tt)
	2nd stage 1
4th	**Flèche Wallonne**
4th	Bicicleta Eibarresa
	2nd stage 4
5th	Trophy Luis Puig
7th	**Vuelta a España**
	4th stage 11
	4th stage 20 (tt)
7th	Criterium International
	3rd stage 3 (tt)
7th	Urkiolara Igoera
9th	Tour of Valencia
	1st stage 5
10th	**Tour de France**
	1st stage 16
	2nd stage 7 (tt)
	2nd stage 14
	4th stage 20 (tt)
12th	**World Road-Race Championship**
12th	**Liège–Bastogne–Liège**
19th	**Amstel Gold Cup**

1991
(Team – Banesto)

1st	**Tour de France**
	1st stage 8 (tt)
	1st stage 21 (tt)
	2nd stage 13
	2nd stage 17
1st	**Tour of the Vaucluse**
	1st stage 1B (tt)
	2nd prologue
	3rd stage 4
1st	**Tour of Catalonia**
	1st Points Competition
	1st stage 5 (tt)
1st	Criterium de Pamplona
1st	Criterium Nocturno, San Sebastian
1st	Criterium Castillon la Bataille
1st	Criterium de Toulouse
1st	Criterium de Alquerias
1st	Criterium de Alcobendas
2nd	**Vuelta a España**
	2nd stage 19 (tt)
	5th stage 8 (tt)
	5th stage 12
	5th stage 16
	5th stage 17
3rd	**World Road-Race Championship**
3rd	Bicicleta Vasca
	1st stage 2
	1st stage 5
3rd	Circuit de l'Aulne
3rd	Criterium de Leves
4th	**Liège–Bastogne–Liège**
4th	Criterium Château-Chinon
6th	Tour of Asturias
14th	**San Sebastian Classic**
17th	**Flèche Wallonne**
43rd	Tireno Adriatico
	2nd stage 5

1992

(Team – Banesto)

1st	**Tour de France**
	1st prologue
	1st stage 9 (tt)
	1st stage 19 (tt)
	3rd stage 13
1st	**Giro de Italia**
	1st stage 3 (tt)
	1st stage 21 (tt)
	2nd prologue
	2nd stage 12
	3rd stage 17
1st	**Spanish Road-Race Championship**
1st	**Tour of Catalonia**
	2nd stage 4 (tt)
	3rd stage 6
1st	Circuit de l'Aulne
1st	Criterium des As, Oviedo
1st	Criterium des As, Fuenlabrada
1st	Criterium de Manlieu
1st	Criterium de Valencia, Rafelbuyol
2nd	Tour of Romandie
	1st stage 4B (tt)
2nd	Criterium Château-Chinon
2nd	Criterium de Alquerias
2nd	Criterium de Alcobendas
3rd	**Paris–Nice**
	2nd stage 1 (tt)
3rd	Tour de l'Oise
4th	Tour of Aragon
5th	Subida al Naranco
6th	**World Road-Race Championship**
15th	Trophy Castilla y Leon
	1st stage 1A (tt)

1993

(Team – Banesto)

1st	**Tour de France**
	1st prologue
	1st stage 9 (tt)
	2nd stage 11
	2nd stage 19 (tt)
	3rd stage 10
	3rd stage 16
1st	**Giro de Italia**
	1st stage 10 (tt)
	1st stage 19 (tt)
	2nd stage 1B (tt)
	2nd stage 14
1st	Vuelta a los Puertos
1st	Trophy Castilla y Leon
	1st stage 1 (tt)/prologue
1st	Criterium de Valladolid
1st	Criterium de Salamanca
1st	Criterium de Oviedo
1st	Criterium de Alquerias
1st	Criterium de Alcobendas
1st	Criterium de Valencia, Rafelbuyol
2nd	**World Road-Race Championship**
2nd	**Spanish Road-Race Championship**
2nd	Criterium de Zaragoza
3rd	Tour of Valencia
4th	**Tour of Catalonia**
	2nd stage 1 (tt)
7th	Clasica de Almería
8th	Grand Prix Gippingen
13th	Tour of the Mining Valleys
	1st Points Competition
	1st stage 2
	1st stage 4
	2nd stage 1
15th	Tour of Romandie
	2nd prologue
16th	Tour of Murcia
	1st stage 6 (tt)

1994

(Team – Banesto)

1st	**Tour de France**
	1st stage 9 (tt)
	2nd prologue
	2nd stage 11
	2nd stage 18
	3rd stage 19 (tt)
1st	Tour de l'Oise
	1st stage 3B (tt)
1st	Criterium Castillon la Bataille
1st	Criterium San Fausto de Durango
1st	Criterium de Fuenlabrada
1st	Criterium de Salamanca
1st	Criterium de Telde
1st	Criterium de Valladolid
1st	Criterium Gran Canaria
1st	Stage 3 (tt) Trophy Castilla y León
2nd	Tour of Valencia
	1st stage 6 (tt)
2nd	Criterium de Tenerife
2nd	Criterium de Alquerias
3rd	**Giro de Italia**
	2nd stage 18 (tt)
	3rd stage 1B (tt)
	4th stage 8
	5th stage 3
	5th stage 5
	5th stage 15
	5th stage 17
3rd	Criterium de Segovia
3rd	Criterium de Zaragoza
3rd	Criterium de Lanzarote
35th	Tour of Romandie
	3rd prologue
41st	**San Sebastian Classic**

WORLD HOUR RECORD:
53.040 kms

1995

(Team – Banesto)

1st	**Tour de France**
	1st stage 8 (tt)
	1st stage 19 (tt)
	2nd stage 7
	2nd stage 9
	2nd stage 10
	3rd stage 13
1st	**World Time-Trial Championship**
1st	**Midi Libre**
	2nd stage 6 (tt)
	3rd stage 1
	3rd stage 3
1st	**Dauphiné Libéré**
	1st stage 3
	2nd stage 1
	3rd prologue
	3rd stage 4
	3rd stage 6
1st	Tour of Galicia
	1st stage 1
1st	Rominger Classic
1st	Tour of la Rioja
	1st Points Competition
	1st stage 1A
	2nd stage 2
1st	Moscow Criterium
2nd	**World Road-Race Championship**
2nd	Colorado Classic
3rd	Tour of the Mining Valleys
	1st stage 4
	3rd stage 1
3rd	Tour of Asturias
	1st stage 1 (tt)
	1st stage 5
4th	Tour of Aragon
	1st stage 4B (tt)
6th	Classic des Alps
6th	**Spanish Road-Race Championship**
9th	**San Sebastian Classic**

1996

(Team – Banesto)

1st	**Olympic Games Time-Trial**
1st	**Dauphiné Libéré**
	1st Points Competition
	1st stage 5 (tt)
	1st stage 6
	3rd stage 2
1st	Tour of Alentejo
	1st time-trial stage
	1st stage 5
1st	Tour of Asturias
	1st time-trial stage
	3rd stage 5
1st	Bicicleta Vasca
	1st Points Competition
	1st stage 5
	2nd stage 3
	2nd stage 4B (tt)
1st	Criterium of Pamplona
1st	Criterium l'Hospitalet

1st	Criterium of Valladolid
1st	Criterium of Valencia
1st	Criterium of Colmar
1st	Criterium of Xativa
1st	Criterium of Fuenlabrada
2nd	Tour of Burgos
	2nd stage 4 (tt)
3rd	Stage 10 Vuelta a España
4th	Tour of Aragon
	2nd stage 2
	4th 4B (tt)
8th	Classic des Alps
11th	**Tour de France**
	2nd stage 20 (tt)
	5th stage 8 (tt)
	5th stage 9
	7th prologue
12th	**San Sebastian Classic**
26th	**Olympic Games Road-Race**
26th	**Amstel Gold Cup**

Compiled by Richard Allchin

The following books are also published by
Mousehold Press and Sport & Publicity
and can be obtained by contacting:
Mousehold Press (01603 425115) or
Sport & Publicity (0207 794 0915):

Mr Tom: the true story of Tom Simpson
by Chris Sidwells

Master Jacques: the enigma of Jacques Anquetil
by Richard Yates

From the Pen of J. B. Wadley
edited by Adrian Bell

A large range of other books about cycling can also be
obtained from Sport & Publicity

Copies of any of Jeremy Mallard's cycling prints
can be obtained by contacting him on: 01746 718 697
or visiting his website: www.presentandcollect.com